TRACK PLANNING IDEAS

from Model Railroader
58 track plans from past issues

SELECTED BY BOB HAYDEN

Art Director: Lawrence Luser
Copy Editor: Burr Angle
Editorial Assistant: Marcia Stern
Staff Artist: Bill Scholz

KALMBACH **k** BOOKS

The material in this book has previously appeared as articles in MODEL RAILROADER magazine

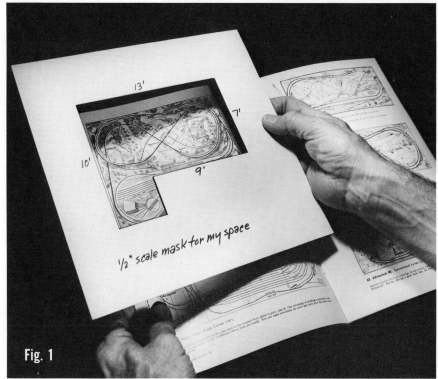

Fig. 1

MR photo by A. L. Schmidt.

Converting track plans from one scale to another

You can build a layout from any published track plan in any scale if you do some simple replanning on paper

By Linn H. Westcott

THIS article is limited to discussing changes one makes to a published track plan to suit it to a larger or smaller scale than was in the layout architect's mind.

Since 70 percent of all model railroaders have been using HO scale for their layouts, most published track plans are designed primarily with the consideration of this scale in mind. You'll find that the shelf areas and table widths are limited to how far a man can reach, from the edge inward, when the layout is built in HO size. Double the layout size for O scale use, and the man is in trouble: his arms are no longer able to reach across. The layout architects weren't forgetful, however: often you'll read their advice to add pop-up hatches or other openings in the middle of the scenery areas if such layouts are built to larger scales, so that you can get to the junction or rerail a car or do some new construction.

Until now this was not too much of a problem for those building smaller than HO. A TT scale railroad took three fourths as much length and width. You could reach across the table nicely.

N scale cuts layout size in half. Now shelves or tables can be ridiculously narrow, whereas space in the actual railroad room could (usually) easily provide for more.

Do special track plans have to be provided for N scale?

Well, some have already been published and more will come; but the difference in scales isn't that great in this hobby, even though it has taken us years to realize how true this is. Only a little of the very same intelligence one needs to build models is needed to make the modifications necessary when changing from one scale to another.

No matter what scale a plan was intended for, it can be useful in all other scales.

This greatly increases the possibilities of each scale, not only in track planning but also in building locos, cars, and structures. With locos, cars, and structures, all you need is a scale rule to convert from one scale to another. However, in track planning there is more give and take, and less need to be precise. An HO track plan is not an exact copy of the prototype, as a locomotive

should be; therefore one can make alterations more freely in copying it, whether building in HO or converting to another scale. When converting to a new size, we can make this freedom work for us, ensuring that railroad operation, scenic effects, and mechanical considerations are all optimum.

Converting a track plan is easy. The scissors, glue, pencil — perhaps a compass — and an architect's scale will be handy for the task. In case you don't know, an architect's scale is a measuring stick divided into scale inches and feet in such scales as 1″ to the foot, ¾″ to the foot, ½″ to the foot, and so on down to around 3/32″ to the foot.

Where do we start?

Most modelers search through back copies of magazines containing track plans; and they certainly should get a copy of the book 101 TRACK PLANS FOR MODEL RAILROADERS. This is available at nearly every hobby shop that handles trains. A number of other track plan books are also available. Most of these others are intended for users of sectional track; they even count for you the number of pieces needed. Such books are well worth studying. Usually the plans cram too much track into their spaces, on the assumption that that's all the space you have; but the tricks used to pack all that track into the spaces are good to know about. They can help you make a layout look less crowded when more space is available.

Usually you will get a better railroad if you consider published plans merely as idea sources. Revise one to suit your tastes — or work out your own plan entirely and have the fun of trying it out. You can't make bad mistakes. After all, this doesn't have to be the only model railroad you're going to build — not if this is a hobby instead of a novelty. What you do on this layout will be fun. What you learn *not* to do on it will help make the next layout fun. Even if you never do build another layout, corrections can be made rather easily on the one you have. Many people don't take advantage of this.

There is one book, however, that will put you a couple of years ahead in layout-planning wisdom if you take the trouble to read it completely. This is John Armstrong's TRACK PLANNING FOR REALISTIC OPERATION. You'll never build a railroad quite the same after you've read it.

What do we look for?

In paging through track plans, regardless of the railroad facilities and scenery, the most important consideration is usually: "Can it be fitted into my space?"

If the published plan is smaller than your space, it can easily be stretched to fit, but if the published plan is a little too large it may be nearly impossible to shrink it. This is because published plans are designed to fit as much track as possible into the given space. One way to check space is to make a paper mask with an opening in it the shape of the space you have: see fig. 1. Make this mask to the same scale as the drawings you are studying. Lay the mask over one plan, then another. If you can see the entire track plan through the mask opening, you can build the plan in your space. Sometimes you can make it fit by turning the mask at an angle to the plan.

Sometimes track plans may not be drawn to the same scale. Then you will need two or more masks, depending on the drafting scale. Let's talk about the scale of the drawing.

Drafting scales are usually ⅜″ per foot for a large HO plan, ½″ for slightly smaller plans, ¾″ per foot for the smallest plans. This is simply because you can fit them on a published page in those three scales. Once in a great while a plan may be reproduced in ¼″ scale or 1″ scale, but we will ignore those extremes here.

Now, if the drawing was made to ¾″ scale when the draftsman was thinking HO, that same track plan can be built in N scale if you think of the drawing as being in 1½″ scale — just double the scale. The ratio goes like this:

DRAFTING SCALES FOR TRACK PLANS
as usually published — inches per foot

Layout space	Modeling size				
	N	TT	HO	S	O
Small	1½″	1″	¾″	½″	⅜″
Medium	1″	¾″	½″	⅜″	¼″
Large	¾″	½″	⅜″	¼″	³⁄₁₆″

Usual spacing of ruled lines across plan

Inches	6	9	12	18	24
Centimeters	15	20*	30	40*	60

*Rounded for convenience in use

This chart is useful in several ways related to making track plans. Suppose you like a plan intended for HO that is drawn in ½″ scale as published, but you would like to build that layout in N scale size. Just find the HO ½″ spot on the chart and read across to the N scale column. You'll find the figure 1″. So you treat the drawing as though it were drawn to 1″ scale instead of ½″ scale, and you have your N scale master plan. You can use the 1″ scale rule on the margin of page 5 to measure the particular drawing and get any desired dimension for your N scale railroad.

Many of the better track plans have lines ruled across the face in both directions. Usually these are spaced as shown on the two bottom lines of the foregoing chart, but in a few cases the spacing is double that much. In either case these lines are helpful in locating things. You can even draw lines to the same spacing on your railroad surfaces for direct locations of track from the plan, thus dispensing entirely with ruler measurements.

The chart assumes that N scale is half as big as HO, that TT is three eighths as big, and so on. Actually they are not quite such convenient ratios. The true ratios are:

N	TT	HO	S	O¼(Q)	O true
.544	.726	1	1.361	1.815	1.936

While these true ratios must be used when converting from drawings of locos, cars, and structures, our track plans are already so distorted to meet model railroad space limitations that rounding off as in the larger chart is quite acceptable.

How about track radii?

If you have a track plan which calls for 22″-radius curves in HO, and you want to build in N scale, you'll need 11″-radius track to fit it the same way.

If you use flexible track this is no problem. If, on the other hand, you use rigid curved-track sections, they are more likely to be of 9″-radius or near it. You will find a little adjusting will be required. The way to go about it is to lay out the straight lines for straight track first, then fit the curves in place wherever they come. Following this method you'll find you'll be adding a short increment of straight track here and there because of the relative compactness of the 9″ curves compared to 11″.

One place you might get into trouble is where one track comes close to another. If in doubt, see that no sharply curved trackage (like we've been talking about) is closer than these distances from any other straight or curved tracks:

SPREAD OF PARALLEL TRACKS
Measured from track center to track center, American practice

		N	TT	HO	S	O
Sharp curves	in.	1.6	2.3	3	4.5	6
	mm.	41	58	76	114	152
Typical straight	in.	1	1.5	2	3	4
	mm.	25	38	50	76	101
Minimum straight	in.	.98	1.30	1.80	2.44	3.46
	mm.	25	33	46	62	88

(The second category is usual spacing for parallel straight tracks in yards. The third category is the minimum for parallel straight track.)

For less sharply curved track, less spacing is needed, but all curves should have at least the spacing shown in the middle pair of lines.

People space

If it weren't for people, you could build a layout just as it comes after making

Fig. 2

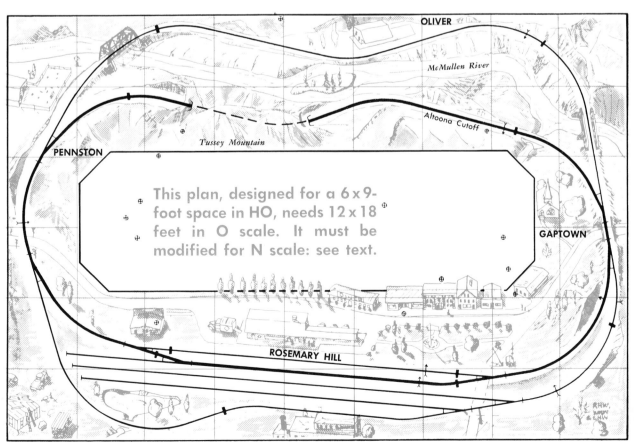

OLIVER

McMullen River

Altoona Cutoff

Tussey Mountain

PENNSTON

GAPTOWN

This plan, designed for a 6 x 9-foot space in HO, needs 12 x 18 feet in O scale. It must be modified for N scale: see text.

ROSEMARY HILL

Scale in feet 24:1 ½″ per foot

15

10

5

0

the appropriate size conversion, but as pointed out before, a man's armlength really determines how far from the table sides or aisleways he can reach into the table area. Typically this is around 24" (60 cm.) for convenience, but in extreme situations — where you can get your hip-level body-bending line above the table edge and where you can rest one hand on some scenery area while you lean inward — you can actually reach to around twice that distance if all you have to do is to adjust a toppled tree or some other simple task. Track should never be that far from the edge unless you have another shorter reach to get at it, either by lifting scenery off a hatch or by providing a ladder or gantry frame.

So, when a track plan is reduced — say from HO to N scale — the space around it for people cannot be reduced. The most serious problem here is when aisle space is either completely surrounded by railroad surfaces, or where an aisle enters into the layout from a side and is surrounded by scenery or track on three sides. Take the track plan in fig. 2 as

an example. It has a surrounded aisle.

This plan takes a room of at least 6 x 9 feet if built in HO size. The only "people space" absolutely needed is in the center area. The shelfwork is only 24" wide.

Reduce this drawing for N scale, and it will fit a closet of only 3 x 4½ feet; but the space in the center will no longer hold people: it becomes only 12" wide.

By this time, however, this particular plan is so small over all that you can still reach any part of it if you keep an aisleway along the front only. So you need a closet 4½ feet long for the layout, and 3 feet deep, *plus* a 2-foot aisleway area. That totals a depth of 5 feet.

The space in the center of the plan can now be closed over with additional scenery — perhaps a lake in this case, to help separate the foreground and background scenes.

This plan can be modified for N scale in another way. This is to enlarge the center area: fig. 3. It makes a nicer layout from the scenic standpoint. On the other hand, it is never too good to have to duck under a part of the layout to get to the operating pit, so take your choice. I think I'd be willing to duck under in this case.

All we did in fig. 3 was to stretch the short sides enough to retain a 24"-wide operating pit. The pit is now only half as long as before, so it's a good idea to stretch the railroad in length, too, if space permits. However, when stretched in width *only*, the overall size is 4'-0" x 4'-4½", so with a center pit rather than with an exterior operating aisle it will actually fit into a smaller closet.

This track plan we have been operating on is plan no. 41 in the 101 TRACK PLANS book. It has the name Quaker State Eastern. Its chief feature is the simplicity of using only a few mainline track switches, but there's nothing to keep you from adding all kinds of turnouts to provide more yard facilities plus a dozen or so industrial spurs to mines, quarries, factories, warehouses, feed mills, racetracks, hot springs resorts, and the like.

It is often better to take a fairly simple plan and stretch it both ways to fit a much larger space, then add yards, spurs, and stations here and there after the main line is completed first. It's easy to cut track and add a turnout where none was before if you do it on straight trackage. Curves are much more difficult, because

Fig. 3

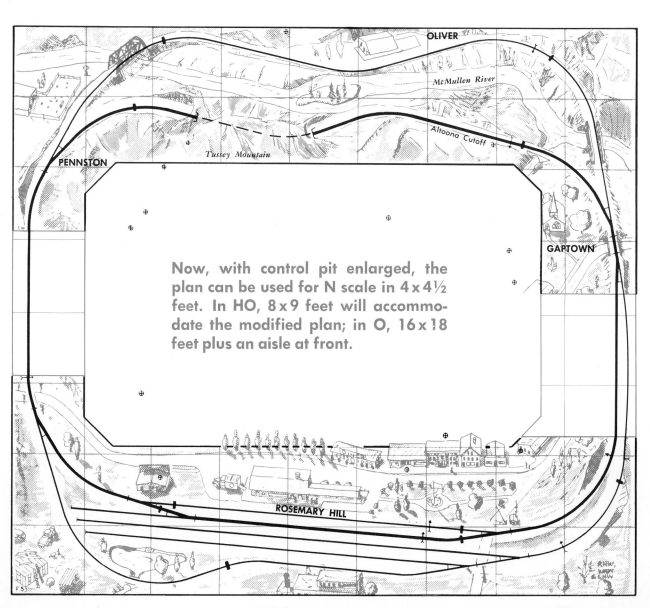

our curves are almost always too sharp to be replaced directly by a switch.

Think crooked

The easiest way to build a dull model railroad that few of your friends will appreciate is to do everything in the obvious way. An obvious model railroad has these kinds of features:

● Track running along the edge of the table.

● Long straight stretches of track unbroken by even the slightest intentional curve.

● Track well away from the edge of the table, but still running parallel to it.

● Curves that make exact 90-degree turns at the corners of the space, or 180-degree turns at the ends.

● All mainline track on the level.

● Upper-level track on another level, not undulating as in real life.

● Obvious ramps between lower and upper levels.

● Main station in the center of everything.

● Main control panel in the center of everything.

● All houses and streets inside the layout running at right angles to the railroad tracks; or, worse, to the table edges.

● Turnouts of too large a number size — unless you have a lot of space to devote to only a little trackwork. These look wonderful in themselves but dwarf the features of the layout around them.

● Turnouts (and other curves) of too small a number size or radius. Here the trouble is in looking toylike. The remedy is to hide parts of any overly sharp curves so you see no more than about 60 degrees of curve at a time. This is a relative thing. A very sharp curve looks its worst when all other visible curves are broader. You can hide 90-degree and 180-degree sharp curves under footbridges, partly in tunnels, partly in deep cuts, and behind warehouses. You can deflect the eye from them by putting interestingly modeled objects nearby, just a little distance from the track. Bad curve situations are also eased when you add scenery to make it look as if the curve *had* to be — for instance, to turn onto a viaduct, to curve around a hill, to approach a grade, or the like.

● Overly bright colors, out-of-scale modelwork, and lack of neatness also lead to making a layout look ordinary.

Not all the things I have listed have to do with track planning, but the matter of making a compromised mess — which a model railroad can be — into a work of art — which can be done in the same space — takes a lot of thinking, some practice, and the willingness to do anything over again anytime.

Well, let's move on:

Aesthetic planning for N scale

Well, we've been talking about how aisle space can't be reduced along with a track plan when converting it from a larger scale to TT or N scale. A similar problem exists with air space.

If you stand with your head, say, 15" above the track on an HO layout, you are seeing it as though from a tower or helicopter 116 feet in the air. If you are that far above an N scale layout, you are seeing it from twice that height. What this amounts to is that you see twice as far in every direction for any angle of downward viewing. You also see over hills, structures, and trees that might otherwise hide some of the compromising done on a larger-scale layout. The result is that you are much more aware of the track plan being an oval, or not much better than an oval. You are conscious of the full sweep of a sharp curve, not just its beginning — and so it goes.

So my suggestion here is a very serious one. If you are building in N scale, try to use the room space that would be three fourths of the space needed for the layout in HO size, instead of only half. Make your curves only three fourths of the HO radius, approximately. Make all other things to about this ratio. It's the ratio shown for TT on the chart near the middle of this story. A TT modeler, by the same argument, would be better with a space seven eighths as big as that assigned to an HO plan. I think you will find this practice will pay great dividends in making any small-scale layout more effective.

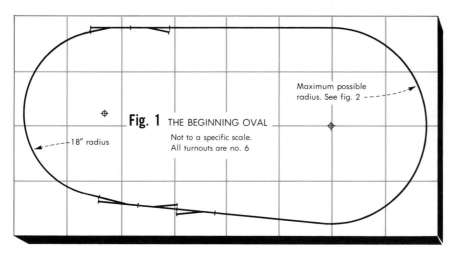

Fig. 1 THE BEGINNING OVAL

Not to a specific scale.
All turnouts are no. 6

18″ radius

Maximum possible
radius. See fig. 2

A small track plan designed for growth

BY ED VONDRAK

ONE of my colleagues is just getting to the point of building a permanent layout, and I volunteered to do some track planning for him. He has quite a bit of space (about 12 x 30 feet), but he wants to start with a simple 4 x 8-foot HO layout that will enable him to get something running soon, and which can be incorporated into a larger pike without having to revise the initial track plan and its scenery. I added the requirements that the initial plan should start out as simply as possible, should be easily improved to provide a reasonable amount of operation, and should nòt become so complex as to be out of character as part of a larger pike.

I consulted 101 Track Plans, Track Planning for Realistic Operation, back issues of Model Railroader, and my own file of ideas and came up with the track plan shown in figs. 1 and 2. At first glance, this plan appears very ordinary. However, it fulfills the criteria I was working with, whereas many other similar 4 x 8-foot track plans would not. Let me elaborate by considering the main criteria again:

• We want to get something running in a hurry. Fig. 1 shows that to get a train running, all we need to lay is a level oval containing five turnouts. Note, however, that we have to be careful where each piece of track is located. This is where long-range planning has its effect.

• The track plan should be easily improved to provide a reasonable amount of operation. Once the initial oval is in operation, a little more track added to three of the existing turnouts provides three spurs for industrial switching. Then some more track plus a few more turnouts adds a passing track, two more industrial spurs, and a small "yard." One of the spurs at the left end of the plan can serve as a locomotive servicing track until the layout is enlarged.

On this small a layout, that long passing track almost makes it a double-track main line, but there are reasons for this design. First, it is possible for a switcher to work the yard while another train is running on the main line. Second, when the layout is enlarged, we will want the passing tracks to be fairly long. You might ask, "Why not just make the whole oval double track?" We don't want to make the initial plan double track all the way around because that would be out of character when the layout is enlarged.

Scenery can be fully developed on the right half of the layout, but I wouldn't put any scenery at the left end unless you can convince yourself to tear it out and revise it later when we enlarge the pike.

Now let's look at one possible master plan into which we could fit our 4 x 8-foot design without changing any of the present trackage. When it comes to ideas for large track plans, there aren't very many different basic concepts. No matter how different they might look at first glance, when they are unwound and stripped of all the frills, virtually all track plans will fit one of the dozen or so basic schemes which are described in most track planning books.

Since I began studying track plans several years ago, I have discovered that all authors (including me) tend toward their one favorite basic scheme most of the time, despite the infinite variety of

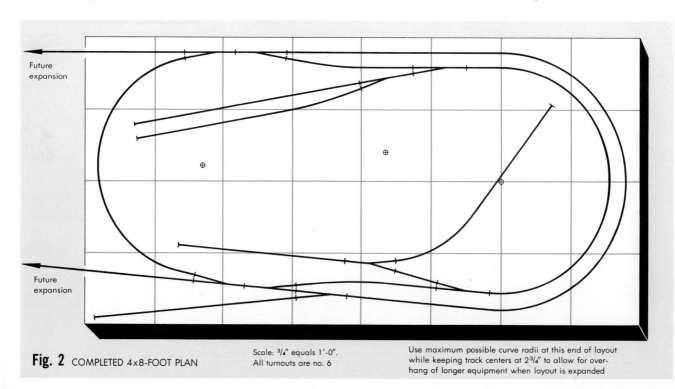

Future expansion

Future expansion

Fig. 2 COMPLETED 4 x 8-FOOT PLAN

Scale: ¾″ equals 1′-0″.
All turnouts are no. 6

Use maximum possible curve radii at this end of layout while keeping track centers at 2¾″ to allow for overhang of longer equipment when layout is expanded

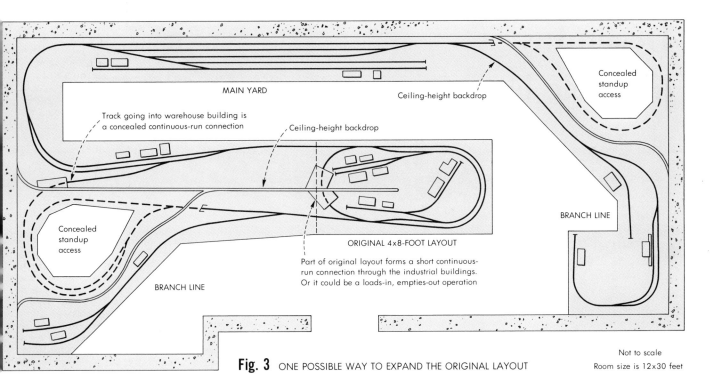

Track going into warehouse building is a concealed continuous-run connection

MAIN YARD

Ceiling-height backdrop

Concealed standup access

Ceiling-height backdrop

Concealed standup access

ORIGINAL 4x8-FOOT LAYOUT

BRANCH LINE

Part of original layout forms a short continuous-run connection through the industrial buildings. Or it could be a loads-in, empties-out operation

Concealed standup access

BRANCH LINE

Not to scale
Room size is 12x30 feet

Fig. 3 ONE POSSIBLE WAY TO EXPAND THE ORIGINAL LAYOUT

twisting, turning, and extra trackage that might be included in the plan. The master plan in this article is no exception. I like the operational possibilities offered by the concept, which is known as loop-to-loop with a division point. Fig. 3 shows how the original 4 x 8-foot track plan of fig. 2 fits very nicely into a loop-to-loop master plan.

Only the most fundamental trackage is shown in fig. 3, just to give an idea of how the initial layout might be expanded. It can be developed into a realistic railroad in many different ways without changing the basic concept of the plan. I have included a couple of specific ideas—a branch line at each end of the layout, and one possible continuous-run connection which, in my opinion, no layout should be without.

Notice how the original "yard" and part of the original oval become more

industrial spurs. Notice also how the left end of the original oval forms a short continuous-run connection through a couple of industrial buildings. This short connection could be used for a "loads in, empties out" kind of operation, and it could also be used when breaking in a new locomotive. It would serve the latter purpose very well, allowing break-in running without disturbing most of the main line.

Another possibility for expanding the track plan of fig. 2 would be to make it part of a large plan like the Santels' Ohio, Michigan & South Shore RR. which was described in the March 1975 issue of MR. With some modifications, my fig. 2 track plan could be put in the Santels' system in place of their towns of Ashville and Mount Sterling.

Perhaps now you can see the reason for including a long passing track in

my fig. 2 plan. It is a respectable 10 feet long (13 feet over the turnouts), which will allow for reasonably long trains in the enlarged version of the railroad.

One thing I would change if I were the one building this layout would be the initial size. I would start with 5 x 9 feet instead of 4 x 8 feet. That would allow a minimum mainline radius of at least 24" instead of the 19" or so required on the passing track in fig. 2. The other thing I would do would be to plan for the ultimate possibility of expanding the master plan to two or more tiers by using techniques which I have described in other articles that have appeared in MR over the past few years. You can't have everything, but I encourage a person to look far into the future and plan accordingly, insofar as possible.

Designing portable layouts

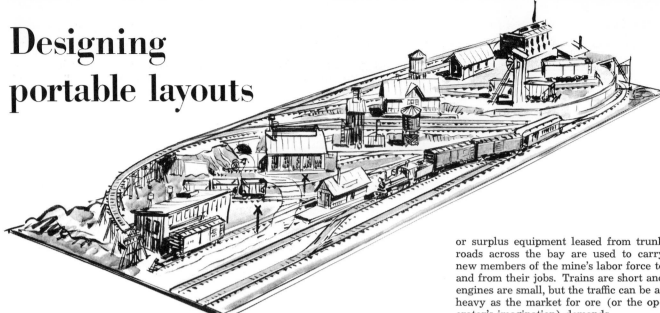

With an argument for eliminating some main lines entirely

By E. S. Seeley Jr.

THE modeler who has no space at all for a typical permanent model railroad system is faced with two alternatives: he can dream — on paper or simply in his mind — toward the day when space will be available; or he can build a portable layout.

A successful portable layout must be easily stored (on end in a closet, under a bed, for example). It must be easy to set up and take down, and it must provide challenging operation. The first two criteria limit the size and shape of the layout board. They also mean that scenery must be minimal or, better still, eliminated entirely: structures and portable layouts really don't mix. Ground cover, if included at all, must be simple and rugged. Thus the physical details of the layout's prototype setting must exist principally in the mind of the modeler. This is fine, since it will make him use his imagination — and imagination is an important part of successful model railroading!

The third criterion — that the layout offer challenging operation — means that the track must provide for certain fundamental concepts. These fundamental concepts apply to all layouts, big or small. They are the secret of effective model railroading. We will explore them in detail in the two portable layouts discussed here.

The Iron Mountain Line

Here is a complete point-to-point switchback line on a compact board. In HO it would be 2 x 7 feet; in N scale, 1 x 3½ feet. It connects the mine at Ferro Peak with the car float at Edison's Cove. Between the two terminals is the tiny hamlet of River Bend where eastbound and westbound trains can pass. Loaded ore cars are hauled to Edison's Cove, where they are rolled onto car floats (for a supposed trip across the bay to the blast furnaces). Besides the empty ore cars going the other way, boxcars and flats loaded with supplies for the mine arrive by car float and are hauled up the mountain to Ferro Peak. Passenger service is provided by a short open-platform combine that makes two trips a day between terminals, perhaps tacked onto the tail of one or two boxcars.

During periods when the mine is working overtime, passenger extras using old or surplus equipment leased from trunk roads across the bay are used to carry new members of the mine's labor force to and from their jobs. Trains are short and engines are small, but the traffic can be as heavy as the market for ore (or the operator's imagination) demands.

As a layout the IM has one very unusual feature — no main line. Two independent terminals, yes; a midpoint siding for meets, naturally; but not a foot — scale or otherwise — of main line. There is a very sound reason for this, which brings us to an important concept of layout design.

We all know about something called *selective compression*. It is one of the magic tools for layout design. We *select* the portions of the prototype we wish to model, then *compress* them to fit our available space. In traditional layouts, selective compression drastically shortens the main line, which is then disguised by scenery and structures to create the illusion of a more realistic relative length. On the IM, selective compression has eliminated the main line entirely.

Why? Because for the modeler whose main interest is in yard switching and train meets, the main line takes up too much space, and requires too much time to build and scenic for the *operating* dividend it provides. Since most of our main lines exist in the imagination anyway, why not eliminate them completely from this sort of portable layout? The space saved can mean better yards or, as with the IM, a smaller overall layout.

This layout design concept can be summarized by a simple rule: "Space is too precious to be devoted to any track that cannot justify its existence with an operational advantage."

IRON MOUNTAIN LINE

Scale: ¾" equals 1'-0"

A — Freight house   G — Station
B — Station   H — Mine warehouse
C — Enginehouse   I — Station
D — Coal   J — Freight house
E — Sand   K — Pit head
F — Water   L — Water

Atlas Snap-Track with 18"-radius curves

	N	TT	HO	S	O, Q
Width	1'-0"	1'-6"	2'-0"	3'-0"	4'-0"
Length	3'-6"	5'-3"	7'-0"	10'-6"	14'-0"
Size of squares	6"	9"	12"	18"	24"
Minimum radius	9"	13½"	18"	27"	36"

Car float

EDISON'S COVE   RIVER BEND   FERRO PEAK

The Bay Street Connecting Ry.

Most large American cities have terminal or belt line railroads that connect all the trunk lines in the area. On these terminal lines, cars are interchanged between the trunk lines and whatever harbor, industrial, and warehouse facilities are available. In New York City, the right of way for such a terminal road happens to be the oily waters of the Upper Bay and the North and East rivers. All day long tugs push barges laden with interchange cars from one point to another. Several destinations served are tiny, self-contained switching lines serving docks and warehouses along the shore. They have no direct rail connections to any other place. The imaginary Bay Street Connecting Ry. represents some features of several such lines in a compact layout that combines plenty of operating flexibility with maximum portability. In HO it would take 14" x 7'-0"; in S scale, 21" x 10'-6".

Freight cars arrive via the float bridge, are switched for proper delivery in the small classification yard, and are spotted on the docks or alongside warehouses as specified in the manifest. Later they are picked up and set out on the storage tracks next to the float bridge to await primary movement to destination by car float. Switching combinations are limited only by the imagination of the operator. Motive power on such a line might consist of one or two tank switchers or Geep diesels. They might leave the line at day's end via car float for servicing at a trunk-line engine terminal for the next day's work.

The real secret of Bay Street Connecting's small size, hence portability, lies in something more than the limited area served by the fictional prototype. Compare the prototype track plan with the layout plan. True, several dock and warehouse spurs have been eliminated in the model plan; but we have also done something considerably more important. We have designed the layout as an *undisguised schematic* of its prototype. Let's examine this term more carefully, for it involves the second fundamental concept of track planning mentioned earlier.

Let's suppose we have built a standard one-lap layout with a yard, engine terminal, and various industrial sidings. We want a control panel that will let us operate the railroad without having to scrutinize each toggle switch and pushbutton mounted on the panel, so we paint a diagram of the track layout on the control panel and mount our switches and pushbuttons at the appropriate places. Each industrial siding and yard track is clearly indicated. So is the main line; but we deliberately avoid showing relative distances, whether between tracks or between points on the layout — because relative distances are not important! All we want to show is each track and what it

connects to: that is the rationale of a control panel diagram. We call this diagram a *schematic*.

On the layout itself we have tried — with clever arrangement of track, structures and scenery — to create the illusion of a real railroad in miniature. We may have succeeded in our own mind, but examined in a rational light, this *is* illusion. A real railroad runs from here to there; ours goes around and around. We overcome this difficulty by giving our station two names. Now in imagination we operate from point to point. Fine! But what about the actual distance the train travels? It is far too short for even the shortest of main lines. We give our main line distance relative to the length of trains and terminal trackage by having the train circle the oval a few times on its trip from terminal to terminal.

This means the layout is a schematic of a real railroad. (A foot-by-foot model would probably take from one end of a college gymnasium to the other.) Our track and structures and scenery help the imagination overcome the unreality of the short oval main line and the two-stations-with-one-name situation: it helps disguise the basic schematic form of the layout. We can call this type of layout a *disguised schematic*.

The layout plan for the Bay Street Connecting Ry. takes us a step further — no structures nor scenery, no physical attempt to disguise the basic schematic form of the layout. This is an *undisguised schematic*. The modeler's imagination must bear the entire burden of creating the illusion of a prototype railroad; but he has gained an important advantage — more track in less space. Thus he can build a layout on a 14" x 7'-0" board that offers a lot of operating challenge, and yet can spend its "time off" standing quietly out of sight in an apartment closet.

There is a rule for this concept, too: "The greater the capability of the imagination for restoring relative distances without physical props, the more track can be fitted into a given space."

Portable layouts offer the chance to model railroad with a minimum outlay of space, expense, and time. They allow us to practice the fundamental concepts of layout design which we will need to understand when the time comes to build that larger, permanent layout.

BAY STREET CONNECTING RY.

Prototype — not to scale

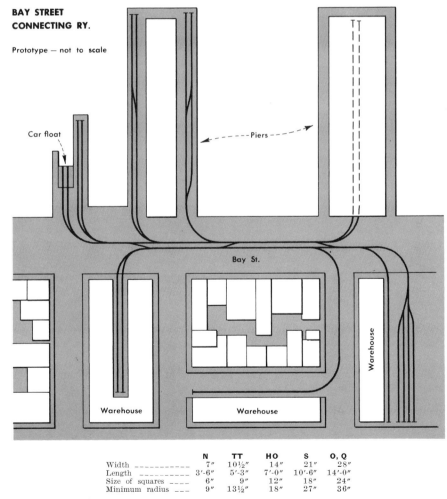

	N	TT	HO	S	O, Q
Width	7"	10½"	14"	21"	28"
Length	3'-6"	5'-3"	7'-0"	10'-6"	14'-0"
Size of squares	6"	9"	12"	18"	24"
Minimum radius	9"	13½"	18"	27"	36"

BAY STREET CONNECTING RY.

Scale: ¾" equals 1'-0"

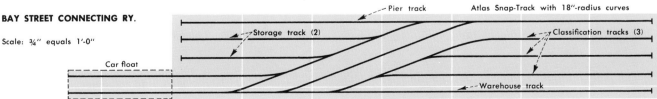

Operations
on the Gum Stump & Snowshoe

Track plan for the man with minimum space

By Chuck Yungkurth

I HAVE no sympathy for the model railroader who says he has no room for a layout. There is *always* room for a layout. It may not be the railroad of your dreams, but it can be something on which you can operate some of your rolling stock. Dock, terminal, and industrial railroads are well suited to small layouts because of their sharp curves and compact switch arrangements.

This belief led me to construct an HO railroad while living in a three-room apartment with my wife and 4-month-old son. There was absolutely no room for a permanent layout. Even the old under-the-bed storage idea was out: I could see the little one approaching the crawling stage already. The obvious place to store the layout was in a closet already occupied by coats, brooms, and other odds and ends. A long, narrow railroad that could be stored vertically in the closet when not in use seemed to be the only answer.

A 1 x 6-foot pine plank was purchased and construction began. I deliberately introduced several complications into the track arrangement in order to lengthen construction time, making it more of a challenge. Among these features were three track levels connected by grades of about 9 percent. I decided to lay the track myself, using tie strip and code 100 brass rail.

The layout, dubbed the Gum Stump & Snowshoe, was described in the September 1963 MR in conjunction with the evolution of my present railroad, the Bellefonte & Snowshoe. The track plan of the GS&S was essentially the same as drawn here, except that on my pike there was another siding at Snowshoe. This has been eliminated to avoid a crossing and custombuilt switchwork. This siding could be worked in if a few more inches were added to the board at the left end, for a switching lead. The layout can be built with sectional HO track, although numerous pieces of track will have to be cut to fully utilize the space on the plank. Flexible track would be simpler.

The perspective sketch is misleading in that it creates a false impression of spaciousness. Things were pretty tightly crammed. One siding at Snowshoe held two standard freight cars, while the other held one. The Gum Stump enginehouse was squeezed between tracks. Instead of embankments, sheer retaining walls had to be provided from rock-carved sheet balsa. The grades also were much steeper than the sketch indicates.

All turnouts were no. 4's except for the no. 6 at the entrance of Gum Stump Yard. I used Atlas switch kits, but most turnouts were "warped" from their original shapes to fit the situation. Some resembled wye switches.

I didn't want to bother with a control panel and track blocks, so I made use of

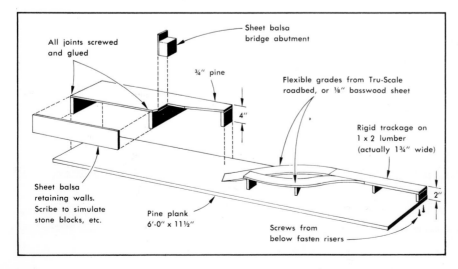

All joints screwed and glued

Sheet balsa bridge abutment

¾" pine

Flexible grades from Tru-Scale roadbed, or ⅛" basswood sheet

4"

Rigid trackage on 1 x 2 lumber (actually 1¾" wide)

Sheet balsa retaining walls. Scribe to simulate stone blocks, etc.

Pine plank 6'-0" x 11½"

Screws from below fasten risers

2"

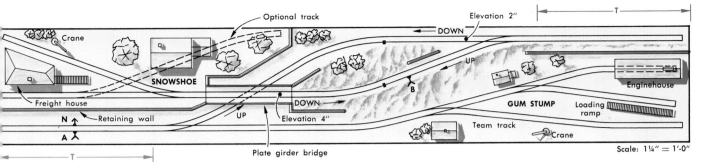

Optional track · Elevation 2″ · DOWN · T · Crane · SNOWSHOE · UP · B · Enginehouse · Freight house · Retaining wall · DOWN · GUM STUMP · Loading ramp · N · UP · Elevation 4″ · Team track · Crane · A · T · Plate girder bridge · Scale: 1¼″ = 1′-0″

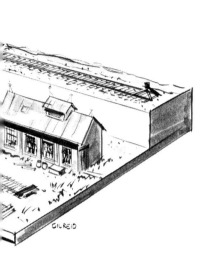

GILREID

the turnout points to direct power to the proper track. [The method is explained in *How to Wire Your Model Railroad*, beginning on page 28.] The drawing differs from my actual wiring, but you can see how simple it can be. Two insulated gaps are needed, and power is connected to the track at points A and B on the S rail, and at point N on the N rail. By throwing turnouts, only one branch or another in the yard and sidetracks gets power.

To me, the most interesting part of operation on the GS&S was that two very short locomotives were needed. There just wasn't any way to incorporate a runaround in the track arrangement without sacrificing virtually all storage trackage. One fellow asked me if it didn't bother me that the locomotives always faced the same direction. My answer was yes, it did; but not nearly as much as the fact that I couldn't run my Bowser Pacific on the railroad.

Operation went something like this: One engine would switch Gum Stump Yard to single out the two cars that would make up a train when hooked up to the four-wheel caboose. The locomotive would then leave the cars on the main and retreat to a spot just under the girder bridge. It was electrically isolated as soon as the turnout to the left was thrown. A second engine from the roundhouse coupled to the other end of the cars. It backed, pulling the three cars into one of the sidings. The other engine then returned to the engine terminal.

Bringing cars into Gum Stump meant a reversal of this procedure. It was common to take half an hour to run a train to Snowshoe and back, including the switching operations at both stations.

The 16″ tails of the switchback (shown as dimensions T on the plan) limited trains to a loco, two cars, and a caboose. I used Ken Kidder's plantation tank locomotives and a very tiny scratchbuilt Huntingdon & Broad Top caboose. (Kadee's logging caboose would do nicely here.) For a while an MEW 44-ton GE diesel was used. A locomotive with a tender was sometimes used to switch Gum Stump, but it was too long to get to Snowshoe with a full train. Shorter old-time cars might possibly have permitted three-car trains.

The layout should present no particular problems even to the beginner. Perhaps the only trouble spot might be the transitions into the very steep grades. It has been my experience that it pays to make these as gradual as possible, both for operation and for appearance. If you use flexible track lengths you can shim and bend the hill trackage until it is smooth. This freedom from joints on the grade is

a big help. Shimming can be concealed with plaster and ballast.

The idea of a 9 or 10 percent grade bothers some people. Steep grades usually present no operation problem with tank engines and short trains. Furthermore, they don't *look* that steep, particularly if you have scenery.

It is somewhat of an art to design and build structures to fit these tight spaces. The odd shape of the freight station at Snowshoe is a good example of what can be done. The enginehouse also would probably have to be built to fit. Buildings can be scratchbuilt, or can be altered plastic or wood kits. Use of lichen should be held to a minimum if the railroad must be moved. A light plywood cover could be made to protect the entire layout if you have much fragile scenery.

With a little careful planning, a layout as small as this one can give many hours of enjoyable model railroading. I feel it is far better than mere armchair model railroading. Also, it keeps you in practice on tracklaying and scenery techniques — valuable experience for the day when you can start work on that dream railroad!

Loco A makes up train consisting of caboose C and two cars.

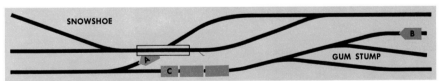

Loco A drops train on main, then backs under bridge.

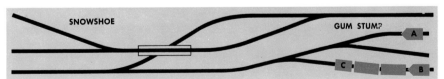

Loco B connects with train, pushes, then pulls it to enter first yard track. Engine A then moves to enginehouse. Engine B can now proceed with train. It is on proper end of train to do switching at Snowshoe.

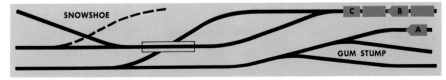

If trailing siding is used at Snowshoe, car for it must be located behind engine.

Thinking big in small spaces

The Pleasant Hill & Sunnyvale RR.: a lot of layout in a 5x8-foot space

BY DON MITCHELL

AT one time or another, most model railroaders find themselves in the quandary of having a special, but large, engine with only a small space for a layout. The favorite locomotive then becomes relegated to running back and forth on a short length of track or, even worse, to static display on the bookcase. The Pleasant Hill & Sunnyvale RR. provides a place where the large engine can get out and stretch its legs occasionally, although most service would be more appropriately provided by small and medium-size engines.

The 5 x 8-foot dimensions of the PH&S result from mating the long sides of two movable modules described in the June 1974 issue of MODEL RAILROADER. Within these dimensions,[1] the PH&S provides a reasonable run which can be extended by continuous lap running; ample car capacity among the small yard and many industry tracks; engine facilities, including a wye for reversing; and enough subtle surprises to keep the switching-problem enthusiast from becoming jaded.

There is no particular geographical locale associated with the PH&S; rather, it is typical of the many short or connecting lines scattered across the country. If that big engine is an articulated, however, it might be prudent to set the

[1]Any modeler building the PH&S should adhere closely to the vertical limit of 12″ between the bottom of the table framework and the top of the highest permanent scenic feature. Exceeding this limit will very likely cause problems when moving the layout.

scene in a benevolent climate, as there is no easy way to stretch the enginehouse tracks to provide for totally covered storage.

In our imaginary setting, Pleasant Hill is both the center point of the line and the center of activity. Here are located the main offices, the yard and engine facilities, and the major concentration of industries. The original builders of the PH&S weren't blessed by these sources of carload revenue, however. Like many other early-day promoters, their prime objective was to provide railroad service to their hometown of Pleasant Hill when the major line in the area elected to route its main line elsewhere.

After the initial euphoria of their success in connecting Pleasant Hill with the main line at Sunnyvale wore off, the builders gradually had reality brought home to them by the small amount of revenue generated by the passenger and farming traffic that used the line on a continuing basis. Despite active promotions of weekend picnic and ballgame specials, the small line looked like it was struggling to a certain demise until the son of one of the owners returned from completion of his studies at a far-off university.

He quickly perceived that an extension westward from Pleasant Hill to Rio Vista Junction would give the PH&S

a route connecting two major lines at quite a saving in time and distance over any existing connection between the two big railroads. In short order the extension was built, and soon large amounts of traffic were flowing between Sunnyvale and Rio Vista Junction. This traffic brought a period of prosperity to the PH&S, and these prosperous times saw the roadbed and motive power upgraded several times to handle the increased traffic, until the PH&S itself was practically a main line.

But time and merger know no bounds, and eventually the two major railroads became one. The sight of a short line waxing profitable by making connections between two points on their own line did not sit well in the corporate offices of the major line, and they soon embarked on construction of their own connection. The day the new bypass opened is remembered by all associated with the PH&S as its blackest day. Traffic dried up almost instantaneously without reducing by one whit the interest payments on money borrowed to upgrade the PH&S so it could handle the previously heavy traffic.

Bankruptcy soon followed—another gloomy day in the PH&S annals, but one which is now looked on as a fortuitous stroke of luck, for bankruptcy brought a far-sighted individual to the little line in the person of the court-appointed receiver. And like the owner's son, who in an earlier crisis saw a way to save the line, the receiver was

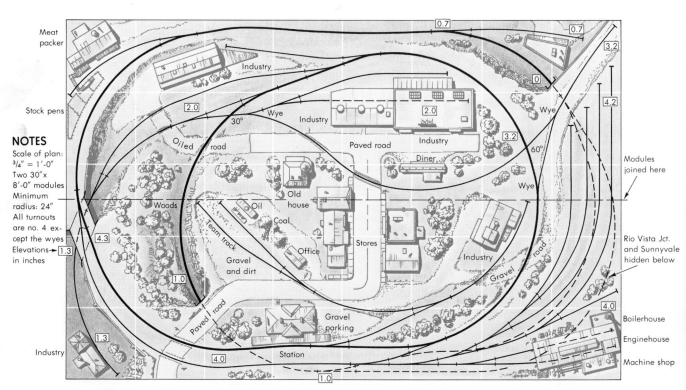

NOTES

Scale of plan:
³/₄″ = 1′-0″
Two 30″x
8′-0″ modules
Minimum
radius: 24″
All turnouts
are no. 4 except the wyes
Elevations
in inches

Meat packer
Stock pens
Industry
Wye
Industry
30°
Oiled road
Paved road
Industry
Diner
2.0
2.0
3.2
60°
Wye
0.7
0.7
3.2
0
4.2
Woods
Oil
Old house
Coal
Team track
Office
Stores
Industry
Gravel and dirt
4.3
1.3
1.0
Gravel road
Wye
Modules joined here
Rio Vista Jct. and Sunnyvale hidden below
Paved road
1.3
Gravel parking
4.0
Industry
4.0
Station
Paved road
1.0
4.0
Boilerhouse
Enginehouse
Machine shop

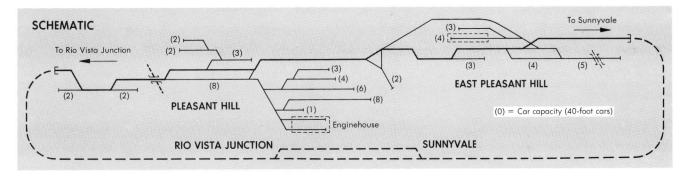

SCHEMATIC

To Rio Vista Junction

(2)
(2)
(3)

(8)

PLEASANT HILL

(2)   (2)

(3)
(4)
(6)
(8)

(1)

Enginehouse

(3)
(4)

(2)

(3)
(4)

To Sunnyvale

(5)

EAST PLEASANT HILL

(0) = Car capacity (40-foot cars)

RIO VISTA JUNCTION

SUNNYVALE

struck by the amount of land the PH&S had acquired at the east end of Pleasant Hill for building a new and bigger yard.

A yard wasn't what the line needed — a source of car loadings was. And what better site could be found than in East Pleasant Hill, and all that railroad-owned land? It wasn't an easy job at first to find companies that were interested in locating, but persistence eventually paid off. Not the least of the talking points was the high-quality transportation offered by the PH&S — good connections and a potentially high-capacity plant, once the deferred maintenance caused by the bankruptcy had been worked off. A combination of real estate sales and leasing and increased carloadings soon had the PH&S back on its feet, and it looks secure for the foreseeable future.

The thumbnail recital of the history of the PH&S should provide accommodation for a wide variety of interests, ranging from old-time steam engines and short cars to modern-day diesels, with intermediate stops at pure branchline operations or representation of a segment of main line. The limiting factor will be how appropriate the short trains (which are limited by the length of the passing sidings and yard tracks) will look to the individual modeler if they are headed by truly big and modern locomotives.

Only relatively small changes in the history of the PH&S would have to be made to turn the line into an interurban turned freight-hauler. Wire-hangers, as well as other modelers, should appreciate the engineering of the PH&S, which has put all turnouts within 18″ of a table edge, for easy construction and maintenance.

Other layout engineering features are

curves plotted at 24″ minimum radius,[2] no. 4 turnouts, 3″ separation between track centers on the main line, and the general location of industrial tracks in front of buildings so that cars can easily be seen while conducting spotting movements. Note, too, that tracks at higher elevations are on the inside of curves when they are near tracks at lower elevation. Any overhang of equipment thus goes into empty air rather than colliding with projecting scenic features.

To my mind, the PH&S would look best if built with small rail. Scratchbuilders have the option of using codes 55, 70, and 83 in order to develop some visual differentiation between primary and secondary trackage. Others should be able to obtain very pleasing results from the many fine code 70 ready-to-lay products on the market in HO gauge.

One caution, however, if commercial components are used — turnout and crossing locations are fairly critical if the design is to be built as shown. In particular, most turnouts will require quite a bit of trimming to maintain the minimum frog-to-succeeding-point spacing that has been calculated on the basis of the dimensions given in NMRA Recommended Practices sheet 12.3.[3]

Another caution should be observed where tracks cross over one another.

[2]While minimum-radius curves are drawn to 24″, actual construction should consist of eased curves of 23″ radius for best results with long equipment. See TRACK PLANNING FOR REALISTIC OPERATION, by John Armstrong, for a full discussion on the benefits to be gained from using eased curves.

[3]The National Model Railroad Association was formed to provide standards that would permit interchange operation of model railroad equipment of a specific scale. The NMRA also issues Recommended Practices for factors not directly involved in interchange operation. Membership is $10 per year, from the NMRA, P. O. Box 2186, Indianapolis, Ind. 46204. Membership entitles the member to a monthly *Bulletin*, among other benefits.

Railhead-to-railhead separation has been engineered at 3″, thus making overhead clearance somewhat under that specified for HO scale in NMRA S7. The exact amount of clearance will depend on the thickness of the material used in supporting the upper track. This limitation is imposed mostly by the grade between the tunnel entrance leading to Rio Vista Junction and the turnout at the west end of the Pleasant Hill passing siding. This grade is calculated at 4 percent, allowing for leveling off at turnout locations. The 4 percent figure is not sacred, especially in view of the short trains likely to be encountered, but the 4.3″ elevation at Pleasant Hill does relate directly to the total height of the layout.

Revising clearances to comply with the NMRA standard will result in changing the grades and elevations at most points on the layout. Other than the 4 percent grade already discussed, the grades elsewhere on the PH&S average around 2 percent. These generally will increase as a result of any attempt to increase over/under track crossing clearances.

As mentioned previously, access to all trackwork is excellent for ease in construction and maintenance. Since a small layout implies lack of a larger space in most instances, one or more sides of the PH&S will likely end up butted against a wall. I would not recommend building this layout, however, unless there is enough space available so that only one of the shorter ends has to be butted against a wall. In the case of the PH&S, this should be the left end, so that there will still be ready access to the hidden trackage, the yard, and most of the industrial trackage.

This same ease of access also makes

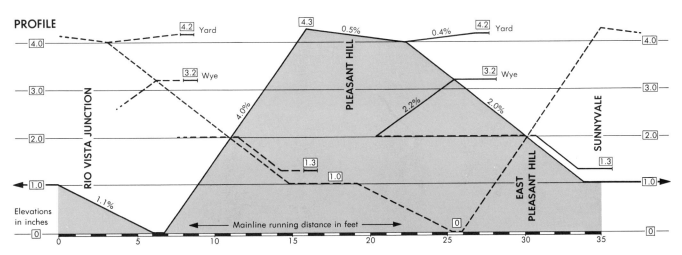

PROFILE

Elevations in inches

Mainline running distance in feet

for ease of operation. Some form of walkaround throttle control would probably give the most satisfaction, while turnout control could be by manual devices except for the hidden trackage representing Sunnyvale and Rio Vista Junction. Electrically operated turnouts would also be advisable at the left end of the layout if it were butted against a wall.

A typical day's operation starts with the arrival of the mainline connection from Sunnyvale. Arriving at Pleasant Hill, the cars are sorted for delivery to local industries or for forwarding to Rio Vista Junction. After sorting, the local switcher starts making deliveries to and pickups from industries in and around Pleasant Hill. Sometime near the end of its endeavors, the connection from Rio Vista Junction arrives. A great deal of hustle and bustle ensues as the pickups from industries and the connecting cars to Sunnyvale are made up into a train and dispatched. The switcher then sorts the remainder of the arrivals from Rio Vista Junction and delivers them to their destinations. While doing this, it makes any remaining pickups of cars for Rio Vista and, returning to Pleasant Hill, puts them in the departing westbound connection. In the meantime, the engine from Rio Vista Junction is turned and serviced. Coupling onto its train, it leaves Pleasant Hill. On arriving at its destination (the hidden trackage), the day's work is completed, and everything is in position to start a new cycle.

Operators will find many little delights hidden among the track patterns. For example, the tail track for the switchback in Pleasant Hill should be just long enough to clear the usual switch engine plus two 40-foot cars. The builder can then let his eyes gleam with delight as he routes one 40-footer and one 50-footer to that area, to the consternation of the unwary operator. Likewise, switching East Pleasant Hill involves use of the runaround and the east end of the wye track. If the industry at the end of this track gets busy

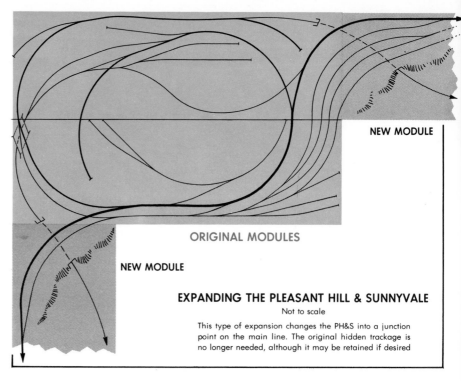

NEW MODULE

ORIGINAL MODULES

NEW MODULE

EXPANDING THE PLEASANT HILL & SUNNYVALE
Not to scale

This type of expansion changes the PH&S into a junction point on the main line. The original hidden trackage is no longer needed, although it may be retained if desired

and more than two cars are spotted there, the whole business of switching in this area suddenly involves many more moves than normal.

If these and the other features not discussed still leave the modeler desirous of more, there is room for additional industries in Pleasant Hill. Adding these will mean taking exception to the 18″ design limitation—something that should not be done lightly. More industry tracks will likewise mean more tracks crossing the boundary between the two modules—a potential source of alignment problems after each move.

Since one of the prime purposes of building modules with the dimensions and limits shown is to preserve the layout through several relocations, some thought should be given to expansion possibilities for that time when space does become available for a larger layout. Expansion is relatively easy, as is suggested in the sketch. The PH&S can be incorporated into a larger layout as a segment of the main line, because the moderately liberal curves and clearances engineered into the original sections permit regular use of most mainline power. If, however, by the time a chance for expansion comes along, the builder has become enamored with the shortline flavor of the PH&S, it can be retained as is by replacing the imagined main line connections with real connections.

And for those modelers who elect to build the PH&S without having or planning to acquire any large motive power, the line's slogan might well turn out to be "The Road to Temptation."

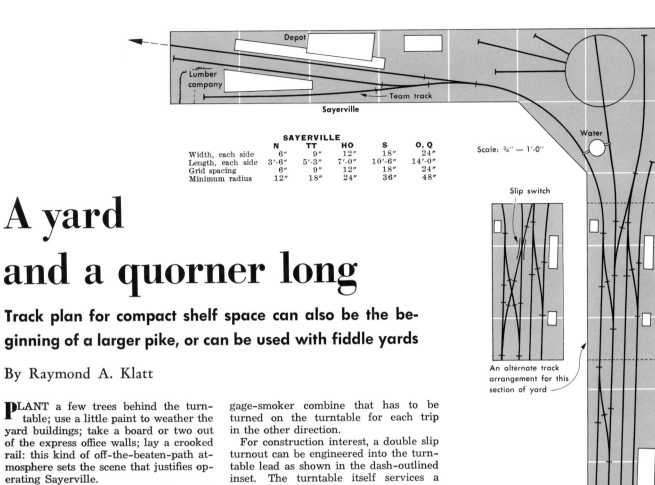

SAYERVILLE				
	N	TT	HO	S	O, Q
Width, each side	6″	9″	12″	18″	24″
Length, each side	3'-6″	5'-3″	7'-0″	10'-6″	14'-0″
Grid spacing	6″	9″	12″	18″	24″
Minimum radius	12″	18″	24″	36″	48″

Scale: ¾″ = 1'-0″

Slip switch

An alternate track arrangement for this section of yard

Water

Freight

A yard and a quorner long

Track plan for compact shelf space can also be the beginning of a larger pike, or can be used with fiddle yards

By Raymond A. Klatt

PLANT a few trees behind the turntable; use a little paint to weather the yard buildings; take a board or two out of the express office walls; lay a crooked rail: this kind of off-the-beaten-path atmosphere sets the scene that justifies operating Sayerville.

Sayerville is a very compact place, well suited to modeling in an apartment, a bedroom corner, or even on a pantry or potato cellar shelf. The shelf is only 1 foot wide if you model in HO, 2 feet in O, 6″ in N. Other scales are comparatively narrow. The shelves extend 7 feet each way in HO, only 3½ feet in N, and so on.

In spite of its settled atmosphere, Sayerville has a team track across from the passenger station, and Cordwell Lumber Co. has a truck there waiting for almost every freight that happens through. The freight station is at the other end of town — as well as on the other side of a three-track yard which is small and confused at best.

A runaround, big enough for two cars, provides a way for the switcher (which could be an 0-4-0T or a Plymouth diesel) to shuffle cars as necessary to distribute them to the local sidings, and to block cars headed for other destinations. That central yard track gets filled with refrigerator cars at harvesting time when fresh lettuce, carrots, and beans are shipped from the nearby farm acreage of the Blue Midget Food Packers.

Sayerville also just happens to be midway between two towns that provide much of the gainful employment of the area, so passenger service for factory and office employees is required in two directions morning and evening. Not *much* passenger service, admittedly — but a couple of cars in a couple of trains a day have to be spotted at the station. One of the trains carries a head-end baggage-smoker combine that has to be turned on the turntable for each trip in the other direction.

For construction interest, a double slip turnout can be engineered into the turntable lead as shown in the dash-outlined inset. The turntable itself services a medium and a long track for loco storage. There is also a very short track for trucks, wheels, a handcar, or what have you — just so it's a bit cluttered around the area. The water tank can be left as it comes, or you can add interest by putting an extra spout on the turntable approach track side of it. The mainline side should have a spout, regardless.

If you ever drop by the railroad facilities at Sayerville, give my regards to the yard foreman. Get him to tell you about the time no. 17 plowed into the water tank when a fishplate gave way on that 24″ radius curve — one of the more exciting moments in somnolent Sayerville.

Scale of both plans: ³/₄" equals 1'-0"

Fig. 1

Curved backdrop

Yard and locomotive servicing

Town

Team track

Two track plans
for an L-shaped space

BY ED VONDRAK

Industries in relief or painted on backdrop

This spur could be an interchange track

Up

Up

Fig. 2

Wharf

Up

Wharf

Down

Part of this spur could be a team track or a locomotive service area

ONCE upon a time there was a need for a track plan for an HO layout to fulfill these criteria: that it fit an L-shaped space, 6 feet overall along one leg and 8 feet overall along the other leg; that the depth of each leg be limited to approximately 18" (but the corner may be deeper); that there be continuous-run provision if at all possible; that there be opportunities for switching; and that there be opportunities for building several different types of scenery.

The brain was put to work, and these criteria were met to my satisfaction by the track plan shown in fig. 1, if one will accept 15" minimum radius, no. 4 turnouts, and grades of 4 percent or 5 percent. (However, all spurs where rolling stock will be left standing should be almost level, unless you use some artificial technique to keep lone cars in place on a grade.)

There are a number of different ways to arrange the turnouts in the runaround and yard throat area. The configuration shown in fig. 1 appeared to be one of the best, allowing the runaround track and the shortest yard tracks to each hold two cars in the clear, and allowing the possibility of setting up some pretty complicated switching puzzles to get cars from one industry to another. The team track crossing would have to be custom-built, but it would add so much operation that it should be well worth the effort to include it. Admittedly, there is a terrible S curve at that point, but that should be no problem if switching is done slowly.

The track plan in fig. 1 also offers ample opportunity for building various types of scenery: a switchyard, small town, waterfront, and bluffs overlooking the lower elevations. Areas requiring steep changes in ground level offer the chance to model rock cuts and/or retaining walls. For those who want to try something fancy, the road disappearing into the background could provide an opportunity to experiment with forced perspective: making the road physically narrower as it recedes, in order to make the background appear to be farther away.

If space is really at a premium, the track plan in fig. 2 might fill the bill. This track plan lacks a continuous-run loop but requires minimal space while still maintaining complex switching opportunities and a chance to model several types of scenery. With only one runaround track in the whole plan, you have to think well ahead in planning switching moves or you may find yourself traveling several miles just to get a car on the other end of the locomotive. If desired, a second, short runaround track could be squeezed in at the upper right by adding a crossover between the industrial tracks. The question of whether or not to include that would depend on what kind of operation you want.

It should be noted that structures on both layouts shown here should be as small as possible while still maintaining believability. As mentioned in MR before, the slogan "Think small and tall" is quite apropos here for both town buildings and industries. Also, a person building a small pike should include as much detail as possible to make the layout seem larger.

Wharf and industry track plan

By Rod Whitmore

Vancouver Power & Transportation Co. offers fine possibilities for operation, track construction, and scratchbuilding of structures

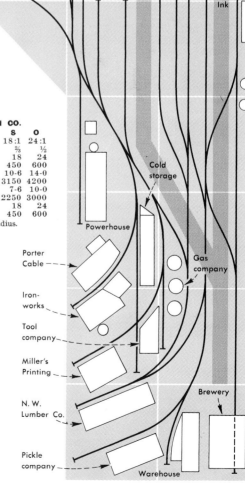

HERE'S a track plan for the man who likes trackwork, operation, scratchbuilding, or any combination of the three. For tracklayers, the crossings and turnouts will challenge the skill of almost any modeler. For the guy who likes experimenting with card order systems and the like, there are enough sidings and industries to keep a dispatcher and a crew of two busy many an evening. Scratchbuilders could spend a winter or two working on structures, cars, and motive power.

This layout interests me for its possibilities for a traction project, although it could also be used just as well with steam dummies or other tank engines, or with short diesels. The Vancouver Power & Transportation Co. is centered in the older industrial part of town built around 1890. I chose Vancouver because its port adds an excellent destination for cars. You could choose any port city: Seattle, New York, Gulfport; or Milwaukee or Chicago on freshwater — or make up your own name.

I strongly suggest using a momentum-type transistor throttle to operate this kind of layout, and to wire the track for cab control with a separate block for

each industry. Block control is described thoroughly in the book *How to Wire Your Model Railroad*.

You can model this layout literally or you can make use of some of its ideas in a version of your own. It can be used as a self-sufficient system or be incorporated into a larger system: for instance, in the manner John Allen combined part of his original small layout with his present larger pike.

VANCOUVER POWER & TRANSPORTATION CO.

	N	TT	HO	S	O
Scale modeled	N	TT	HO	S	O
Drawing reduction	6:1	9:1	12:1	18:1	24:1
Scale of drawing per foot, in.	2	1⅓	1	⅔	½
Spacing of rulings ___in.	6	9	12	18	24
mm.	150	225	300	450	600
Length ___ft.-in.	3-6	5-3	7-0	10-6	14-0
mm.	1050	1575	2100	3150	4200
Width ___ft.-in.	2-6	3-9	5-0	7-6	10-0
mm.	750	1125	1500	2250	3000
Minimum radius ___in.	6	9	12	18	24
mm.	150	225	300	450	600

Turnout size: no. 4, all scales. Use curves of uniform radius.

Destinations unlimited: a compact layout

By Michael R. Welch

THE major problem facing a modeler with minimum space for a model railroad is: what kind of a track plan will fit the space and also provide maximum operating interest? Two alternatives might be the belt line of minimum radius versus the shelf layout with parallel tracks interconnected by complicated switchwork, but both of these ideas suffer from the same complaint: after completion, the train doesn't go anywhere; whether round and round or back and forth, it remains in the same locale.

This is not realistic. Railroads exist, for the most part, to move goods and passengers from one place to another. To represent this in model form, the train at least must *seem* to travel from Here to There, even if There is only a few actual feet from Here. Two basic operations are involved in prototype railroading: yard switching (making up and breaking up trains) and along-the-route switching, and through train movements. The first offers the most detailed maneuvering; the second, the most colorful action. Faced with the compromises demanded by limited space, complex operation seems to me the preferred choice; yet there is always the thought that occasionally it would be nice to see a heavy mainline coal drag fighting its way up a mountain grade, or a red ball reefer hotshot flashing across the plains.

This combination of both industrial switching and mainline operation is the idea that guided the development of the Greenbrier Central. It is a coal road that connects the coalfields of West Virginia with the steel mills and generating plants of the Midwest via a wharf on Lake Erie. Despite having a main line of about half a scale mile, the impression that the road traverses some 500 miles is created.

Station names help create this effect. The Blue Ridge mine area has a name representative of the mining country. Cumberland logically represents the interchange point with the Baltimore & Ohio. The main line continues through western Pennsylvania to northeastern Ohio, to the second major town of North Euclid (located outside of Cleveland) and to the coal-unloading pier at Port Erie.

Cumberland and North Euclid are industrial towns. Each has a half dozen industries which should be chosen to provide rail traffic between the two cities as well as to interchange with the B&O. Possible industries to generate this cross traffic might be: grain elevator, furniture factory, metal fabrication plant, building supply yard, container factory, hardware maker or supplier. A general merchandise supply house might be located at Cumberland, a farm machinery plant at North Euclid. Each town also has a team track to service industries not on line. And since almost all types of industry can be reached via the B&O interchange, any type of freight car might logically appear on GC tracks.

Some of the major traffic commodity, coal, is shipped from the mine to on-line industries and coalyards. More of it goes to the B&O interchange; trainloads go to Port Erie destined for the Detroit and Gary steel mills, some possibly for translake shipment to Canadian ports. This moves in solid hopper car drags made up in Cumberland. There can also be some shipment of low-grade coal from the B&O interchange to Port Erie. The unloading pier at Port Erie is a steel trestle with undertrack storage bins from which coal is chuted directly into the holds of the lake carriers.

The minimum radius is held to the figures shown for each scale in the track plan data table to allow for a heavy train of hoppers plus an engine of appropriate size. The two passing sidings are approximately six carlengths long. Shortness is an advantage here: the short main line can be kept busy with many train movements of shorter trains rather than longer and fewer trains. Normally cars move directly from the industries of one town to their destination, so no storage yard is provided (primarily due to lack of space), but one of the passing siding tracks can be used for temporary storage when necessary. If there is room to add one more track beside both the Cumberland and North Euclid runaround tracks, car variety can be increased considerably. The lack of space dictates the minimum engine facilities at Cumberland: water tower, sand bin, ashpit, and a conveyor for loading coal into tenders.

Passenger service on the GC would be minimal. A single baggage-coach combine, normally stored on the Cumberland team track, would suffice. It could travel unceremoniously at the rear of a way freight or, with a locomotive of its own, make its way grandly along the line, possibly as the Black Diamond Limited.

- B&O

5.0

No need to have straight borders around the layout if your construction method is sufficiently flexible. Let needs of track and operators determine final boundary

CUMBERLAND

Team track

Station

5.3

5.3
1.7

NORTH EUCLID

BLUE RIDGE

Tipple

22"
26" 30"
24"

5.2

0
3.5

0   PORT ERIE

Team track   Station

GREENBRIER CENTRAL RY.

Scale modeled		N	TT	HO	S	O
Drawing reduction		8:1	12:1	16:1	24:1	32:1
Scale of drawing per foot, in.		1½	1	¾	½	⅜
	per meter, mm.	125	83	63	42	31
Spacing of rulings	in.	6	9	12	18	24
	mm.	150	225	300	450	600
Width, over all	ft.-in.	5-3	7-11	10-6	15-9	21
	meters	1.60	2.40	3.20	4.80	6.40
Length, over all	ft.-in.	5-5	8-1	10-10	16-2	21-8
	meters	1.65	2.48	3.30	4.95	6.60
Minimum radius	in.	11	16.5	22	33	44
	mm.	280	420	560	840	1120
Turnout size		No. 4 or no. 4½, all scales. No. 4½ shown.*				
Multiply elevations by for in.		.5	.75	1	1.5	2
	for mm.	13	19	25	38	50

*Some turnouts labeled no. 4 are actually 4½. Commercial turnouts differ in length and diverging angle. Track location adjustments may have to be made accordingly.

SCALE MODELED	N	TT	HO	S	O
Drawing reduction 1:	6	9	12	18	24
Normal turnout size	No. 4, all scales				
Maximum grade, main lines	2.9 percent, all scales				
SIZES IN INCHES					
Spacing of rulings	6	9	12	18	24
Length of space	60	90	120	180	240
Width of space	22	33	44	66	88
Minimum radius, as drawn	9	13.5	18	27	36
Track center spacing	1.0	1.5	1.9	2.7	3.5
Multiply elevations by	.5	.75	1	1.5	2
SIZES IN MILLIMETERS					
Spacing of rulings	150	225	300	450	600
Length of space	1500	2250	3000	4500	6000
Width of space	550	825	1100	1650	2200
Minimum radius	225	338	450	675	900
Track center spacing	25	38	48	68	89
Multiply elevations by	13	19	25	38	50

Tennessee Southern track plan

BY MICHAEL R. WELCH

THE Tennessee Southern provides operations quite similar to those of the Greenbrier Central, which I described in the May 1968 issue, but the Tennessee Southern has a more compact shape, fitting a room or corner only six or seven times the track radius in length. In the HO size it is 120" or 3 meters.

The layout features one turnback curve plus a double switchback into a hidden storage yard. A train can thus make a run of nearly four times the length of the space per trip.

The concept of operation is to provide a connection from the region on the upper tier with an interchange station at Waynesboro Junction. Here the TS meets the Illinois Central for interchange. The IC itself enters from a dummy tunnel at the top and leaves via the tunnel at the right center to reach the hidden trackage. Either of two Illinois Central trains can be run to the junction for interchange, then back into the tunnels.

This whole complex can be built as shown, or the branch line could be added to a corner of an existing layout along the lines outlined in the At the Throttle editorial about branch lines in the June issue, allowing a variety of trains to appear at Waynesboro Junction.

From Waynesboro Junction the TS winds its way out of the valley through Scragg's Cut to reach Hollow Rock. Here a spur serves a small phosphate strip mine. The railroad continues to Humboldt, the terminal.

Both Waynesboro Junction and Humboldt have four or five industries and a team track. The industries are chosen to concentrate primarily on cross traffic. For instance, the Natchez Natural Phosphate Co. owns a string of ore cars which it uses to transport phosphate to the Maygrow Fertilizer Co. processing plant at Waynesboro via the TS. (These cars serve the purpose of providing special-consist trains on the Tennessee Southern.)

Since there is relatively little track to be built, the TS offers the opportunity to build very well detailed trackwork. This means the use of scale-size rail such as code 70 for HO, individual ties, and proper attention paid to the level of the terrain surrounding the track. Remember that track actually level with the surroundings is almost never seen. Most of the prototype railroads are elevated slightly above the surrounding terrain. Even track in a cutting is raised above the drainage ditches at each side.

Enginehouse

HUMBOLT

Team track

Illinois Central

WAYNESBORO JUNCTION

Custom turnout; or use a wye switch

Interchange and team track

HOLLOW ROCK

Phosphate strip mine

Fertilizer plant

SCRAGG'S CUT

Elevations in inches

Illinois Central

The Buckley & Onarca RR.
a compact plan

Practical design for the man who wants operation in a minimum of space

Track plan and drawings by Bill Baron

THE Buckley & Onarca RR. is a compact plan with both good operating and scenic potential for the modeler who wants a layout in a minimum of space; yet it offers equally good possibility for expansion later should the desire and space become available.

The layout could be built to any scale. The proportion of the drawing matches HO Snap-Track, and it calls for the following components: twenty-three 18″-radius, six ⅓-18″-radius curved sections; forty-two 9″, three 6″, three 3″, one 1½″ straight sections; seven right-hand and eight left-hand turnouts.

As conceived, the Buckley & Onarca represents a typical short line of the early part of the century, with small locomotives and cars servicing the industries in a compact area. The track plan consists of two interlocking ovals with a short stretch of common trackage at the entrance to Buckley Yard. With two control cabs, two trains could be operated: one on the lower level that tunnels under Onarca Hill, the other on the upper level servicing the various industries. The train on the lower level might be considered a mainline run from the trunkline railroad interchange which delivers cars to, and picks them up, at Buckley. When not on the model scene it could go "on the spot" in the tunnel until time for its next appearance.

An exact pattern of operation is not possible in discussing this layout plan, because obviously the type of operation depends to a large extent on the industries actually selected. The mine on the upper level suggests that a daily mine run might be considered to keep the mine furnished with hopper or gondola cars necessary to maintain production. On the other hand, the lumber facility on the little pond might ship only a car every other day. On this comparatively small railroad there are six spots to drop and pick up freight cars.

Passenger service on such a railroad would be minimal: possibly a combine attached to the first train each day to carry workers to their jobs; or for a separate passenger operation, a loco and a single coach could be used.

Scenically, with the hills and valleys shown in the bird's-eye view, the basic framing calls for L-girder construction: this will make the modeling of the undulating terrain easier. Roadbed construction of the plywood-Homasote type used in past MR projects should work well.

The bridges and trestles offer a field day to modelers. The two curved trestles on the right and the one at the lower left are especially challenging. The pile trestle carrying the lumber industry spur across the pond is a type not often seen on layouts. Note that the outlet of the pond is a dam, with the access road to the lumberyard on top.

Note also the use of trees as background scenery and to separate the various tracks at spots where the two lines come comparatively close together.

Should space become available for expansion, the B&O could be used as the central portion of an around-the-walls layout. The switching lead to the lumberyard, angling off to the upper right, would be one point to start expansion. The line could return by way of the upper-level spur at the upper left-hand corner.

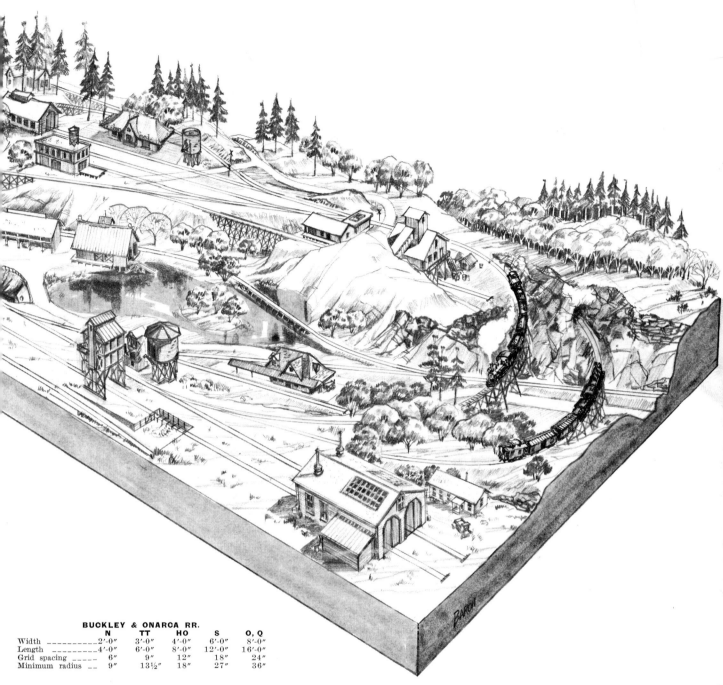

BUCKLEY & ONARCA RR.					
	N	TT	HO	S	O, Q
Width	2'-0"	3'-0"	4'-0"	6'-0"	8'-0"
Length	4'-0"	6'-0"	8'-0"	12'-0"	16'-0"
Grid spacing	6"	9"	12"	18"	24"
Minimum radius	9"	13½"	18"	27"	36"

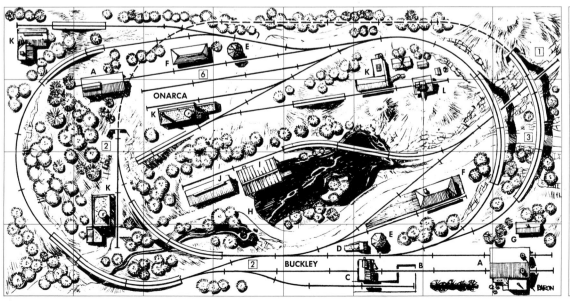

A	Engine-house
B	Ashpit
C	Coal
D	Sand
E	Water
F	Station
G	Office
H	Dam
I	Sawmill
J	Lumber
K	Industry
L	Mine

The Jefferson, Memphis & Northern

A simple, scenic 5 x 9-foot table layout with a Deep South setting

BY ANDY SPERANDEO

THE JEFFERSON, Memphis & Northern is an HO scale railroad which uses a simple track plan to allow as much scenic realism as possible in a 5 x 9-foot space. The idea is to use John Armstrong's principle of "scenic vignettes" and build one simple, railroadlike scene on each side of a central scenic divider. Using sectional track and plastic kit structures, the basic railroad could quickly be brought to apparent completion, so the JM&N would be a good project for someone's first railroad.

However, because it is planned to be scenically satisfying, it can also be a source of lasting enjoyment as scenic effects, structures, details, and rolling stock are refined along with the builder's growth in the hobby. Also, despite the simplicity of the track plan, the Jefferson Yard area can be operated in an interesting and quite realistic manner.

In concept the JM&N represents a portion of a small north-south class-one railroad connecting the Mississippi Gulf Coast with Memphis, Tenn., and perhaps points farther north as well. It is trying to compete with the giant Illinois Central in much the same way as the old Gulf, Mobile & Northern (later merged with the Mobile & Ohio to form the Gulf, Mobile & Ohio, itself later absorbed into Illinois Central Gulf). The particular locale is in northern Mississippi, where there are hills sufficiently rugged to provide justification for the high ridge which divides the layout into two distinct scenes.

Jefferson is a small but important town, perhaps a county seat, where the JM&N connects with the St. Louis-San Francisco (Frisco) line's main line from Memphis to Birmingham, Ala. Jefferson also boasts a small textile mill, which is the major non-agricultural employer in the county, and a few other small industries.

Frenchman's Bend is little more than a hamlet grown up around a general store and a country schoolhouse. The JM&N, which even in the diesel era is a timetable-and-train-order operation, has a small train-order office at the south end of its passenger siding here. There are no living quarters for the operators, so presumably they board with nearby families.

The structures shown are all readily available plastic kits, and most of them are used as their designers intended. A little simple kitbashing is indicated, however, in order to have buildings which fit the theme of the JM&N. The Jefferson feed store, for example, is a Tyco freight station, and the Frenchman's Bend train-order office is an Atlas trackside shanty, both fitted out with new signs and details to serve their new purposes. The Southern Oil Company's bulk depot is a combination of three of the

same Life-Like kits, in order to come up with a facility a bit more imposing than a single tank. The mill is represented by a Heljan warehouse and a Vollmer machine shop painted in matching dusty brick colors and joined on the layout, perhaps adding a moderately tall smokestack.

No effort has been made to fill the available space with structures, just as the track has been kept to a minimum. When something more impressive than the plastic buildings is desired, they can be replaced with kits or with scratchbuilt substitutes rather than filling more space with additional buildings. This approach allows an uncommonly large area for scenery and avoids the overcrowding which is the bane of small layout design.

The scenic treatment shown is meant to be interesting in itself and not merely a collection of tricks to hide an excessive concentration of track. The layout should be built for near-eye-level viewing, either for a standing operator (good) or for an operator seated in a comfortable chair (best). This will allow a central ridge of no more than 8 or 9 inches high to effectively separate the scenes.

Cuts are used to carry the end curves across the ridge, partly because the hills represented aren't big enough to justify tunnels, and partly because tunnels are far too common on small model railroads. The location of the cuts on curves and the road overpass will be more than enough for the needed separation.

The layout could be built on a flat-top table initially, but in that case an early improvement should be to either lower the tabletop, or cut it away (except for the area directly below the tracks) and use open framing under the Frenchman's Bend area. This would allow the creek to run in a steep little valley and would also allow the railroad to be supported on a fill above the creek's floodplain and the hamlet.

Fills, embankments built with material removed from cuts, are a common feature in real railroad construction but are too rarely modeled. A fill is an excellent display setting for watching and photograph-

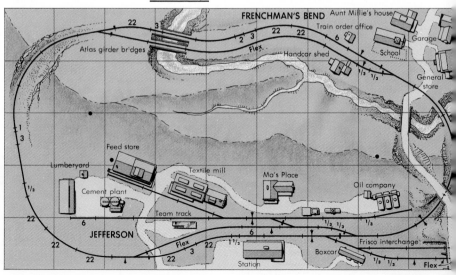

JEFFERSON, MEMPHIS & NORTHERN RR.

Grid lines are 12" apart

Unnoted track sections are either 9"-straight or 18"-radius curved

Gap in one rail

Gap in both rails

Track feeders

R.

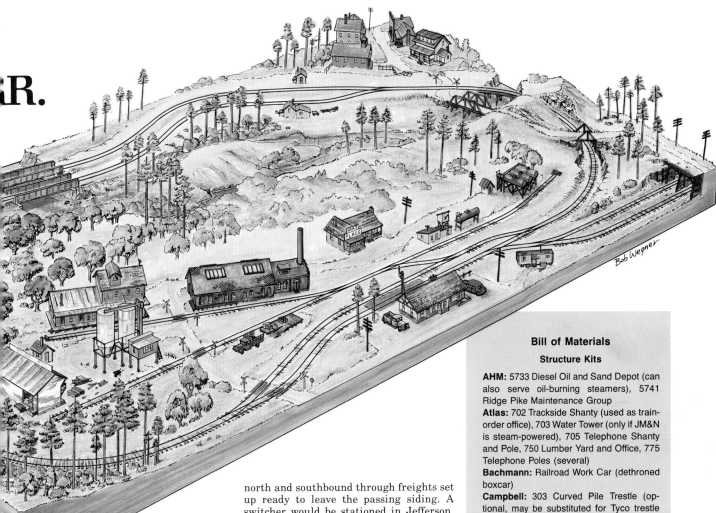

Bob Wegner

ing trains, and is perfectly logical in this location between two cuts.

The ridge spur shown would break up the outline of the main ridge and keep it from being so obviously a scenic divider. It also gives the opportunity to model a small branch flowing into the main creek. The hills would be covered with trees; the locale dictates pines, for which there are several commercial kits.

Locomotives and rolling stock, whether of the steam or diesel eras, should be small and conservative. Ten-Wheelers and Consolidations would be appropriate steam types, and GP7s or RS-2s would serve in more recent times. Although 22″-radius curves are used where possible, the main line has several 18″ curves. It would be best to operate freight service only and to limit even modern cars to a 50-foot maximum length.

The conventional rule says it is possible to operate two trains simultaneously in opposite directions on this layout, because there are two passing sidings on its lap of single track. In practice, however, this would be a pretty dull business of stopping at every siding to meet the other train.

It is possible for one operator to enjoy "serious" operation with a scheme which is at once more relaxed and more realistic. This would use the Frenchman's Bend side of the layout only as a staging area, with

north and southbound through freights set up ready to leave the passing siding. A switcher would be stationed in Jefferson, and the day's work would begin with this engine getting cars out of the industry tracks and the Frisco interchange for the southbound through freight.

When these cars are blocked and spotted in the clear on the Jefferson passing track, the switcher would "go on the spot" (wait) on the engine service track. This would clear the main for the southbound to roll in, pick up the waiting cars, and set out cars for Jefferson and the Frisco. Once this freight was out of town (and back in the Frenchman's Bend siding), the switcher would return to work, spotting the new arrivals and getting out the northbound cars to have them ready for the other through freight.

This sequence could be repeated as many times as desired and would effectively represent the working of a busy through station along a single-track mainline railroad. Even passenger service could be represented by adding a short combine to the through freights in the manner of the Georgia RR. When even this level of operation becomes too strenuous, the JM&N should provide some pretty places to just watch the train roll by.

The Jefferson, Memphis & Northern is a deliberately simple track plan. Because of its small area it doesn't try to do everything, but what it does try to do, it tries to do well, including scenic opportunities, structure settings, and even operation. A newcomer to model railroading could learn a lot about the hobby and his interests with the JM&N, have fun doing it, and come up with a layout of creditable — if not overwhelming — appearance.

Bill of Materials

Structure Kits

AHM: 5733 Diesel Oil and Sand Depot (can also serve oil-burning steamers), 5741 Ridge Pike Maintenance Group
Atlas: 702 Trackside Shanty (used as train-order office), 703 Water Tower (only if JM&N is steam-powered), 705 Telephone Shanty and Pole, 750 Lumber Yard and Office, 775 Telephone Poles (several)
Bachmann: Railroad Work Car (dethroned boxcar)
Campbell: 303 Curved Pile Trestle (optional, may be substituted for Tyco trestle set)
Con-Cor/Heljan: 361 Appliance Warehouse (main building of textile mill)
Kibri: 9950 Cement Towers
Life-Like: 01349 Southern Oil Co. (3 kits), 01351 Al's General Store
Revell: 986 Country Schoolhouse
Tyco: 907 Trestle and Bridge Set (use trestle bents only), 7761 Arlee Station, 7776 Aunt Millie's House, 7779 Ma's Place, 7785 Freight Station (used as feed store), 7793 Speedy Andrews Repair Shop (garage)
Vollmer: 5612 Workshop (boiler house for textile mill)

Atlas Track Required

No. 21 9″ straight — 20
No. 22 6″ straight — 3
No. 23 3″ straight — 4
No. 33 18″-radius curve — 9
No. 35 1/3 18″-radius — 8
No. 36 22″-radius curve — 8
No. 42 Terminal Joiners — 6
No. 47 Track Assortment — 1
No. 52 Remote LH Switch Machine — 1
No. 53 Remote RH Switch Machine — 1
No. 55 Plastic Rail Joiners — 1 pkg.
No. 56 Switch Control Box — 2
No. 85 Through Plate Girder Bridge — 2
No. 100 3-foot length cork roadbed — 16
No. 104 Curvable Track (Brass) 3 feet — 2
No. 121 #4 Custom Line LH Turnout — 3
No. 122 #4 Custom Line RH Turnout — 6
No. 215 Selector — 2
(Control Jefferson switches manually with 3 Caboose Industries no. 204 high-level switchstands for mainline switches, 6 no. 202 ground throws for all others)

Railroad in

WHAT appears to be a large but relatively unobtrusive coffee table can well turn out to be a fairly extensive railroad. Apartment dwellers, or warm-climate dwellers living in slab-on-grade houses, do not have use of a basement and rarely have an attic or spare room for railroad activities — so why not turn a liability into an asset and bring the pike smack into the living room where family and guests may enjoy it too?

This pike is 6'-6" in diameter, which makes for a handy low table when the railroad is covered and allows for a railroad in any small scale with up to 36" maximum radius possible. Many interesting track plans chock-full of operating possibilities can be developed in this circular format. Size does not necessarily need be as generous as shown; smaller-diameter pikes could be developed using minimal radii.

The drawings show a method of construction using screws and glue. This can be varied to suit your own pet methods.

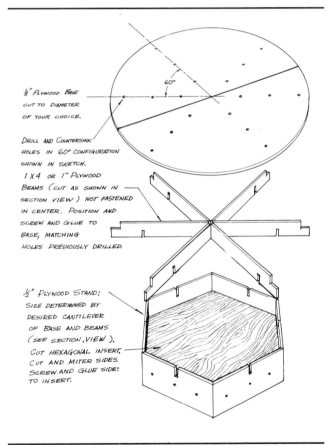

½" PLYWOOD BASE CUT TO DIAMETER OF YOUR CHOICE.

DRILL AND COUNTERSINK HOLES IN 60° CONFIGURATION SHOWN IN SKETCH.

1 X 4 OR 1" PLYWOOD BEAMS (CUT AS SHOWN IN SECTION VIEW) NOT FASTENED IN CENTER. POSITION AND SCREW AND GLUE TO BASE, MATCHING HOLES PREVIOUSLY DRILLED.

½" PLYWOOD STAND: SIZE DETERMINED BY DESIRED CANTILEVER OF BASE AND BEAMS (SEE SECTION VIEW). CUT HEXAGONAL INSERT. CUT AND MITER SIDES. SCREW AND GLUE SIDES TO INSERT.

WALNUT (OR OTHER WOOD) PLY AND FORMICA GLUED TO ½" PLYWOOD TABLETOP

TABLETOP SCREWED AND GLUED TO BARREL CONFIGURATION (SEE SECTION VIEW)

PLY GLUED TO BARREL CONFIGURATION

1 X 4 UPRIGHTS KNOTCHED TO MATCH ½" PLYWOOD STRINGER

UPRIGHT

STRINGER

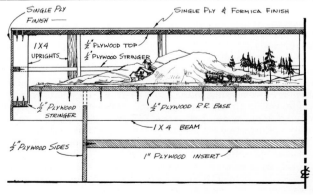

SINGLE PLY FINISH

SINGLE PLY & FORMICA FINISH

1 X 4 UPRIGHTS

½" PLYWOOD TOP
½" PLYWOOD STRINGER

½" PLYWOOD STRINGER

½" PLYWOOD R.R. BASE

1 X 4 BEAM

½" PLYWOOD SIDES

1" PLYWOOD INSERT

coffee table?

By Bill Baron

A compact track plan

THE Somers Junction RR. was conceived to fit a 2'-6" x 6'-8" flush door if built in N scale. The flush door provides a rigid yet relatively thin (1⅜" to 1½") structure on which to build a railroad in 160:1 proportion. A flush door of this size is available at builder's stores or lumberyards. The door can be set atop sawhorses, bricks, concrete blocks, or prefabricated decorative legs. Do not screw legs into the hollow core, however, for there is nothing but cardboard or Celotex inside. Screws won't hold. Bolts going all the way through will hold if extra-large washers are used top and bottom.

The best wood for railroad purposes would be birch or mahogany. Seconds or rejects can be purchased at considerably lower prices than perfect flush doors. The damage on these seconds is barely noticeable in most instances, and since you're going to build a pike atop the door, it doesn't matter if its face is scarred or the corners are nicked.

A hollow-core door, as opposed to a solid-core door, is better to use for railroad purposes because it weighs less. It also allows you more freedom in building scenery. Most hollow-core doors have a Celotex, cardboard, or cardboard-tube core. This means you could cut into the face, remove the core material in that area, and put in a scenic cavity for a pond or a highway underpass. You could also bury a switch machine, or build a downgrade to a quarry or the like, and so on.

Care must be taken not to destroy the structural characteristics of the door by removing too much of its facing or core, however.

The 2'-6" width would be ideal for an apartment dweller. It could become the base of a coffee table if a glass or Plexiglas cover were built to fit over it. With some modifications the door could also be hinged to fold against a wall either horizontally or vertically (allowing for ceiling clearance, of course).

The track could be mounted directly to the face of the door, but it would be much better to add ballast strips for a more realistic appearance. The track could all be on the level, too, but if the track were mounted on ballast boards throughout, grades (developed of ¼" plywood and supports) could raise the rear track to an elevation of 2" (27 scale feet) as indicated on the plan.

Somers Junction Yard is one piece of ¼" plywood supported on 1 x 2's with the track fastened directly to it. It is important to remember that the elevations shown are for track only. The rivers and some of the roads are to be built below the 0" elevation indicated for the track.

Controls for this railroad could be made portable on the ends of cables and tucked into a drawer beneath the layout. Wiring could be installed beneath the scenery, in channels cut out of the door face, or could be bound into cables and tucked beneath the supported track before scenery is finished.

By Bill Baron

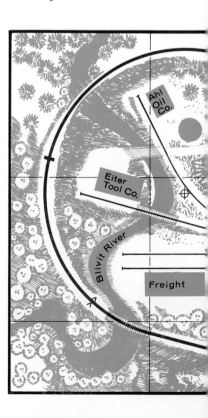

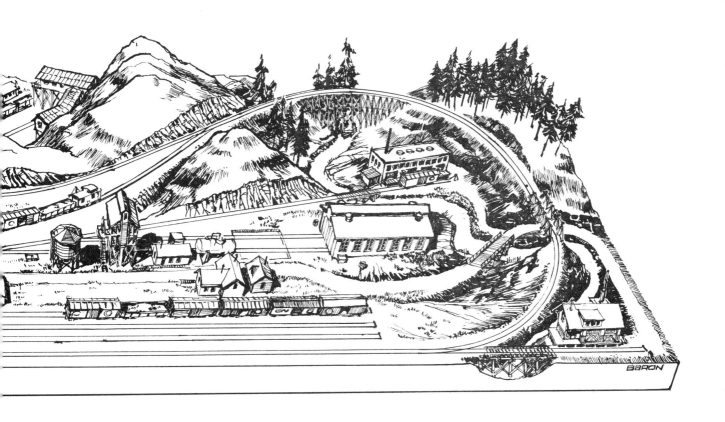

SOMERS JUNCTION RR.

S and O scale layouts will require hatches in the scenery for access to turnouts that are far from table edges.

Different makes of track and turnouts will require moderate adjustments in positions of turnouts and spacing on ladders.

	N	TT	HO	S	O, Q
Scale of drawing to the foot	1½″	1″	¾″	½″	⅜″
Spacing of rulings	12″	18″	24″	36″	48″
Curve radius	12″	18″	24″	36″	48″
Table length	6′-8″	10′	13′-4″	20′	26′-8″
Table width	2′-6″	3′-9″	5′-0″	7′-6″	10′-0″
Multiply elevations by	½″	¾″	1″	1½″	2″

Turnout size: No. 4 or sharper, all scales.

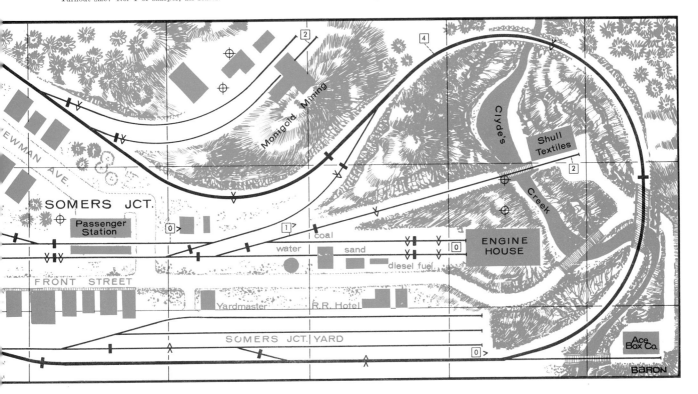

The Texas Subdivision in N Scale

A modern Kansas City Southern-theme track plan for a small space

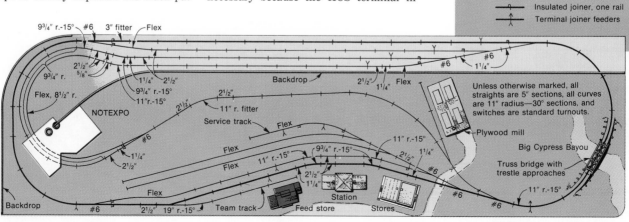

BY ANDY SPERANDEO

MODERN, heavy-duty railroading is, as we all know, impossible to model in a small space. That's why I picked a modern, heavy-duty theme for this 2½ x 9-foot track plan designed to fit along one wall of a bedroom. Using N scale helps a lot, of course, as does picking a prototype carefully.

The Kansas City Southern is the line I chose, specifically a piece of the Dallas, Tex., to Shreveport, La., Texas Subdivision of KCS subsidiary Louisiana & Arkansas. The KCS was featured in a two-part article by Fred W. Frailey in the August and September 1979 issues of TRAINS. The second installment deals in part with current operations on the Texas Subdivision and describes train movements which would be both interesting and practical on a small model railroad. I designed the Texas Subdivision track plan to be able to stage the same kinds of train movements that the KCS does and to give some sense of the prototype's locale. The plan does not attempt to exactly duplicate the track patterns or geography found in the prototype.

The principal through freights on the Texas Sub are numbers 53 and 54, which run between New Orleans and Dallas via Deramus Yard in Shreveport. See the accompanying map. The interesting thing about these trains from a model standpoint is the way the KCS handles them to avoid terminal congestion in both Dallas and Shreveport. The 54, even-numbered because its timetable direction is northward, is scheduled to arrive in Hunt Yard at Greenville, Tex., at 8:00 p.m. daily. There the road crew that brought the train from Shreveport goes off duty, and the yard job begins sorting the cars — blocking them, it's called — for delivery in Dallas. This is necessary because the KCS terminal in

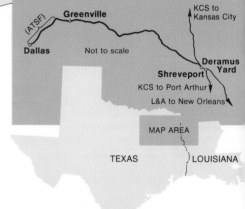

Scale of plan: ¾" equals 12"

⊣⊢ Insulated joiner, one rail

⊥ Terminal joiner feeders

Dallas consists of two tracks leased from the Rock Island and reached over 38 miles of the Santa Fe under a trackage-rights agreement.

When 54 is ready to go to Dallas (scheduled departure from Greenville is 12:30 a.m.), another road crew working a turnaround job out of Hunt Yard takes it in and leaves it on one of the leased tracks, then they pick up whatever cars the connecting lines have left on the other track and return to Greenville as no. 53. Hunt Yard then blocks the train for easy setouts and pickups at Shreveport to keep from tying up busy Deramus Yard. Number 53 is scheduled to leave Greenville at 4:00 p.m., usually with the same crew that brought in 54 the night before.

Hunt Yard is actually a partially dismantled ex-Missouri-Kansas-Texas (Katy) facility and has only three tracks. It thus offers division-point activity in a limited space and can well serve as the focal point of the Texas Sub layout. It's not just a two-train-a-day operation either, at least when business is good. When traffic warrants, KCS adds nos. 55 and 56 to the timetable and runs extras as required. As the TRAINS articles explain, after a period of decline the KCS is upgrading itself and aggressively seeking new business. Which brings us to the coal trains.

KCS salesmen have been promoting the virtues of Wyoming coal to utilities along their line, with the result that several unit coal trains are received from the Burlington Northern at Kansas City for delivery to generating stations on the KCS. One of these run-through unit trains, hauled by a mixture of KCS white and BN green diesels, serves a powerplant at Welsh, Tex., which is east of Greenville on the Texas Sub. It requires only a little modeler's license to locate the North Texas Power & Light Co. power plant just northwest of Greenville and serve it with a similar operation. There isn't really a power plant there, but Thomas S. Carter, KCS president, would be happy if there were.

The prototype Texas Sub also offers another coal train option. White KCS F units, with boosters rebuilt as engineless slugs, haul unit trains of lignite from a strip mine near Sulphur Springs, Tex., to a connection near Pittsburg, Tex., with an automated electric railroad serving a Texas Utilities Generating Co. (TUGCO) power station. The NOTEXPO facility on the model could be a lignite burner, then, and be served by an all-KCS operation. It should be only one or the other, however, as power plants don't generally switch back and forth from bituminous to lignite.

The track plan is a simple loop, with offstage holding tracks to provide through trains to be worked in Hunt Yard. A spur serves the power plant, with more holding tracks connecting with the loop behind the scenes to allow an empties out/loads in unit-train operation. There are a couple of industry spurs to give the Hunt Yard switcher some work between trains, serving businesses typical of the area. More spurs could be added, but I wanted to avoid overcrowding, a common fault of small-layout designs.

The layout as shown uses mostly Atlas sectional track, with some flextrack curves in locations where the parallel sectional track can be used for reference. Of course flextrack could be used exclusively, but there is a certain advantage to the sectional-track approach. A new model railroader could get the basic trackwork for the Texas Sub down very quickly and so have something running while he worked on rolling stock and scenic effects. If you decide to use flextrack, see the third part of Gordon Odegard's Clinchfield series in the January 1979 MODEL RAILROADER for a guide to successful trackwork.

Smooth operation of the Texas Sub layout will require reliable control of trains on the hidden staging tracks. My friend David Barrow, of Austin, Tex., adopted the simple expedient of hanging mirrors near the ceiling so he can see trains behind a backdrop on his railroad. If you would prefer to solve this problem electronically, there are now simple and dependable optical-detection devices available off the shelf which can show where trains are on hidden tracks and even align switches automatically. Although hidden, the staging tracks will be easily accessible from above for cleaning, maintenance, and accident adjustment.

The scenery should suggest a transition from the wooded country of East Texas to the more open farmland and prairies around Dallas. The backdrop will be very

important in this respect, as well as in hiding the offstage trains. Don't be put off by the need for a backdrop. Photographic detail and definition are not required and, in fact, will hurt the layout by drawing the eye from the railroad scene in the foreground. The forest and open, rolling countryside landscape needed would be best done in a sketchy and impressionistic style and wouldn't require any great feats of perspective.

The forest scene at the east end of the layout should be dense enough to hide the trains as they duck through the backdrop — we don't want anything that looks like a tunnel portal in this part of the country. The truss bridge with its low trestle approaches crossing Big Cypress Bayou will be a scenic attraction in itself. You can add to the Texas flavor of the layout by pronouncing the word "bayou" as "bye-oh" (Texans have never learned to deal with this Louisiana word).

Hunt Yard will be the center of interest, of course, but there is room just in front of it for a bit of Greenville's main street to run parallel to the railroad. Such an arrangement, with stores and small industries flanking the railroad station, is common in small towns in East Texas and North Louisiana. The yard will need some engine service equipment and the usual railroad outbuildings, but be sure to keep these facilities as simple as possible. An important theme to capture in representing many modern railroads, particularly the KCS, is economy through simplification of facilities. The fancy name for this is "plant rationalization," and as the terminal situation suggests, it's a definite factor on the Texas Subdivision.

The NOTEXPO generating station will dominate the west end of the layout, and if it seems like a big industrial structure to be stuck out in the middle of nowhere, that's just what modern power plant locations are like. Some kitbashing or scratchbuilding is in order here to allow the coal trains to run through an unloading facility on their way to and from the holding tracks; trains on the main to Dallas will exit to the left by curving around behind the power plant. Tall smokestacks can terminate this end of the freestanding backdrop, and if there's a choice, the rear corner at this end is the one to put into the corner of the room.

If the layout were ever to be expanded, the best bet would be to extend it east from Greenville. Another town or two could justify running a "dodger," or local freight turnaround job, out of Hunt Yard. The lignite strip mine connection could also be included. From a modest beginning, the Texas Sub might well become a fairly extensive system, with enlarged staging tracks for longer and more varied train consists. If your ambitions are large and your space is small, it would be nice to be able to build a small layout with potential for development.

Even as a small layout, however, the Texas Subdivision gets a lot done. It represents a modern, competitive, class-I railroad and one of the areas it serves. It performs some interesting operations in a manner very much like the prototype's. It's a simple plan and offers no great construction difficulties, but many more-complex layouts can't do as good a job of looking like a railroad.

Commuter track plans

Take your pick of the Vicksburg & Eastern RR. or the Union Metropolitan Transit Authority

PLANS BY MICHAEL WELCH

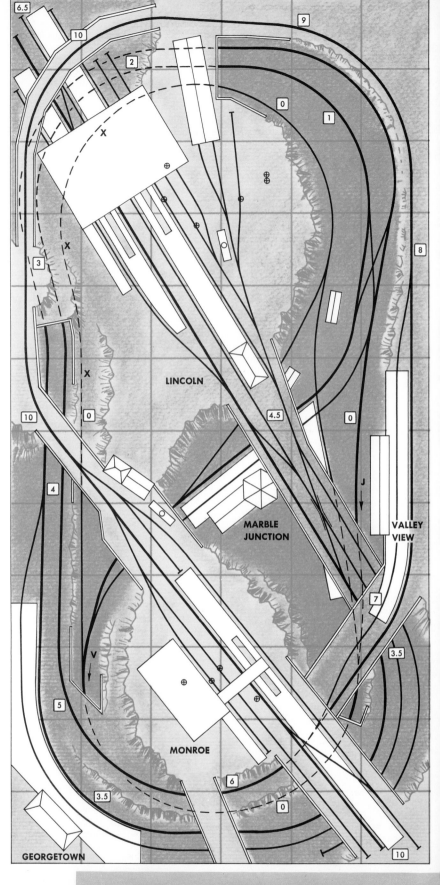

MODEL railroads in tight places usually offer limited operation, such as running round and round or switching freight cars into too-few industrial spots. But if a man wants a lot of action, and if he likes being a towerman operating an interlocking plant just as much as being an engineer or freight conductor, then the commuter railroad provides a fine challenge.

Typically a commuter railroad begins at a multiplatform terminal. Trains swing left and right through the throat switchwork; and there, or as often farther along the line, they take branch tracks to any of several suburban destinations. A few commuter lines such as the Long Island, the Hudson Tubes, or (at one time in the past) the New Haven have a second downtown terminal so that some trains go to one, some to the other. This makes for interesting routing at the junction of the two main lines. Sometimes a commuter line had a line that split to reach some remote place by either of two routes—which rejoined farther out. Each splitting or rejoining of routes provides interesting interlocking plant problems, especially if the junction has more than two diverging branches in each direction.

Commuter trains are often long but they can be short. They usually use double or multiple track, but there are single-track systems. They often have high station platforms, but they can use low platforms with steps provided on the cars. They can operate by steam, electric, or diesel power; with locomotives or self-propelled cars. Self-propelled cars save space on a model railroad but the servicing and turning of locomotives adds a lot of interest if space permits it.

The two track plans on this spread were designed by Michael Welch to fit near-minimum spaces. He had HO in mind. If the same plan were adapted to a space

VICKSBURG & EASTERN RR. or UNION METROPOLITAN TRANSIT					
SCALE MODELED		N	TT	HO	S	O
Drawing reduction 1:		8	12	16	24	32
Maximum mainline gradient, percent		3	3	3	3	3
Normal turnout size, number		4	4	4	4	4
SIZES IN INCHES						
Length of space	ft.-in.	6-0	9-0	12-0	18-0	24-0
Width of space*	ft.-in.	3-0	4-6	6-0	9-0	12-0
Spacing of rulings	in.	6	9	12	18	24
Parallel straight track spacing		1.0	1.5	2.0	3.0	4.0
Parallel curved track spacing		1.5	2.25	3.0	4.5	6.0
Minimum mainline radius		11	16.5	22	33	44
Multiply elevations by	in.	.5	.75	1	1.5	2
*Access hatches will be needed in HO and larger sizes.						

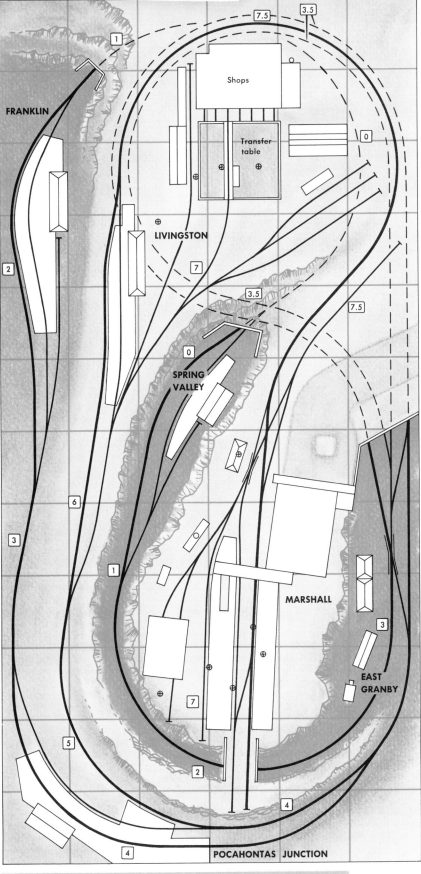

three quarters as long and wide, and then N scale were used, an even more intriguing system could be developed.

VICKSBURG & EASTERN (left plan) serves residential and industrial areas from its main terminal at the city of Lincoln. From this four-track station trains follow the main stem to Marble Junction. Here they can loop back to the terminal or continue on to the more remote town of Monroe. If desired, one can consider that Marble Junction has two more branchings. Trains entering tunnel portal J can be considered as continuing on to an unseen destination, Johnstown. Actually they are held in the tunnel at XX or else run around the lap through XX several times to build operational mileage before returning to Marble as another train. Likewise, trains entering portal V can be considered as going to the suburb of Vicksburg by the same holding or looping manner. Without too much alteration, tunnel XX could be double-tracked to provide a holding track as well as a run-by track so that Vicksburg and Johnstown trains would not block other operations.

Note also that trains from Monroe can loop back to Monroe at Marble or also go on to Johnstown or Vicksburg. The permutations are such that seven different train routings are possible from the two main terminals.

Traffic density? A little scheduling by sequences will provide fairly heavy traffic. Three trains can arrive in quick succession at Lincoln and it will still have an empty platform for another. Additional arrivals can be held along the double track between Lincoln and Georgetown should all platforms be occupied. The looping arrangements through Marble can take trains end to end, and there is a second track plus a side platform besides.

Some of the parallel single trackage of the railroad has been arranged to look like double track in keeping with commuter-system expectations.

When building a pike like this, one should be sure to provide a way to maintain any turnouts that are in hard-to-reach locations. A good plan, also, is to build the lower tiers first, get them performing well, and then add upperwork.

UNION METROPOLITAN TRANSIT (right plan) has a large downtown terminal that is not modeled. Trains thread a tunnel as far as the junction at East Granby. (Actually they are held on trackage within the tunnel until arrival time at EG.) From the junction they diverge to any of three destinations: Franklin and beyond, Spring Valley and beyond, and Livingston, the latter line being modeled to its end at Marshall. The system's motive power shops are at Livingston, while Marshall has a small engine service terminal. Platforms are short, and perhaps RDC's or single electric cars would make up all but the "longest" trains on this system.

When desired, the outer track of the long tunnel can be kept clear; and then trains can be run in lap fashion continuously on this railroad. The inner track can still be a holding track. Gaps divide it into three blocks so trains can be held independently, end to end.

VICKSBURG & EASTERN RR. or UNION METROPOLITAN TRANSIT					
SCALE MODELED	N	TT	HO	S	O
Drawing reduction 1:	8	12	16	24	32
Maximum mainline gradient, percent	3	3	3	3	3
Normal turnout size, number	4	4	4	4	4
METRIC SIZES					
Length of space, centimeters	184.5	277	369	553.5	738
Width of space, centimeters*	92.25	138.5	184.5	277	369
Spacing of rulings, millimeters	150	200	300	400	600
Parallel straight track spacing, millimeters	25	37.5	50	75	100
Parallel curved track spacing, millimeters	37.5	56.25	75	112.5	150
Minimum mainline radius, millimeters	275	412.5	550	825	1100
Multiply elevations by, millimeters	12.5	18.75	25	37.5	50

*Access hatches will be needed in HO and larger sizes.

The Wawbeek & Sunmount Ry.

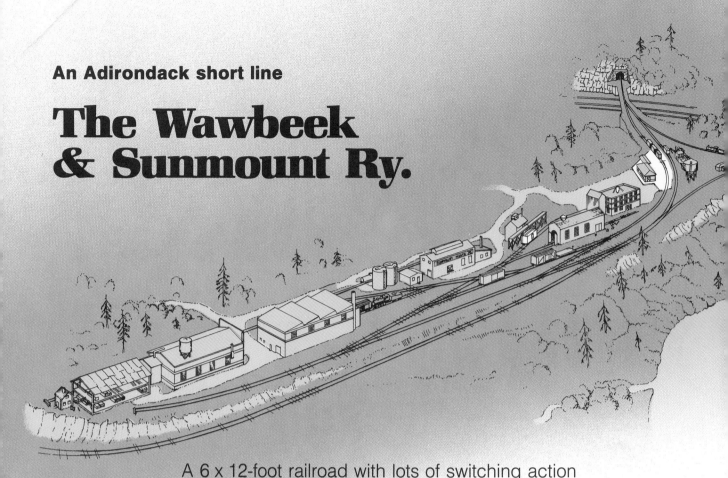

A 6 x 12-foot railroad with lots of switching action

BY LEONARD BLUMENSCHINE

OIL your swivel stool and let's take an HO scale ride on the Wawbeek & Sunmount Ry., from the valley town of Wawbeek around and up the pine-covered hillsides to Sunmount, the western terminal of this mythical mountain short line. I'm partial to Adirondack country, as the place names show. But the W&S would be just as much at home in arid Southwest highlands, the Rockies, or West Virginia hill country — whatever area you're partial to.

I've dotted the many sidings with a variety of customers, but the W&S could just as well specialize in a product like iron or timber. I prefer mixed-traffic business myself, because even on a small road with five- or six-car trains you can still run a colorful mixture of cars. The fun on the W&S lies in the switching and train makeup at the ends of the line, and a single-commodity theme would dampen that.

Wawbeek is sanely laid out with a Delaware & Hudson interchange, industries, a small flat yard, and an engine terminal which can handle most medium-bulk locomotives. Sunmount is a different story: a switchman's paradise, or nightmare, depending on his temper at the moment.

Let's roll. An 0-6-0 has just made up a train on the Wawbeek arrival/departure track and is tacking on a wooden caboose. Something like a venerable Consolidation, or even a small Mikado, comes off the turntable headfirst. After clearing the three-way switch, the road engine backs into the drill track. From there it heads onto the main line to disappear briefly and run

around its waiting train, finally backing in off the main line to couple up. Since Wawbeek is the eastern terminal, all trains leave westbound (to the left) and, naturally, return eastbound.

With a loaded stockcar, a tank car, an empty hopper, and a couple of boxcars behind our engine, we take the curve skirting Wawbeek's industrial district and duck into Long Tunnel. Upon emerging at Saranac we start up a steady 3 percent grade which takes us through the short, curved Saranac Tunnel and on into White Pine. We have some work to do here, so we head into the passing siding and leave the train spotted on the level.

Running around the train via the main, we exchange the empty hopper for a loaded one at the iron mine (both iron and titanium are mined in the Adirondacks). Maybe the *Wawbeek Wailer* will pass us while we're switching here — this local passenger run consists of a combine and a coach pulled by a 4-4-0 with a melodious voice.

We've come about a scale half mile to this point, or once around the layout, and a choice is at hand. Since we pulled into the pass at White Pine, we can take the switch to the left at Madawaska and then head up a final, short 4 percent grade into Sunmount. This strictly point-to-point run would be about 4/5 of a scale mile. But much of the fun of operating the W&S is its continuous-run main line. Depending on your inclinations, the W&S is either a twice-around plan treated as point-to-point

or a point-to-point treated as a twice-around.

But let's not debate it. We haven't seen all the main line yet, so we'll take the crossover route at Madawaska and keep on going downgrade and around. On this second circuit we miss Wawbeek completely, as if it were not there. Since the main sneaks around it behind the upper level scenery, we can think of Wawbeek as being miles behind.

Threading the tunnels and climbing again, we return to White Pine, now a scale mile and a half out of Wawbeek. We again enter the siding and this time take the Sunmount switch at Madawaska. Our old kettle gets a last, brisk workout on the short hill and pulls up just beyond the Sunmount station.

When the main line is treated this way, taking advantage of its detached, continuous-run feature, Sunmount is close to 2 scale miles from Wawbeek — even more if you want to keep taking either the main at White Pine or the crossover at Madawaska. I like this capability of keeping a freight or passenger run making laps on the main line while switch engines work the terminals; the maintracker won't run over a foot of track the switchers need, except when the Wawbeek job has to pull the D&H interchange.

Meanwhile, watch your step at Sunmount, where the yard is laid out to please aficionados of switching puzzles. After the road engine cuts off and backs into the west leg of the wye to wait for servicing, the

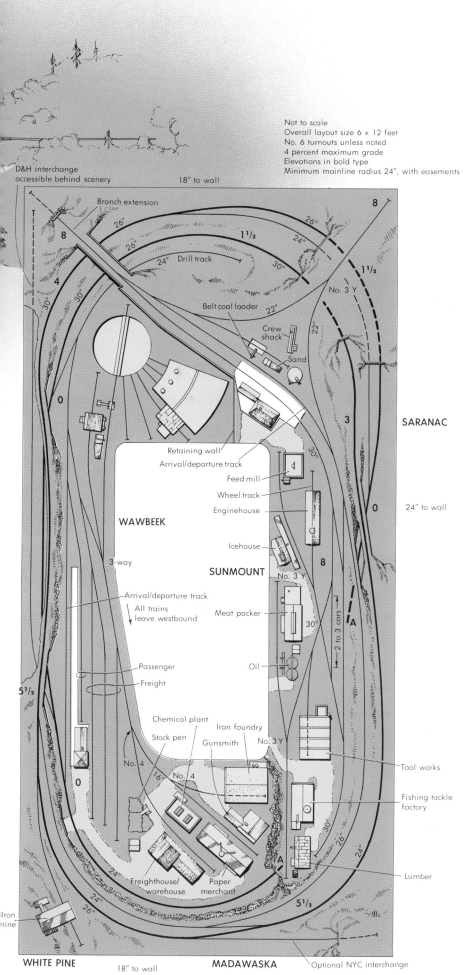

Not to scale
Overall layout size 6 x 12 feet
No. 6 turnouts unless noted
4 percent maximum grade
Elevations in bold type
Minimum mainline radius 24", with easements

D&H interchange
accessible behind scenery

18" to wall

Branch extension

8

26"

26"

26"

24"

1 1/2

8

8

4

Drill track

24"

30"

1 1/2

4

30"

30"

No. 3 Y

Belt coal loader

22"

Crew
shack

22"

Sand

SARANAC

0

Retaining wall

30"

3

Arrival/departure track

Feed mill

Wheel track

24" to wall

Enginehouse

WAWBEEK

0

Icehouse

SUNMOUNT

8

No. 3 Y

3-way

Arrival/departure track

All trains
leave westbound

Meat packer

A

2 to 3 cars

30"

Passenger

Oil

Freight

5 1/2

Chemical plant

Iron foundry

No. 3 Y

Stock pen

Gunsmith

Tool works

No. 4

No. 4

0

Fishing tackle
factory

30"

A

Freighthouse/
warehouse

Paper
merchant

Lumber

24"

26"

24"

Iron
mine

24"

26"

5 1/2

WHITE PINE

18" to wall

MADAWASKA

Optional NYC interchange

Sunmount goat sets the cabo[...]
leg of the wye near the crew s[...]
to work on the train. What [...]
back-and-forth, back-and-forth dance with
a car or two at a time. The outbound cars
from the Sunmount industries must be
pulled and set on the track nearest the depot, as the new arrivals are spotted, to keep
the switchbacks and short runaround reasonably fluid.

I'll pause for a moment while you study
the interlaced industrial spurs and the
end-to-end runaround tracks. If you enjoy
switching, Sunmount is the place to be,
and when your shift is over you'll find a
highly recommended resort/sanitarium not
far up the road.

When the arriving train has been broken
up and spotted, the cars for the next eastbound should be standing on the station
track. This leaves the arrival/departure
track clear for the road engine to complete
its turn around the wye and pick up the
caboose. After setting the caboose on the
train, the engine can top-off at the coal,
sand, and water facilities. It can then couple up to its train and get the whole outfit
onto the arrival/departure track with a
switchback move up the tail track behind
the Sunmount Lumber Co. Or it could re-
tire momentarily to the east leg of the wye
and wait while the switcher moves the
train out; this would allow the switch crew
to sort the train into the proper order. One
way or another, the train ends up ready to
drop down the hill to Madawaska and take
the main line east back to Wawbeek.

Smaller railroads don't have to be duller
railroads — at least when it comes to
switching. I grant that the W&S is pretty
well packed with track at the expense of
scenery, but there is some space where I
could have drawn in another passing siding
and more industrial spurs. I don't advise
adding much more than what's shown, and
in fact, you might not build all the spurs
shown until you feel you want them. What
I wanted in planning the W&S was to get a
lot of long-term operating pleasure in a
comparatively small space.

The way I figure it, the W&S, built in
HO, can easily go into an 8 x 15-foot area.
This might be an end of a basement or attic, part of a garage, or even the bedroom
Junior just abandoned for State U. — if
you can talk his mother into it. In an 8 x 15
space the Wawbeek side of the layout can
butt against a wall and an 18" access
passage can be left at each end. Most of the
railroad can be reached from the central
operating position, but the end passages
will be handy for construction, maintenance, and emergencies. The 2-foot aisle
along the Sunmount side provides a little
viewing space for visitors, or a second operating position could be established in front
of Sunmount so you can share the fun with
a friend.

The Wawbeek & Sunmount is a railroad
to be enjoyed. Plop a swivel stool in the
middle, keep your elbows in, fire up the old
2-8-0, and forget the gas crisis, inflation,
nuclear meltdowns, and your daughter's
orthodontia. What really matters is getting those two carloads of dressed meat
down from Sunmount in time to make the
midnight connection with the D&H.

Walk-in track plan ideas in 6 x 13 feet

BY ED VONDRAK

ONE family that visited my Quanta RR. expressed surprise at some of the geometry of my layout. Since they were just beginning to plan a layout of their own, I volunteered to assist them in working out a track plan for their pike.

They had a 6 x 13-foot room, with a door at one end of one of the long walls. They wanted to run modern equipment in HO scale, including some big 86-foot boxcars, so their initial thought had been to use a track plan with broad curves which would fill the room, leaving two pop-up access hatches roughly centered in the layout.

If one wants to have that kind of a layout, I think a good way to proceed is to choose one of the 4 x 8-foot track designs in the book 101 TRACK PLANS, enlarge it, and add pop-up access hatches. This procedure will yield 30″-radius curves with ease. However, this is not the approach which I advocate, as you have probably already guessed from the title of this article. I prefer a walk-in layout plan over any other type of plan, and I am so sold on walk-ins that some people must leave my house wondering why they ever considered anything else.

To fit a walk-in plan into 6 x 13 feet sounded like quite a challenge, but I thought I'd try it. For initial brainstorming you can't beat John Armstrong's "by the squares" procedure, so that's how I started.

For those who are not familiar with Armstrong's "squares" process, let me briefly describe it. A "square" is defined in terms of the minimum radius you plan to use. The size of a "square" is also affected somewhat by the required clearances between concentric circles of track. These clearances depend on both the radius of the curve and the type of equipment which you plan to operate.

A square is defined by making a complete circle of concentric double track fill a space 2 squares by 2 squares with appropriate clearances, as shown in fig. 1A. A 90-degree turn then takes 1 square (fig. 1B), and a track looping back on itself requires a space about 2 squares by 3 squares (fig. 1C). Minimum aisle width is usually about 1 square, but this may vary. For more details, I refer you to John Armstrong's book TRACK PLANNING FOR REALISTIC OPERATION.

Two basic approaches can be used with the squares method. You can set your standards (minimum radius, minimum clearances), design your layout, and then use squares to see how big your layout is going to be; or you can try fitting various patterns of various-size squares into your allotted space and then see what track plans will fit into the different squares patterns, and what minimum standards will be required in each case. In general, you may have the most success by using a combination of both techniques.

In the 6 x 13-foot space under consideration here, it is convenient to try 2-foot squares. The space is then 3 squares by 6½ squares. A 2-foot square means using relatively sharp 18″-radius curves. Although they might look a bit odd, you can still run 86-foot boxcars as long as you leave almost 3″ center-to-center clearance between concentric curves. I prefer to sacrifice large radii for more operational possibilities and easier access.

At any rate, let's see what will fit in 3 squares by 6½ squares. An oval or waterwings along one long wall will obviously fit, as shown in fig. 2A. What about that long wall next to the door, though—maybe a yard or branch line there? We'll tackle that later. First, let's experiment further with the main line. *Voila!* A folded dogbone should just barely make it, as shown in fig. 2B, and where a folded dogbone will fit, so also will the more interesting twisted figure eight, as shown in fig. 2C. With these basic possibilities, let's try filling in some details.

My friends wanted mountains, and I told them they should also have at least a small yard, one or two passing tracks on the main line, and some industrial spurs. I figured that a branch line was in order for the mountain area, and the yard area could be part of a large city to justify shunting some big cars around.

It was Dr. Roy Dohn who said in an MR article 10 years ago that if he had only three spurs they would be a team track, an interchange track, and a wharf, to provide maximum operation. I tried to heed his advice as I planned the spurs in the layout designs presented here. The results are shown in figs. 3 through 7.

Fig. 3 shows the waterwings with all of the details added. A fairly good-sized yard results when it is placed along the other long wall, and bringing the yard lead off the far side of the oval makes it possible to work the yard without fouling the main line. Two reverse loops are provided by the X pattern in the center of the waterwings. To figure out how to wire such a track plan, I refer you to Linn Westcott's book HOW TO WIRE YOUR MODEL RAILROAD.

Mountains are included at the left end of the waterwings in fig. 3, with the branch line in the mountains probably serving mining and/or logging operations. If desired, one could eliminate the high mountain backdrop and make a mountain over the whole left-hand loop of the waterwings. Access to the hidden turnouts would then have to be from underneath the mountain scenery. The long spur which originates inside the mountain and ends next to the door at the left end of the room could be considered as another branch line.

The fig. 3 layout could be put into operation fairly rapidly by laying just the waterwings first. The remaining trackage could be added at whatever

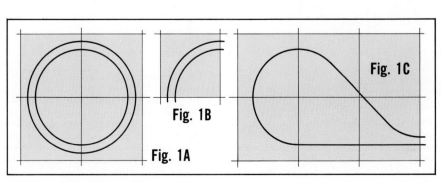

Fig. 1A

Fig. 1B

Fig. 1C

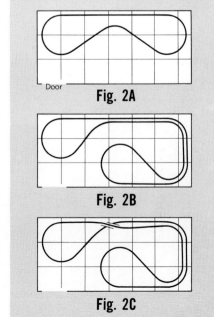

Door

Fig. 2A

Fig. 2B

Fig. 2C

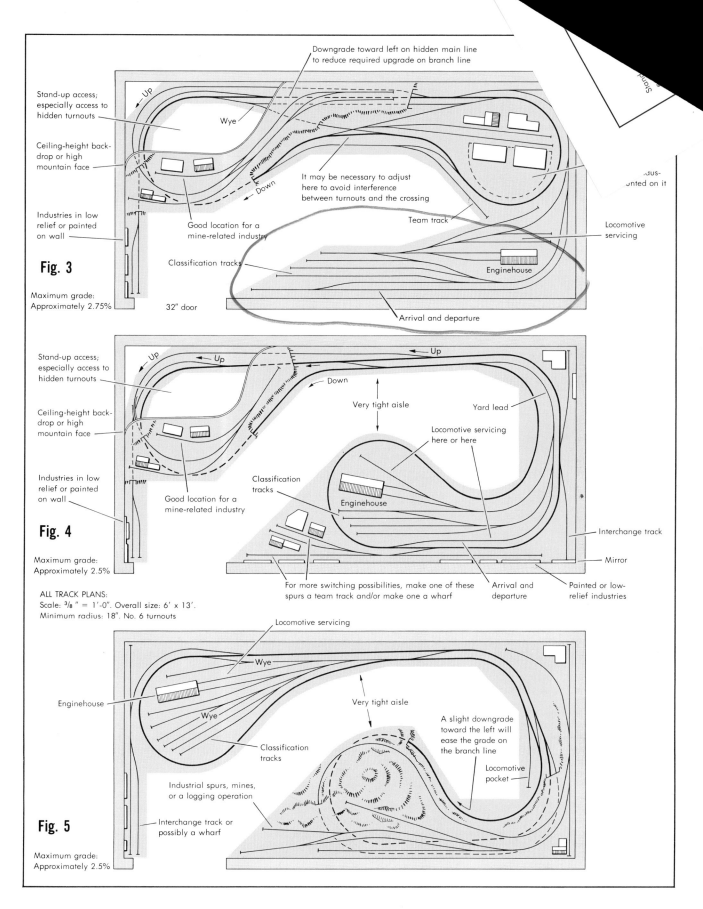

Fig. 3

Stand-up access; especially access to hidden turnouts

Ceiling-height backdrop or high mountain face

Industries in low relief or painted on wall

Maximum grade: Approximately 2.75%

Downgrade toward left on hidden main line to reduce required upgrade on branch line

Up

Wye

Down

It may be necessary to adjust here to avoid interference between turnouts and the crossing

Team track

Good location for a mine-related industry

Classification tracks

Enginehouse

32" door

Arrival and departure

Locomotive servicing

...us-...nted on it

Fig. 4

Stand-up access; especially access to hidden turnouts

Ceiling-height backdrop or high mountain face

Industries in low relief or painted on wall

Maximum grade: Approximately 2.5%

ALL TRACK PLANS:
Scale: 3/8" = 1'-0". Overall size: 6' x 13'.
Minimum radius: 18". No. 6 turnouts

Up

Up

Up

Down

Very tight aisle

Yard lead

Locomotive servicing here or here

Classification tracks

Good location for a mine-related industry

Enginehouse

For more switching possibilities, make one of these spurs a team track and/or make one a wharf

Arrival and departure

Interchange track

Mirror

Painted or low-relief industries

Fig. 5

Locomotive servicing

Wye

Enginehouse

Wye

Classification tracks

Industrial spurs, mines, or a logging operation

Interchange track or possibly a wharf

Maximum grade: Approximately 2.5%

Very tight aisle

A slight downgrade toward the left will ease the grade on the branch line

Locomotive pocket

pace you choose. If you like to watch trains run, one disadvantage of this plan is the short main line, and especially the short exposed portion of the main line. Also, the passing tracks on the main line are pretty short, and that fact puts severe limitations on the

lengths of trains that can be operated.

Fig. 4 shows a folded dogbone with the yard and branchline trackage placed rather similarly to that in the waterwings plan. The main line is considerably longer in fig. 4 than it is in fig. 3. Two reverse loops are provided: one

via the yard lead/receiving and departure track, and one via the crossover in the middle of the plan. The access aisle turns out to be pretty tight. The mountains above the left-hand loop could be modified as suggested for fig. 3 if so desired.

35

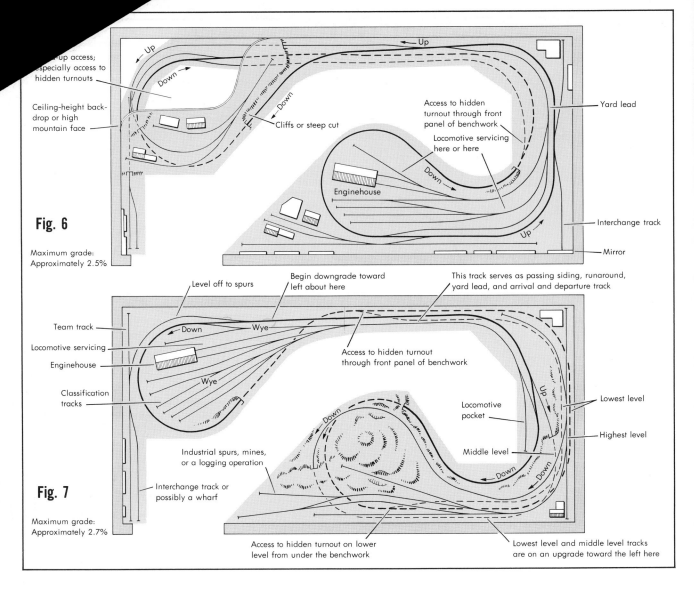

Fig. 6

Maximum grade:
Approximately 2.5%

Fig. 7

Maximum grade:
Approximately 2.7%

Fig. 5 shows the folded dogbone again, but with the yards and mountain branch line moved to the opposite ends of the layout. Again there are two reverse loops via crossovers, and again the access aisle is pretty tight. On this plan there is no yard lead independent of the dogbone main line.

The fig. 5 plan makes much more of the branch line and mountains than do figs. 3 and 4. Several spurs are shown on the branchline trackage, but only to indicate how much space is available. If the mountains were going to be made more rugged, then some of the spurs shown on the plan should be omitted.

One could begin building either the fig. 4 or the fig. 5 pike by laying just the dogbone, but one should plan ahead for various clearances, and some slight grades are called for.

Fig. 6 appears at first glance to be similar to fig. 4, but there are a couple of very fundamental and important differences. Fig. 6 has a twisted figure-eight main line rather than the folded dogbone of fig. 4. This leads to less flat area on the layout. Also, the track plan in fig. 6 has one-direction operation. There are no reverse loops. This simplifies the wiring, but it means that the only way to run trains the opposite di-

rection is to run with the locomotive going backwards.

Fig. 7 appears to be similar to fig. 5, but again there are important differences. The plan in fig. 7 is a twisted figure eight. It is similar to the main line in fig. 6, but has the opposite twist. The plan in fig. 7 is unidirectional, as is the fig. 6 plan.

The fig. 6 and fig. 7 main lines would take the longest time to get into operation because of the grades involved. This is especially true in fig. 7, which has the trickiest clearances in the mountain area at the lower right. However, the twisted figure-eight plans in figs. 6 and 7 both have these desirable features: a yard lead independent of the main line, two long passing sidings on the main line, and the possibility of using the hidden passing siding as hidden storage or a layover track to provide more interesting operation.

It would be possible to add reverse-loop cutoffs to the twisted figure eights in figs. 6 and 7, but it would make the aisle space in fig. 6 impossibly narrow, it would also infringe on the aisle space in fig. 7, and the grades in both cases would be pretty steep—probably of the order of 6 percent. It should be noted, however, that it would be possible to

operate in such a way as to always take the 6 percent downgrade. If one had a bit more room—say, 7 x 14 feet—it would be easy to add return-loop cutoffs to both of the twisted figure-eight plans using grades of no more than about 2.7 percent. In either case, one cutoff would connect the two end loops by going around the inside edge of the figure eight along the aisle, and the other cut-off would join the two loops by going around the outside of the figure eight, along the wall.

I have been conservative in using no. 6 turnouts throughout all of the plans presented here, and I have used 18" radius as a minimum standard on both the main and branch lines. One could gain some space advantages by using no. 4 turnouts and by cutting the branch-line radius down to perhaps 15".

Well, so much for my ideas. There are other things that one could try in 6 x 13 feet. A point-to-point track plan would fit very easily. Other more complicated plans are also possible. The sky's the limit, and it really boils down to one question: What do *you* want to do with *your* space? I hope I have given you some ideas from which you might progress to the layout design that you like best.

Lehigh & Ohio track plan

BY TOM PICK

SHORTLINE railroading provides a good theme for small and medium-sized model railroads because of the unscheduled type of operation and frequently short trains. The Lehigh & Ohio RR. is a short line placed in a setting of the rolling farmlands of southern Ohio, where it serves a number of small towns and local industries. For a short line, the L&O is a fairly busy outfit, so a look at the operations are in order.

Train operations are centered in the main yard at Bourne, where cars are distributed and engines are serviced. The main office of the company is located in the station, facing the company shops on the other side of the yard. The motive power consists of a Ten-Wheeler, a couple of light Consolidations, and a small switch engine (all bought secondhand from one of the larger connecting roads). A couple of wood cabooses are also on the property, along with a standard steel baggage car, a railway post office, and a coach for the local passenger train.

Operations begin with the arrival of an interchange run with cars for distribution to the local industries along the L&O. The yard switch engine then makes up local trains to run in both directions from the yard, handling local work in the towns along the way. A short two- or three-car passenger train can be used to handle the milk and mail business after the local freight's return. Once the passenger train leaves, all of the outbound cars from the local freight runs are combined and run out of town in another interchange run, possibly meeting the passenger local on the way.

This layout is a two-lap arrangement, meaning that trains make two circuits of the layout area before retracing their original route. Since there are passing tracks at three of the four stations, meets between trains are possible to keep traffic moving. The short sidings will limit train length, but this is a normal situation for shortline operations, so it is in keeping with our original concept. Cab-control wiring would be needed for this type of operation.

The L&O layout can be built in any scale but aisleway locations will have to be modified in the larger scales. If it is built in a size that takes a space more than two arm's reaches wide, meaning about 5 feet or more, then some other means of access will be necessary. These access hatches could be provided inside the layout somewhere. If one of the long sides is located along a wall, additional access hatches will be needed unless it is built in Z or N scale, where one can reach over the entire layout from one side.

While this layout can be built in the space indicated for Z and N scales, it would be much better to use the space and radius figures given for the next larger scale to provide more room for increased curve radii and scenery. If such larger-scale dimensions are used, track centers should remain the same as was indicated for your particular scale.

Train length may also be limited by the 4 percent grades, especially with light locomotives that do not have traction tires. But, with our shortline idea, the small trains will fit in nicely.

Tom Pick worked out this design years ago but never built it. We have modified it to allow the use of commercial track radii and regular no. 4 turnouts.

LEHIGH & OHIO RR.

Scale modeled	Z	N	TT	HO	S	1/4"
Drawing reduction ratio 1:	6	8	12	16	24	32
Maximum gradient	2.5 percent, all modeling scales					
Normal turnout size	No. 4, all modeling scales					
SIZES IN FEET-INCHES						
Length of space	5-2 1/16	6-10 3/4	10-4 1/8	13-9 1/2	20-8 1/4	27-7
Width of space	2-0 3/16	2-8 1/4	4-0 3/8	5-4 1/2	8-0 3/4	10-9
Spacing of rulings	0-4 1/2	0-6	0-9	1-0	1-6	2-0
Minimum mainline radius	0-8 1/4	0-11	1-4 1/2	1-10	2-9	3-8
Multiply elevations by	0-0 3/8	0-0 1/2	0-0 3/4	0-1	0-1 1/2	0-2

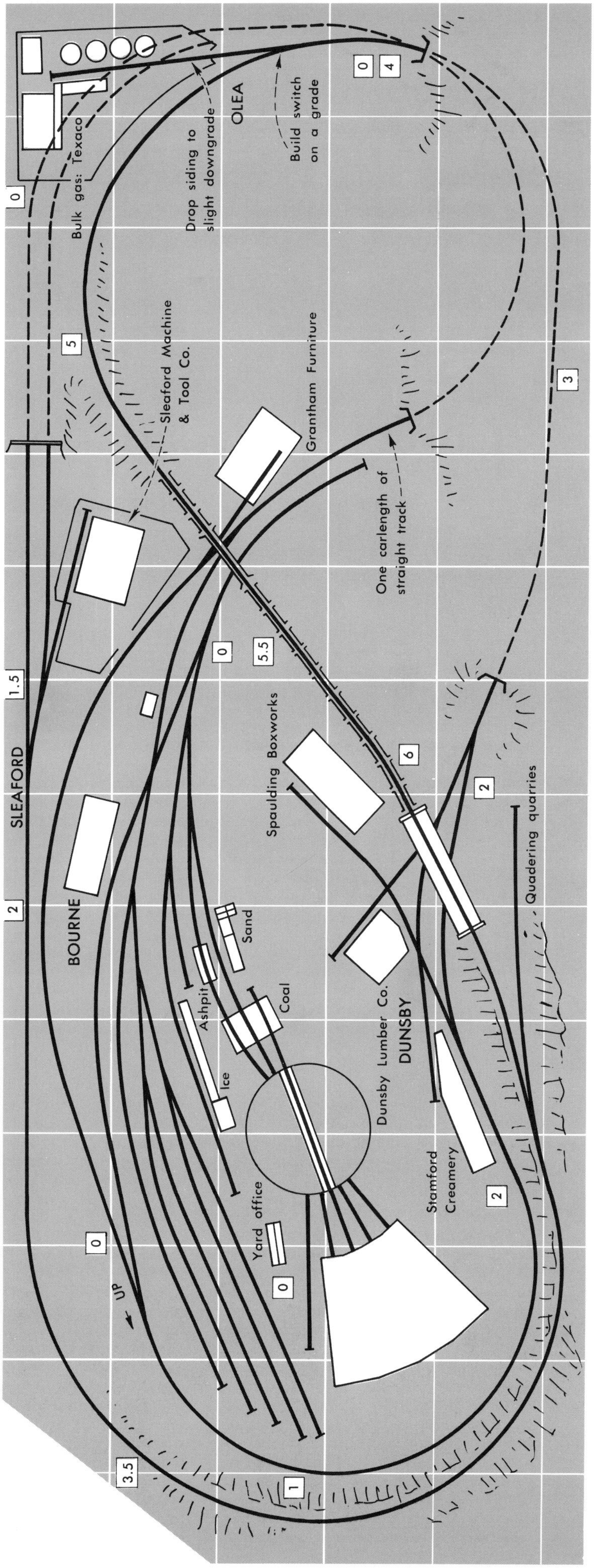

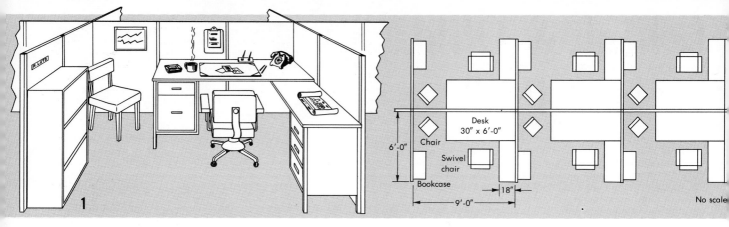

Figure labels within image: 1, 6'-0", Chair, Desk 30" x 6'-0", Swivel chair, Bookcase, 18", 9'-0", No scale

Cubicle railroads—with two track plans

Your hobby space doesn't have to be any larger than your work space

BY ROBERT J. LUTZ

THE idea for cubicle railroads was born one afternoon during a coffee break from a lengthy and tedious set of calculations.

I am employed in a large engineering office at an east coast shipyard where each engineer and draftsman is assigned to his own cubicle. The cubicles are separated by steel partitions arranged in rows as shown in fig. 1. The perspective sketch shows a typical arrangement of an engineer's cubicle measuring 6 feet deep and 9 feet wide—about 1.8 x 2.7 meters.

As I sipped my coffee, the old noggin began to wander to model railroading, as it is prone to do on many occasions. The "idea lamp" came on and, says I to myself, "I wonder what kind of a model railroad could be fitted into this cubicle?"

By the time I had finished my coffee I had rough-sketched a layout to fit the space. Since management would frown heavily on a railroad in the office, I took the cubicle idea home and finished working on it there. Real estate for a model railroad is hard to come by in many a household, so maybe this idea might be an answer to the space problem of other modelers. A cubicle would fit nicely in a corner of the basement or attic room either in just this size or in a slightly altered space.

Besides providing for a layout with operating challenge, the space should accommodate a workbench, parts storage, tools storage, and all within reach of a swivel chair. A way to frame the space is shown in fig. 2, although other methods could be substituted.

The storage equipment will be underneath the railroad framing, perhaps looking much as in fig. 1. Here, the set of drawers to the right would be handy for storing rolling stock, kits under construction, and parts. The drawers to the left would serve as a place to store tools. Many variations of small drawer cabinets are available from unpainted furniture stores, or you can build your own from plywood leftovers. A pullout work surface fitted with self-supporting extendable kitchen cabinet hardware

is located under the 18" wing to the right. Railroad controls can be located under the layout, in front of the chair.

After the framing is completed, one should install the background board before laying track. The sky background can be painted upon ⅛" Masonite, which will readily bend to the 12"-radius corners. Prime-paint the Masonite with several coats of flat white paint. Then apply a final finish coat of a very pale blue to simulate a clear sky background. Sky is darker at the top, nearly white at the horizon. The Masonite should extend below the intended background scenery profile. Hold the top edge of the Masonite in place with an outside corner cap molding or a U-channel type of molding. Scenery contour cleats made of scrap lumber can be fastened to the plywood and Masonite with glue and screws.

I designed track plans of two different concepts to fit the cubicle.

The Valley Western, fig. 3, a high-density-traffic, trunkline railroad, is an example of fitting a maximum of railroad into a minimum of space. If done in N scale it should fit the 6 x 9 cubicle, but, of course, it could be built in larger or smaller scales just as easily if the space is proportionately larger or smaller.

The other railroad, the Short Hills & Eastern, fig. 4, will fit the same space in HO.

Since I work on and enjoy ships, both layouts have a marine influence. Prototype railroads, too, have been influenced by water, with many a mile of track hugging the shores of rivers and bays. Considerable interchange traffic comes from marine service, and from a modeling standpoint it offers a somewhat different approach for scenery treatment.

I am also partial to passenger train operation, so both layouts are geared to it; but I have also tried to strike a reasonable balance by including some intricacies of freight train operation.

Valley Western

The Valley Western is a single-track trunk line with numerous passing sidings. It is basically a point-to-point bridge-traffic system. Its western terminal is Rine Cliffs. Here an interchange point is found high on a plateau. It has an engine terminal with turntable. The main line descends from the plateau, runs through the Rine Valley, and then rises to Queenstown on another plateau. Queenstown has a stub terminal fitted inside a return loop. The return loop is used to turn locomotives, observation cars, and sometimes complete trains. Out-and-home operation from Rine Cliffs is possible by using the loop.

Stations are relatively close together, so geography in the form of the river, low mountains, and rocky cliffs with cuts, tunnels, and bridges provides natural separations between towns. There is some European influence which is the result of my watching German railroads operating on both banks of the river in the Rhine Valley.

Passing sidings are deliberately kept short to add to the operating problems. This keeps trains short, creating an illusion of distance. Freight trains ought to be 12 to 15 cars long. The stub terminal tracks at both Rine Cliffs and Queenstown can accommodate six-car passenger trains. A combine, two coaches, diner, parlor car, and observation car would make a typical limited consist. There are many prototype precedents of name-train consists just like this example.

In the 1930's and 1940's the Reading Co. ran frequent Philadelphia to New York three-car "Clockers" consisting of a beautiful high-wheeled Pacific, two coaches, and a heavyweight cafe car. They were a pretty sight and they rolled fast. This is the intent here. The passing sidings do not allow two six-car passenger trains to meet, but these shorties can oppose the limiteds successfully. Double-tracking the main line from Kessart along the shore of the bay to Donnaburgh would alleviate this situation, for those who would prefer it.

Donnaburgh represents a fair-sized city. The station has a spur for a sleeper or diner drop. Also located here are seven industrial sites and a small yard, warranting the assignment of a full-time yard switcher. The way freights and through freights can drop and pick up cars by the block, with the local switcher doing the industrial switching.

All told, 23 industrial sites are scattered throughout the system. This will keep way freights on the line for quite a time. I've made no attempt to define the specific industries, but the nature of freight traffic should be general mixed in keeping with trunkline bridge traffic.

With the use of a few local control panels, several people could operate this railroad together. Motive power can run the gamut, as long as the overall wheelbase of single-end locomotives and cars does not exceed the 96-foot turntable at Rine Cliffs.

Scenery is important to the illusion on this layout. Low rolling mountains provide a logical geographic separation of tracks and towns without being excessively high. At Rine Cliffs and Queenstown the cities are above track level, partly supported by a stone retaining wall. At Rine Cliffs this wall should be just a few feet higher than a standard passenger car. Rine Cliffs station is an ancient three-story frame structure with a waiting room at track level, a ticket office at street level, and division offices in an attic having twin dormers.

At Queenstown, the street level and the stone retaining wall must be high enough in elevation to clear the hidden portion of the return loop. The station is a multistory red brick structure similar to that at Rine Cliffs. The road's general offices are on the upper floors, and a square clock tower tops the building.

Short Hills & Eastern

The Short Hills & Eastern is a point-to-point shortline railroad. It has no turning facilities for locomotives, but it contains a hidden lower-level "fiddle yard" which adds considerably to the operating fun.

The road represents a wholly owned island subsidiary of a major mainland trunk line. It is located some 2 hours' sailing time from the mainland. Interchange by car float and car ferry arrives at Seaford Harbor. These ships sail alternately to the mainland. Train operations are scheduled to the arrivals and departures of the two marine units.

The major source of freight traffic comes from Hoozitts Mining Co. at Short Hills. It exports a rare and extremely heavy material known as wattchamacallit that is hauled in ore trains that roll onto the car float to reach mainland refining plants. The balance of freight service is hauling general merchandise to and from industries along the line.

Cliff Castle, at Short Hills, is a model of a medieval castle that was built in the early 1900's by a wealthy mining magnate and is now operated as a luxury tourist hotel.

Bay Pier is a popular stop for sport

fishermen. Many fishing party boats operate from its pier.

Passenger traffic is frequent to satisfy the tourist traffic, sport fishermen, and the miners at the Hoozitts Mine, who work very short shifts due to the great weight of wattchamacallit.

The two marine units are kept deliberately small to avoid overpowering the model railroad by sheer size. The design of the car ferry, fig. 5, was checked by a naval architect friend of mine, and it is well within the realm of practicability as a diesel-powered ship. The car float is a typical two-track railroad car float with a specially strengthened hull to carry the great weight of the ore cars.

Both units are waterline models with hulls to be carved out of white pine and the superstructures built up of multiply Strathmore board. The car ferry is 182'-0" long, the car float is 152'-0" long, and both have a beam of 43'-6" and a car deck freeboard of 10'-0". Both hulls are fitted with a pocket in the car deck at the stern which receives the outboard end of the ferry bridge. To keep my story plausible, let me specify that tidal variations at Seaford Harbor are only a few feet and there is always a slight decline over the ferry bridge to the stern of the hulls.

The ferry bridge is of heavy truss construction. Realism will be enhanced if it is made to operate. It could be motor-driven with a double-ended motor and gearing located in the control room atop the lifting bridge, or it could be operated by a small hand crank. It should be raised and lowered to correspond with the docking and undocking of the hulls.

The ore trains are limited to eight cars because of their great weight. They are operated as unit trains, never mixed with general-service cars. The car float has a capacity of six 50-foot cars or

eight ore cars. Ore trains are handled on alternate sailings; loaded cars are pushed aboard two at a time, first to port, then to starboard, with a light idler car ahead of the locomotive.

The car ferry carries general-service freight cars only, plus passenger cars. It also has day accommodations for 81 passengers in the upper cabin. It has a capacity of six 50-foot freight cars or four 50-foot freight cars and one 80-foot pullman or coach. The one-car passenger interchange is made on alternate sailings.

After unloading and reloading, either hull is lifted out of the slip by hand (simulated sailing) and placed in its proper slip on the lower-level fiddle yard.

The fiddle yard lends itself to the man with more rolling stock than the railroad can accommodate. This makes for variety in interchange and can be made as elaborate as one may wish. It provides for a traffic pattern diagramed in fig. 6. Since the fiddle yard trackwork is hidden under the layout, so is purely functional, I'd suggest using flexible track and no. 4 switches.

The mine interchange track of the fiddle yard eliminates the bothersome sight of loaded ore cars returning to the mine. Two sets of eight ore cars are used. One set is always empty; the other carries simulated loads.

Empty ore cars move from fiddle yard to car float, float to Seaford Harbor, over the road to Short Hills; are pushed through the minehead and down into the fiddle yard. The loaded cars travel in the opposite direction starting from the minehead.

Set your own period in time; a large variety of small motive power and passenger rolling stock is available, both modern and old-time.

If you choose the steam era, keep in mind the lack of locomotive turning

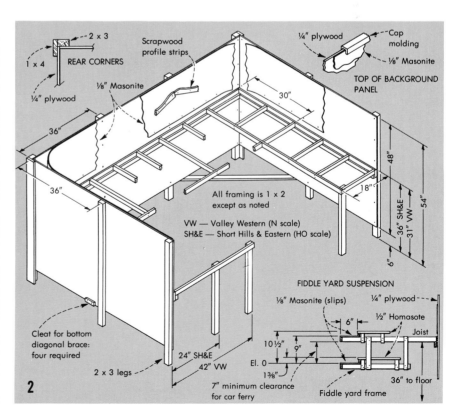

2

39

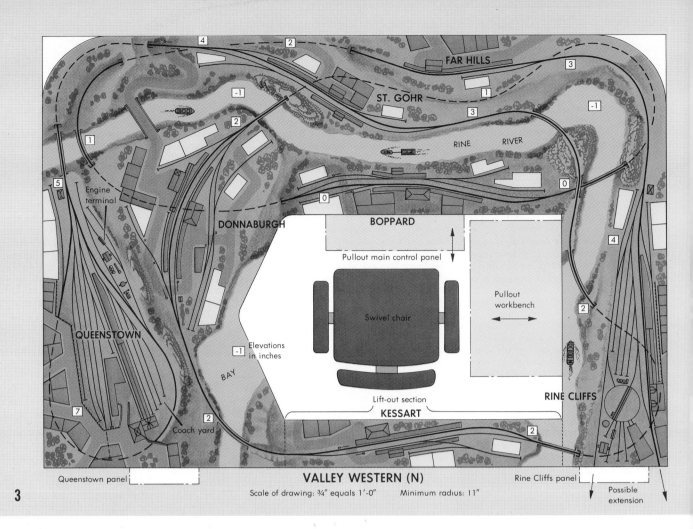

3   **VALLEY WESTERN (N)**

Scale of drawing: ¾" equals 1'-0"   Minimum radius: 11"

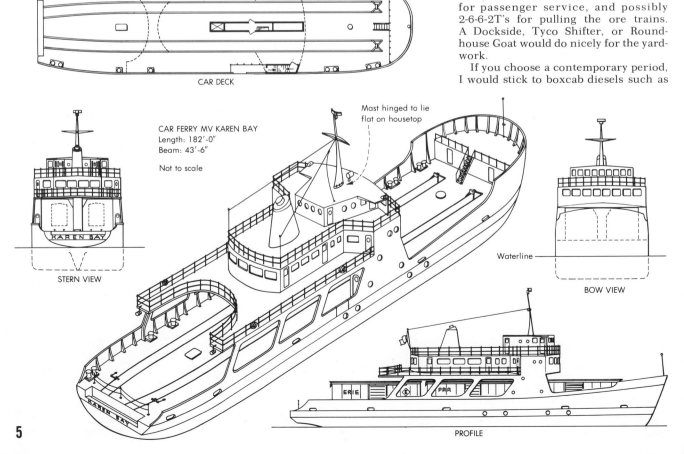

facilities. I would lean toward tank-type locomotives such as 4-6-4T's or 4-6-6T's for passenger service, and possibly 2-6-6-2T's for pulling the ore trains. A Dockside, Tyco Shifter, or Roundhouse Goat would do nicely for the yardwork.

If you choose a contemporary period, I would stick to boxcab diesels such as

CAR DECK

CAR FERRY MV KAREN BAY
Length: 182'-0"
Beam: 43'-6"

Not to scale

Mast hinged to lie flat on housetop

STERN VIEW

Waterline

BOW VIEW

PROFILE

5

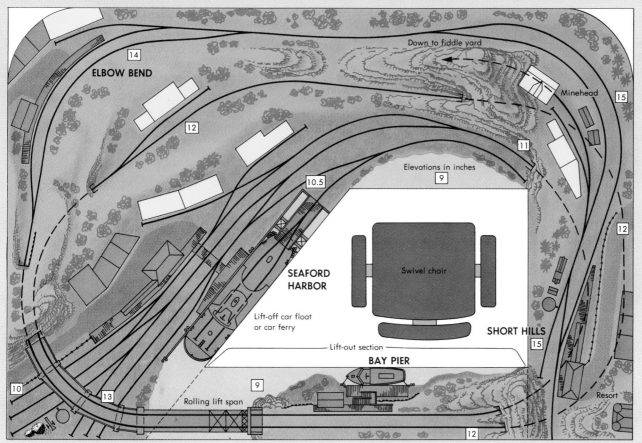

ELBOW BEND

14

12

10.5

Down to fiddle yard

Minehead

15

11

Elevations in inches

9

Swivel chair

SEAFORD HARBOR

Lift-off car float or car ferry

SHORT HILLS

15

Lift-out section

BAY PIER

9

Rolling lift span

Resort

10

13

12

SHORT HILLS & EASTERN (HO)

4 Scale of drawing: ¾" equals 1'-0"
Minimum radius: 18"

EMD's BL-2 or any of the Geep locomotives. An Athearn Hustler or a Plymouth diesel would be nice for the switching chores.

The Short Hills & Eastern owns only two passenger cars: a combine and a day coach. The interchange cars should include at least one 80-foot pullman sleeper, modern or standard, and several coaches. These should all be lettered for foreign roads.

I'd suggest powering one track on the car float through a set of contacts on the ferry bridge so you can occasionally bring different motive power from the fiddle yard. The car float is designed to carry the weight because the Short Hills & Eastern's locomotives are serviced at the parent road's shops on the mainland.

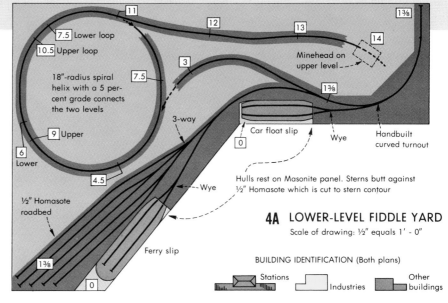

11

7.5 Lower loop

10.5 Upper loop

18"-radius spiral helix with a 5 percent grade connects the two levels

7.5

9 Upper

6 Lower

4.5

½" Homasote roadbed

1⅜

0

12

13

1⅜

14

Minehead on upper level

3

1⅜

3-way

0

Car float slip

Wye

Handbuilt curved turnout

Wye

Hulls rest on Masonite panel. Sterns butt against ½" Homasote which is cut to stern contour

Ferry slip

4A LOWER-LEVEL FIDDLE YARD

Scale of drawing: ½" equals 1' - 0"

BUILDING IDENTIFICATION (Both plans)

Stations   Industries   Other buildings

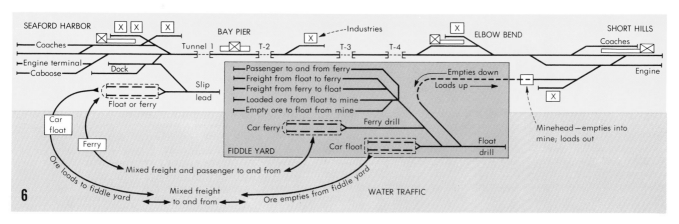

SEAFORD HARBOR   X X   X   BAY PIER   ←── Industries   X   ELBOW BEND   SHORT HILLS

Coaches   Tunnel 1   T-2   T-3   T-4   Coaches

Engine terminal   Dock   Slip lead   Passenger to and from ferry   Empties down   Engine

Caboose   Freight from float to ferry   Loads up

Float or ferry   Freight from ferry to float   X

Car float   Loaded ore from float to mine   Minehead—empties into mine; loads out

Ferry   Empty ore to float from mine

Car ferry   Ferry drill

FIDDLE YARD   Car float   Float drill

Ore loads to fiddle yard   Mixed freight and passenger to and from

6   Mixed freight to and from   Ore empties from fiddle yard   WATER TRAFFIC

Saranac & Wol

Let 'em rip on the main line while you're busy upstairs shiftin

BY LEONARD BLUMENSCHINE
PHOTO BY MARTIN SHAMES

IT'S sort of like packing a pair of long pants into a short suitcase. You put the cuffs against one end and accordion-fold the rest, first to the right, then to the left.

The bottom tier of the Saranac & Wolf Pond Ry. is a straight and narrow dogbone, mated at the middle with facing turnouts that form passing sidings and also act as direction reversers. Around the back, a branch takes you climbing up the first fold to end at the Saranac passenger and engine terminals perched over one loop. From here a switchback movement shunts you in the opposite direction into the freight yard and industrial tracks. These are built over the left end of the dogbone.

Wolf Pond, not much of a burg in anybody's book, is represented on the main line by a pair of sidings. One track feeds a stock pen and slaughterhouse, plus a grain and coal mill (the former a Frank Ellison project [May 1950 MR], the latter George Allen's famous Mifflinburg Mill [July 1952 MR]). The other boasts a closet-size passenger stop with a boxcar freight house and a sawmill. Additional industries backdropping the upper-tier freight yard go in for grain elevatoring, boxmaking, furniture building, and reefer icing.

The Saranac terminals can muster half a dozen assorted passenger cars for the summer Adirondack tourist trade (twenties to thirties style) and handle an equal number of engines in a good-sized service facility that includes Eric Stevens's clas-

sic coaling station [October 1951 MR et seq.], an oil fuel rack, an ash hoist, and a 116-foot turntable big enough to take on everything, including a visiting Challenger engine which comes mammothing in from the Alleghenies every once in a while.

In designing the plan I have tried to select the various industries so that the Saranac plants feed the Wolf Pond edifices, and vice versa. This calls for a lot of switching, freight peddling, and out-and-backing. But the four- or five-car shorties had better watch out, because the dogbone is meant to be shared main line.

Although it's no great shakes in length, and the sort-of easemented curves narrow to 22" radius (if in HO) in the tunnels, there's still enough to allow some parading, New York Central style, plus some interchanging at Wolf Pond.

Operated at its simplest, one-man fashion, you can let 'em rip on the main line while you're busy upstairs shifting cars, making up trains, and pampering locomotives. What interested me most was that each of these operations uses the full 16½-foot span of the benchwork. Instead of compacting the service and yard areas inside the loops, the accordion-folding allows each to spread right out to the edges, creating, in a way, two layouts in one: a continuous-run job and a shelf-switcher.

Like so many plans, this was drawn to fit a particular space: a 9 x 25-foot ground-level playroom abutting a garage. One end of it is ruined for railroading by opposing doors to the garage and the basement, a stairway, a clothes-storage closet, and a perpetually out-of-tune console piano. The S&WP is meant to fill what is left and still leave space to get at bookshelves, hi-fi equipment along the wall at the operator's back, and a pair of win-

dows 18" away from the turntable end of the benchwork.

Anyway, I fancied the plan enough that I decided to see what it would look like in miniature. The color photograph (by an advertising photographer friend, Martin Shames) shows the model. It was built in the scale of the original drawing, 1" to the foot. For fun I assembled it as if I were building the actual layout.

Underneath the track and scenery is L-girder benchwork cut from balsa strips: 1/16" x 3/16" and 1/16" x 1/4" for the girders, joists, and risers (as close as I could get to 1 x 3 and 1 x 4 lumber), plus 1/8" x 1/8" lengths for the 2 x 2 legs. I followed Kinnickinnic Railway & Dock Co. methods [January 1972 MR], particularly for the five rear triangular support brackets. These are spaced to be screwed to studs in the paneled playroom wall.

The track plan was traced onto and cut from mat board. This was white-glued to 1/32" balsa sheet, resulting in a sandwich resembling plywood-Homasote roadbed. I didn't intend to go beyond this skeleton-framework appearance of roadbed on risers over benchwork, but a visitor to the office (that's where it was built during a month of pleasant lunch hours) allowed as how scenery and buildings would be nice.

Ordinary textured men's room paper towels proved helpful, just as they are for zip-texture scenery on full-size layouts. First I cut and tried pieces, often many times because the scale is so small. Then, before gluing in place, I applied color from broad- and narrow-tipped felt markers in a range of the usual earth, stone, and greenery colors. After each scenic element was glued and dry, I trimmed any excess with a single-edged blade. The result was startling. Although I gave up trying to make 1/4"-tall trees,

Pond Ry.

rs, making up trains, and pampering locomotives

the felt tips tended to raise fibers on the paper when applied and thus make what look like shrubs and weeds in several places. Also, the pebbled texture of the towel, rubbed lightly with the felt markers so as not to flatten it, made a dandy stone retaining wall which faces much of the upper yard and terminal tier.

The buildings were a challenge, but turned out to be the most fun. One-ply Strathmore paper was just right. First, I laid out all four walls on a flat, after making series of parallel lines at door, window, and roof heights. Felt pens and color pencils did the rest, giving me, among others, a pullman-green station, a weatherbeaten roundhouse, and a rusty corrugated-sheet grain elevator

and sawmill. Once the flats and roofs were cut out with single-edged blades (I must have used two dozen), they were folded and white-glued together. It was even possible to cut open a few stall doors on the roundhouse and make the turntable turn via a wheel mounted beneath the benchwork.

So much for an exercise in 16½". I wouldn't recommend doing it for every plan you conceive, but it's certainly a nifty way to create a conversation piece and to visualize, in three dimensions, that favorite layout you've always wanted to build. My only letdown: the citizen who eyed the model in the office one day and asked, "So, okay. Where are the choo-choos?"

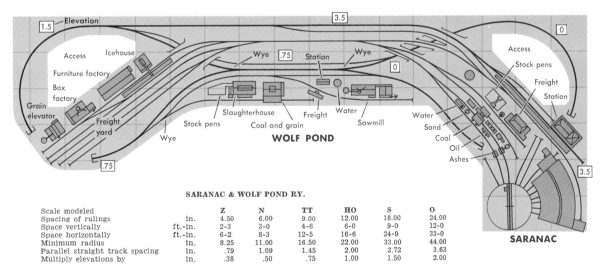

SARANAC & WOLF POND RY.

Scale modeled		Z	N	TT	HO	S	O
Spacing of rulings	in.	4.50	6.00	9.00	12.00	18.00	24.00
Space vertically	ft.-in.	2-3	3-0	4-6	6-0	9-0	12-0
Space horizontally	ft.-in.	6-2	8-3	12-5	16-6	24-9	33-0
Minimum radius	in.	8.25	11.00	16.50	22.00	33.00	44.00
Parallel straight track spacing	in.	.79	1.09	1.45	2.00	2.72	3.63
Multiply elevations by	in.	.38	.50	.75	1.00	1.50	2.00

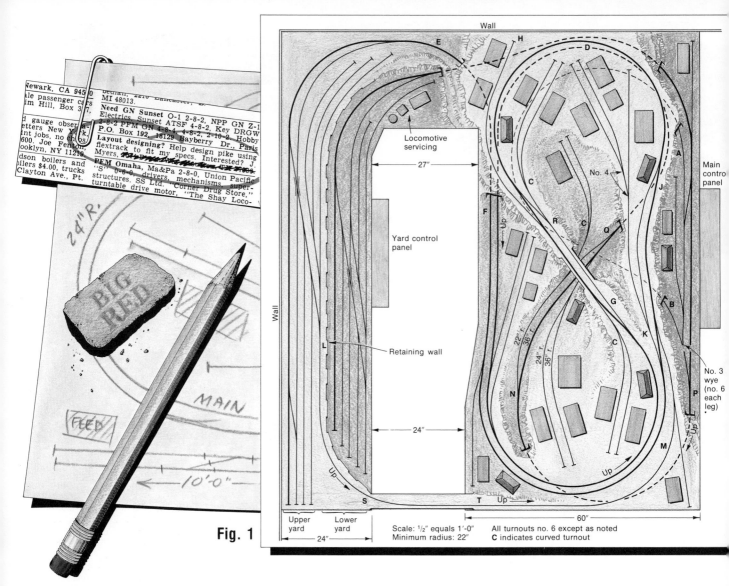

Fig. 1

Locomotive servicing

27"

Yard control panel

Retaining wall

24"

Wall

Main control panel

No. 4

22" r.
36" r.

24" r.
36" r.

No. 3 wye (no. 6 each leg)

Up

Up

Up

Up

Up

Upper yard | Lower yard

24"

60"

Scale: 1/2" equals 1'-0"
Minimum radius: 22"

All turnouts no. 6 except as noted
C indicates curved turnout

Three track plans for the JM&j Lines

Builder and planner got together via our classified ads

BY ED VONDRAK

THIS STORY actually begins in the classified ads section of the March 1977 issue of MODEL RAILROADER. I enjoy reading the classifieds once in a while, usually just out of curiosity, and in that issue an unusual WANTED ad appeared. Jim Myers of Houston, Tex., was looking for someone to help him design a track plan. Curiosity got the better of me and I wrote to Jim. Here is the list of requirements that came back in the mail a few days later.

Scale: HO

Space available: 9 x 10 feet, with walls along two sides and no windows.

Layout style: Walk-in, but aisles can be bridged. Few, if any, hidden access hatches.

Construction: Prefer solid table to open grid. Track plan should be adaptable to progressive construction over a period of a few years.

Levels: Up to three or four track levels, but no stacked benchwork à la John Armstrong.

Wiring: Diagram desired for installing cab control.

Features: Two or three major cities with large yards, plus at least five other towns with industrial spurs. All cities and towns to have some space for streets and structures.

Traffic: Heavy freight traffic, but some passenger operation too.

Emphasis: To be on switching rather than scenery.

Setting: Contemporary southwestern United States.

Special trackwork already owned: three no. 6 double-slip switches, three left-hand 22"/18" curved turnouts, six right-hand 22"/18" curved turnouts, two no. 4 wye turnouts, two crossovers, and a variety of other no. 4 and no. 6 turnouts.

Minimum mainline radius: 24" or larger.

When I wrote back to Jim I told him it would probably not be possible to do all he wanted in the space he had available, but

he replied, "Not to ask is not to receive." I had to admit he was right. Here was a challenge I couldn't resist.

I was pretty sure from the beginning that the track plan would have to be what I call a "bowl-of-spaghetti" design. How else could so much operation fit in such a small space without using stacked benchwork? I personally do not like spaghetti-bowl track plans, and I would not build one for myself, but here was an opportunity to find out whether or not I could design such a pike.

I also told Jim that I don't do wiring diagrams, because I don't like to force my style of wiring on anybody. Wiring diagrams are like computer programs — you are not really certain everything is going to work correctly until you actually do it and test it. The subsequent "debugging" is hard enough firsthand, much less trying to do it via letters or the telephone.

TRACK PLAN NO. 1

I started sketching some ideas, and the plan that emerged and seemed best to fit the bill for Myers is shown in fig. 1. It is

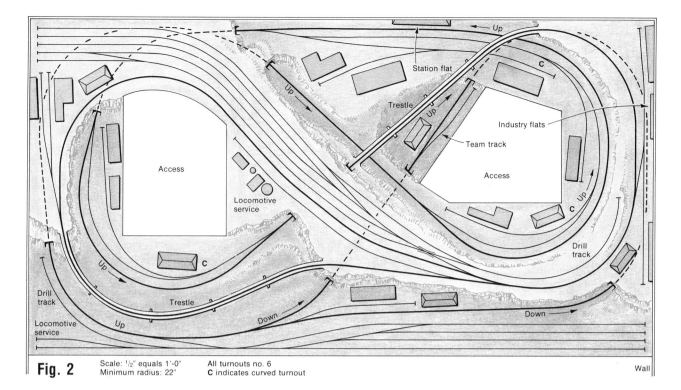

Fig. 2 Scale: ½" equals 1'-0" All turnouts no. 6
Minimum radius: 22" **C** indicates curved turnout Wall

crowded, the passing tracks are terribly short, and the minimum radius is 22" instead of 24", but this plan has some interesting features.

The two main yards are placed along the left-hand wall with the upper yard about 4" higher than the lower yard. A city backdrop would be painted on that wall. Visually there is only one large city, but from an operations standpoint there are two large yards, one at each end of the main line.

The layout can be operated in point-to-point fashion between these yards, with switching opportunities at several small towns along the way. The very short double tracks at the towns serve as runarounds, but not as passing sidings.

The pike can also be operated as a loop-to-loop layout. One loop is the hidden trackage that connects points A and B on the lowest level, and the other loop is formed by the upper yard lead together with the connection LSTM that bridges the aisle.

The first plan is well suited to progressive construction. The layout's first stage would include the two main yards along the left-hand wall, the town at ABP along the right-hand side, and the town at NQ in the center of the table. A temporary connection from D to E would complete the main line. Those two points are at the same elevation, making it easy to add the temporary connection.

With this configuration, the layout would be strictly point-to-point. If the hidden reverse loop connecting points A and B were included on the lowest level, then there could be point-to-loop operation out of the upper yard. There would not yet be a bridge across the aisle at ST.

At some later date the connection DE would be removed, and both of those tracks would be extended around toward F and continue on up to the upper loop GRHJKM. That would also be the time to bridge the aisle and add the connection LSTM to complete all of the trackage as shown in fig. 1.

You could modify this track plan to get reasonably long passing sidings by double-tracking the main line all the way from ABP to NQ and from GR all the way around the loop to JK. One might also be tempted to install a single or double crossover at F. That would allow much more varied operation, but it might be an electrical nightmare because eastbound on one of those tracks is westbound on the other.

I chose 22" as the minimum radius for the plan in fig. 1 for two reasons. One was that it allowed the use of reasonable dimensions for both the aisle and table widths, and the other was that Jim already owned a number of curved turnouts whose larger radii were 22". Hence, he could literally just drop in a turnout and run an industrial spur off the inside of any of his mainline curves.

TRACK PLAN NO. 2

Just about the time I finished the plan in fig. 1, I received an apologetic letter from Jim. He was building a new house and the projected railroad location had changed. The new space measured 13½ feet long and about 8 feet wide, with walls on three sides. I told Jim that change is the name of the game in model railroading and started sketching new ideas. I kept trying to keep the yards together as they had been in the first track plan, but I wasn't happy with any of the plans that resulted. Finally I tried a new approach altogether and came up with the plan shown in fig. 2. This one was inspired by some of the layout ideas in Linn Westcott's book, 101 TRACK PLANS.

This layout, like the first one I designed, can be operated point-to-point or loop-to-loop. It could also be built in progressive stages by starting with the reverse loop and yard on the lowest level and temporarily bringing the track back to meet itself as each ascending figure eight is added. This would require some rebuilding of the benchwork to readjust the grades each time more mainline track is added,

but in the meantime the layout could be operated either point-to-loop or loop-to-loop at every stage of construction.

The lower yard is shorter than the upper yard, and the track plan includes no cutoff track for the locomotives of trains pulling directly into the lower yard. Such a cutoff would make the lower yard very short indeed, and it is probably better just to use the lower reverse loop all the time and always back the trains into the yard.

On this second track plan I made the passing tracks reasonably long so they could actually be used as passing tracks and not just serve as runarounds for switching purposes.

In this plan I accomplished a couple of other things that I had not been able to bring off in the first. While the minimum mainline radius is again 22", one mainline route has a minimum radius of 24". I accomplished this by making all the single-track curves at least 24" in radius and by making the *inside* radius 22" on the double-track curves. Hence if a train takes the outer track on all the curves, the smallest radius encountered is 24". At the same time the 22" radius curves on the inside passing tracks would allow Jim to use some of his curved turnouts.

Some problems occur with the track plan in fig. 2. Almost the entire main line is on a grade, so one would have to use some artificial means of holding loose rolling stock in place during switching moves. Otherwise cuts of cars would take off for the lower yard every time the locomotive was uncoupled. Because of the grades I located the industrial spurs in the downhill direction at all the towns out along the line. This leads to lopsided operation, although the switchback spurs help out in that regard.

Except for the two large bridges, scenery is at a premium in this track plan, but Jim had said earlier that that would be all right. A couple of things did bother him about this plan, though. What had started out as one or two aisles had degenerated into two access holes, and that wasn't what

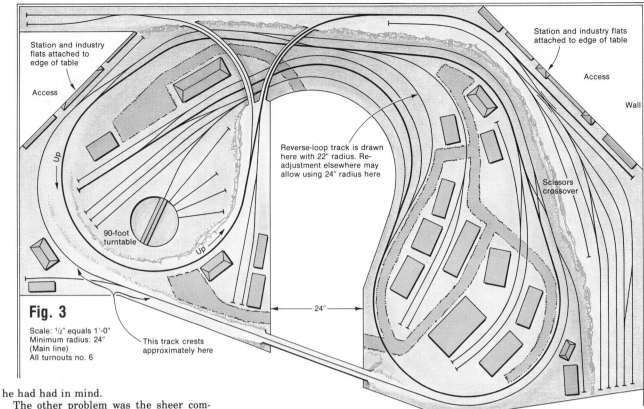

Station and industry
flats attached to
edge of table

Access

Up

Up

90-foot
turntable

Fig. 3

Scale: ½" equals 1'-0"
Minimum radius: 24"
(Main line)
All turnouts no. 6

This track crests
approximately here

Reverse-loop track is drawn
here with 22" radius. Re-
adjustment elsewhere may
allow using 24" radius here

Station and industry flats
attached to edge of table

Access

Wall

Scissors
crossover

24"

he had had in mind.

The other problem was the sheer complexity of the plan. I had just kept stacking up figure eights until I got the number of towns Jim wanted. The result was four track levels at the center of the layout. With that many levels and all the grades, the plan in fig. 2 is not well suited to the solid-table style of construction that Jim wanted.

The plan is presented here because it has some good features and some MR reader might be inspired to try building a pike along these lines. For Jim Myers, however, it was back to the old drawing board.

TRACK PLAN NO. 3

Jim asked if we could try a U-shaped plan and not worry so much about being able to reach across the table. I usually try to hold the maximum reach to about 30", but I thought I would try doodling some ideas for a G-shaped or U-shaped plan with wide wings as Jim suggested. The result is shown in fig. 3. This one struck Jim's fancy and is the layout he is now building.

The track plan in fig. 3 is basically point-to-point with a continuous-run option. One long passing track is located about midway along the run, and the continuous-run connection that crosses the aisle can also serve as a passing track. This feature may not be obvious, but it can be seen by "running" three trains, play-acting style, out of the yards towards each other. Then I think one can see how the continuous-run connection can be used as sort of a passing track or alternate route to allow the last train that left the yard to arrive at the opposite yard first.

I drew this plan with 24"-minimum-radius curves, except for the one reverse loop connection that Jim wanted to add near the lower yard. That one turned out to be 22" in radius. There is a lot of flexibility in the industrial area within the loop on the right-hand side of the plan. I sketched in some ideas, but that area could be made much more complex if one desired. In fact,

there is probably enough room there to fit in some variation of the Timesaver switching puzzle, one of my favorite track configurations and one which I discussed in the February 1979 issue of MODEL RAILROADER.

Jim plans to make one major change in the plan. He is going to omit the wye on the upper level. He wants to sacrifice the turnaround capability for a couple of reasons. The railroad will be much easier to wire without the wye there, and he also decided that he wanted a branch line, so what was to be the left leg of the wye will now become a branch line going to a mine at the upper left-hand corner of the pike.

It was an interesting project to design a track plan for the JM&j Lines. I found out that I could draw spaghetti-bowl-style plans, and three interesting layout ideas were generated, all because Jim Myers decided to place a classified ad in MODEL RAILROADER.

The San Jacinto District

An HO switching railroad for a 9 x 12-foot room

BY ANDY SPERANDEO

ONE way to model a big railroad in a small space is to represent only a piece of the large system. A section of busy main line would be nice if you want to sit back and watch trains roll, but if you like challenging switching, a branch line serving a number of industries is a better choice. This track plan takes the branch line approach and applies it to the Atchison, Topeka & Santa Fe Ry. in Southern California.

The prototype San Jacinto District is a branch which leaves the Santa Fe's Los Angeles Division (Third District) main line at Highgrove, about 6½ miles south of San Bernardino, and heads south, east, and finally north up the San Jacinto River valley. The line as far as Perris was built as part of the old California Southern's main to San Diego, but the same landslides in Temecula Canyon which led to the Santa Fe's takeover of the CS cut this line back to a branch extending to a terminal in the small town of San Jacinto.

The track plan does not attempt to represent the San Jacinto District precisely, but it does use certain features of the prototype to develop the Santa Fe theme. One of these is the ornate brick combination station at Perris, a well-known building now used by the Orange Empire Trolley Museum. Drawings of the Perris station appeared in the November 1969 MODEL RAILROADER and are reprinted in Kalmbach's RAILROAD STATION PLANBOOK; the book's cover features a Gil Reid painting of the Perris station. The track plan is designed to incorporate a model of this station as one of its focal points; besides being interesting in itself, this model would help identify and authenticate the layout's prototype.

Another important prototype feature is citrus fruit traffic. The San Jacinto District is at the eastern edge of a large Southern California orange-growing area, and the track plan includes three fruit packing houses, a refrigerator car icing plant, and a packing crate factory among its industries. As well as being characteristic of the plan's locale, this kind of traffic is closely identified with the Santa Fe. The model San Jacinto District's main business will be getting empty reefers iced and spotted for loading, then carrying the loads up to the main line to be forwarded east. (Pre-icing of empties was really concentrated at San Bernardino, but spreading some of it out increases the operating interest of this layout.)

The track plan is designed to fill a 9 x 12-foot room with HO railroad. Its point-to-point line runs from a three-track fiddle yard representing Highgrove, around the walls through Perris, and into the small yard at San Jacinto. A spur line reaches

the Hemet industrial district on a peninsula into the center of the room. (See the illustration for an idea on making this peninsula stable.)

I started out trying to fit 22″-radius curves but decided to settle for 18″-minimum radius to provide more switching opportunities. The large arcs of minimum radius are located so that they can be seen only from inside the curve, and this will make their sharpness less apparent, particularly if the layout is built near eye level. Where a curve of some length is seen from the outside, at Hemet, I used a 26″ radius.

The turnouts are mostly no. 4s for the same reason that the curves are sharp, but I did use no. 6s at certain points. The 6s at the ends of the Perris passing track are meant to enhance one of the railroad's nicer scenes. The others on the San Jacinto icehouse spur and in crossovers at Perris

and Hemet are there to ease S curves: no. 4 crossovers have too much of an S curve even for small engines and 40-foot cars. The crossover in front of the packing crate factory is not really necessary, but it does offer some useful and interesting ways to shuffle cars between the two tracks.

The structures are very important on this kind of railroad, because they are both a large part of the modeled scenery and the justification of the operating scheme. The plan is scaled to provide space for the particular buildings listed, which include plastic kits, craftsman kits, and two scratchbuilt models. If you aren't fully confident as a modelbuilder, the range of kits shown will allow you to start simply and develop skills as you go along. Everything on this railroad is close to the front edge — a major advantage of walk-in track plans — so there is plenty of opportunity to work up a high state of detail.

At Perris, the stores, gas station, and stockyard are to be used as the manufacturers intended. The Campbell Seebold & Sons Mfg. Co. will make a creditable packing shed with appropriate signs and details. The station is admittedly a big project, but it will give you something to look forward to. I'd advise building a cardboard or styrene mock-up of the station model to act as a placeholder in the scene until the model itself is ready.

At Hemet there is no station, only a signboard. The operating interest here is on the spur, where I envision two parallel tracks reaching into the middle of a city block. Most of the industries along these tracks are oriented to face the cross streets, an arrangement which is common in the prototype but not often seen on model railroads.

The bulk oil dealership and the cement supply yard are composed of plastic kits with little or no modification, although fences, trucks, and other small details would help them look more complete. The lumberyard and the San Jacinto St. packing shed are plastic kits with a little kitbashing: the Heljan Edison Laboratory would need loading doors, signs, and a simplified front to become a packing shed; and one of the two Atlas kits used for the lumberyard should be cut down to eliminate its loading door and platform, making its right-angle position to the track appear more logical.

The Campbell Richmond Barrel Works would be built as designed but detailed to represent a maker of orange crates rather than barrels. (Its location at a turnout is intended to create complications when a car is left there.) The Sunkist packing plant would use the Suydam no. 83 kit for its street end and the corrugated-metal kit no. 1 as a packing shed extension. The freight station would be a scratchbuilt model of the Santa Fe freight station in Hermosa Beach, Calif., as described in Kalmbach's SCRATCHBUILDING & KITBASHING MODEL RAILROAD STATIONS. Such a model would be worthwhile to gain a bit more Santa Fe atmosphere, and it fits the street frontage situation perfectly.

I've shown the Campbell Skull Valley Station and wood water tank at San Jacinto because both are models of Santa Fe prototypes, and the Classic Miniatures branch line oil tank is similar enough to Santa Fe structures to be useful. Engines were actually turned on a wye at San Jacinto, but a Diamond Scale Models 75-foot turntable will do the job in a lot less space. The icing plant uses a Suydam kit no. 566 as its starting point: the building would be cut down to fit between the backdrop and the track, the platform extended with

47

stripwood, and signs installed labeling it as a railroad facility.

The scenery would be mostly gentle, grassy hills with a few scrubby trees and occasional orange groves. I've worked in a bit of the San Jacinto River between Hemet and San Jacinto, with the tracks crossing on Campbell curved pile trestles. A well-done backdrop would go far toward making this small railroad look a lot larger. The backdrop could enlarge the towns and show more of the hills and orange groves, and it would be highlighted by 10,805-foot San Jacinto Peak rising above the town of San Jacinto.

The fiddle yard would be best kept out of sight but readily accessible. One easy way to do this is shown in the illustration: mount another shelf above the yard shelf and hang lift-up doors from it. It's worth keeping the offstage trains hidden to help maintain the fiction that they are running another 18 or so miles to reach the Third District at Highgrove.

If I were building the San Jacinto District, I'd set the period in the late 1940s, for three reasons. Until the 2650 class GP7s began arriving in 1949 the Santa Fe didn't have much diesel power available for low-mileage branchline work, so the railroad could use 2-8-0 steam engines. In fact, even a light 4-6-2 would be appropriate, and the Key Imports 1226-class Pacific can take 18"-radius curves with ease.

Also, this period predates mechanical refrigerator cars on the Santa Fe, and the need to precool reefers at the icing plant before switching them out to the packing sheds adds an enjoyable complication to the railroad's operation.

Finally, the sharp curves will work best for an era when there were few freight cars longer than 50 feet. If you prefer diesels, stick to the early 1950s and use zebra-striped Geeps for power.

The Santa Fe's 1947 Los Angeles Division employees' timetable shows the San Jacinto District being served by daily-except-Sunday mixed trains nos. 505 and 506, second-class trains between San Bernardino and San Jacinto which ran via the Third District between Highgrove and San Berdoo. The 505 was scheduled to arrive in San Jacinto at 11:40 a.m. (San Jacinto is *west* of San Bernardino by timetable direction), and the 506 was to depart at 12:01 p.m. These runs could be the basis for the model San Jacinto District operations and would provide both freight and passenger service.

The mixed trains will need a passenger car which can take the layout's sharp curves, and the Santa Fe had the perfect prototype in its 46-foot, open platform combines, nos. 2309 and 2314-2320. The cars were built as steel drovers' cars in the 1930s and during World War II were rebuilt as baggage-coach combinations (nos. 2593-2599) for service as rider cars on mail trains. After the war they were repainted mineral brown — the Santa Fe's version of boxcar red — and renumbered as above for mixed-train service. The combine would normally run as the next-to-last car in the train, with a regular caboose behind for the train crew. Since the original drovers' cars had many parts in common with Santa Fe's standard steel caboose, a reasonable model of the mixed-train combine could be built from Athearn caboose kits. Drawings and photos of these cars appear in *Caboose Cars of the Santa Fe Railway* by Frank Elling-

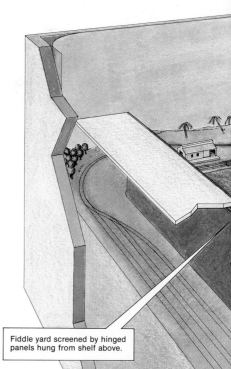

Fiddle yard screened by hinged panels hung from shelf above.

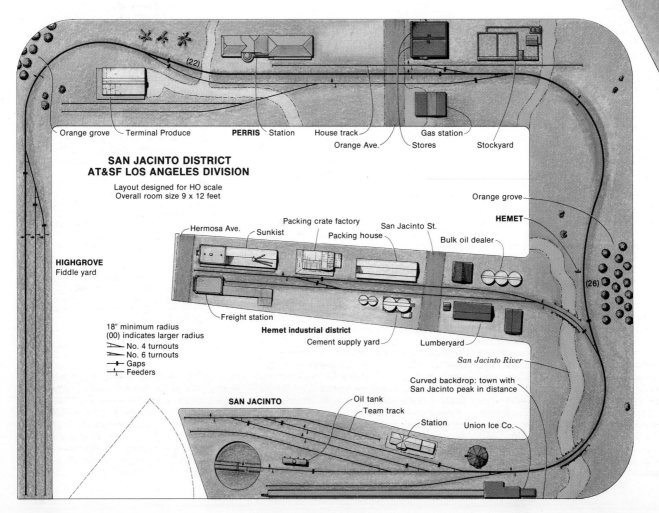

Orange grove — Terminal Produce
PERRIS Station — House track — Gas station
Orange Ave. — Stores — Stockyard

**SAN JACINTO DISTRICT
AT&SF LOS ANGELES DIVISION**

Layout designed for HO scale
Overall room size 9 x 12 feet

Orange grove

HEMET

Hermosa Ave. — Sunkist
Packing crate factory — San Jacinto St.
Packing house
Bulk oil dealer

HIGHGROVE
Fiddle yard

Freight station

18" minimum radius
(00) indicates larger radius
— No. 4 turnouts
— No. 6 turnouts
— Gaps
— Feeders

Hemet industrial district
Cement supply yard — Lumberyard

San Jacinto River

Curved backdrop: town with
San Jacinto peak in distance

SAN JACINTO
Oil tank
Team track
Station — Union Ice Co.

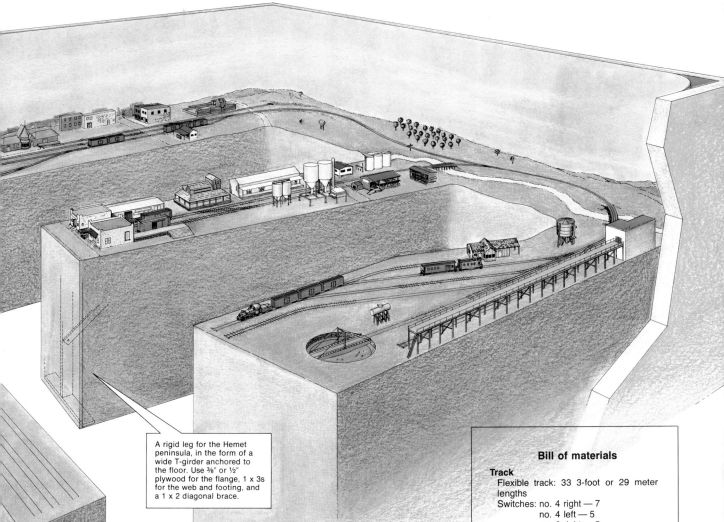

A rigid leg for the Hemet peninsula, in the form of a wide T-girder anchored to the floor. Use ⅜" or ½" plywood for the flange, 1 x 3s for the web and footing, and a 1 x 2 diagonal brace.

ton and published by Railroad Car Press.

The mixed-train operation would make for a leisurely evening of switching for one man, using either a simple switchlist or card order system of car distribution. I wouldn't pay too much attention to the short scheduled turnaround time at San Jacinto, as second-class branchline schedules were used mainly to provide trains with running authority without the need for train orders. If you wanted to share the operation with a friend, a switcher could be stationed at San Jacinto and given the task of having outbound cars ready from that town and Hemet so that 505 could quickly become 506. The mixed trains would switch only Perris under this scheme.

For more intense operations, the San Jacinto District can stage a pretty fair fruit rush to simulate orange-harvesting season. The three tracks in the fiddle yard would allow setting up two extra trains of empty refrigerator cars, in addition to the regular mixed, to be iced at San Jacinto, spotted for loading, and dispatched east with fresh citrus.

Such a rush might be spread over several operating sessions. To start, the mixed train would begin bringing more empties onto the San Jacinto District than are needed immediately, stashing the excess reefers in the pass at Perris and the storage track at San Jacinto. Then you could

have a very busy session or two with extras bringing more empty reefers in and hauling loaded ones out, with all tracks crowded to capacity. Finally, the end of the rush would be signaled by a session in which only the mixed train brings any cars in, with perhaps an extra coming in as a caboose hop to take out the last cars of the harvest. After this the San Jacinto District would settle back to its quiet mixed-train running until the next crop comes in.

The fiddle yard is the key to this operating flexibility, since by rearranging trains there between operating sessions, you can vary the intensity of the traffic and control the number of cars actually on the railroad. Storage shelves above or below the staging tracks would be handy for holding extra reefers and other freight cars.

I have shown gaps and feeders on the track plan for conventional block control, but if more than one operator is to work the San Jacinto District, a command control system would be worth considering. Command control allows completely independent control of locomotives on electrically continuous tracks, and while it requires that each locomotive carry a receiver, either the CTC-16's or any commercial system's receiver will easily fit inside an HO Santa Fe steam engine tender. This kind of control would make it easy to invite someone else to share the fun, since there would be no complex controls or block limits to learn. When the railroad is really busy, command control will allow interesting cooperative switching, which would be almost impossible with conventional wiring.

Bill of materials

Track

Flexible track: 33 3-foot or 29 meter lengths

Switches: no. 4 right — 7
no. 4 left — 5
no. 6 right — 5
no. 6 left — 1

Cork roadbed: 42 3-foot lengths

Structures

Perris: station, scratchbuild from drawings in RAILROAD STATION PLANBOOK; Terminal Produce Co., Campbell no. 377; stores, Con Cor/Heljan no. 902; gas station, Evergreen Hill Designs no. 206; stockyard, Campbell no. 400.

Hemet: lumberyard, two Atlas no. 750 with modification; bulk oil dealership, Williams Brothers no. 500 and no. 501; cement supply yard, Kibri no. 9950 and no. 9952; packing house, Con Cor/Heljan no. 915 modified; crate factory, Campbell no. 422; Sunkist packing plant, Suydam no. 83 with no. 1 as extension; freight station, scratchbuild from Hermosa Beach freight station construction story in SCRATCHBUILDING & KITBASHING MODEL RAILROAD STATIONS; San Jacinto River trestles, two Campbell no. 303.

San Jacinto: station, Campbell no. 367; water tank, Campbell no. 356; icing plant, Suydam no. 566 modified; oil tank, Classic Miniatures no. 31; turntable, Diamond Scale Models 75-foot single-span model.

If the San Jacinto District could be built in a slightly larger room, I would nevertheless advise keeping it simple. The first priority for using additional space would be enlarging the aisles, followed by increasing the minimum radius and allowing more space for scenery. Good operating railroads don't have to be crowded, and this one is meant to be comfortable.

The Rowland Springs RR. layout

Its unbelievable history provides clues to the selection of rolling stock and structures. Once it was 2-foot gauge, then interurban, and now it is standard gauge with self-propelled cars

BY LINN H. WESTCOTT

WITH the sudden fuel shortages of the mid-1970's, North American lifestyle was greatly changed. There were disasters, as we well know. But also, back in those years, came the beginnings of some delightful developments: results of Yankee ingenuity, Southern perseverance, Western vigor, and Canadian candor in combination. One of the instances that exemplifies this occurred in the region around Trondheim down in Maine. The story occurs in four eras which I will not take in chronological order. Suffice it to say, for the moment, that today Trondheim is a thriving community as it was also in the early 1900's; but in between it had decayed what seemed hopelessly.

The bad years were much the result of the automobile. The interstate highway was not built close enough to Trondheim to help it; yet it was near enough to siphon away most of Trondheim's small factories. Even the little woodworking plant that made the famous Curvable Flyer sleds for youngsters had gone. The Grand Chunk Ry., coming up from Portland, threaded its main line through Trondheim; but passenger trains had been withdrawn, the freights rattled through without stopping, except for the local. It came on Thursdays in alternate weeks only. Main St. was a row of stores, many of them boarded up. Behind were the once lovely homes, some in good repair, others not. Most of the younger people had moved away from their family homes to Portland, Boston, or farther. This is the way it was nearly 20 years ago when the fuel shortages began; but before we come to the present, let's backtrack to the early 1900's.

Then, Trondheim was alive. It was building new schools. Factories were enlarging their quarters. And in those days, being a county seat was also considered beneficial.

But overall, the reason for Trondheim's prosperity was because it was the gateway to Rowland Springs, some 17 miles to the south. That's 27 kilometers in case you have forgotten the old measures. Rowland Springs rivaled such watering places as Saratoga, French Lick, and Manitou. It was fashionable for the people of Boston, from Beacon Hill, Back Bay, and even as far west as Newton Highlands, to vacation at the Rowland Springs Hotel and Spa, playing tennis on the lawn, canoeing on Mousemabroomtic Pond in front of the hotel, drinking or swimming in the spring water, or getting lost and finding oneself again in the great maze beside the pond. The maze was a network of footpaths separated by tall hedges of yew that kept seven gardeners busy pruning them. It was said to be a copy of a similar maze at Clematis Brook, near Boston, and that one was a copy from Hampton Court in England.

The hotel building was like a castle and a chateau combined. It had a grand central dining room, a glass veranda looking down upon the pond, and several wings of rooms with large windows and handmade lace curtains. The grounds were lovely, sloping down in all directions to a moat which had been dug around the foot of the hill. By deed, no roadway was ever to cross the moat and intrude upon the tranquility of the estate.

An exception was made for the interurban cars, for they were built with especially quiet gears. They crossed a trestle onto the hotel lawn where guests could descend under a glass-roofed shelter. Except for a footbridge, the interurban was the only approach to the hotel.

At the north end of Mousemabroomtic Pond was the Rowland Spa bottling works, connected to the interurban with a short spur track. From here carloads of bottled water were shipped to every state and six of the provinces. Some of the wetter states ordered the water by the tank car load; and for these the interurban trestles had to be specially reinforced. The trademark of Rowland Spa Water was beautifully lithographed on every bottle label: a mermaid in the pond looking up at the flag-topped towers of the hotel. In the hotel's east wing there

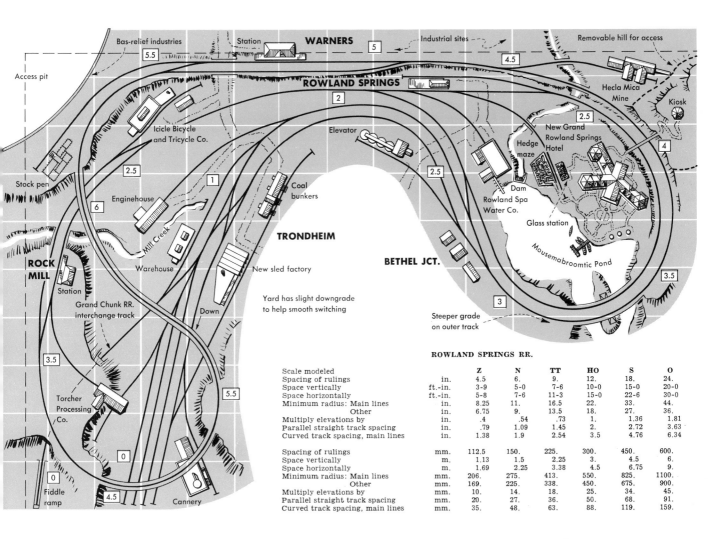

ROWLAND SPRINGS RR.

		Z	N	TT	HO	S	O
Scale modeled							
Spacing of rulings	in.	4.5	6.	9.	12.	18.	24.
Space vertically	ft.-in.	3-9	5-0	7-6	10-0	15-0	20-0
Space horizontally	ft.-in.	5-8	7-6	11-3	15-0	22-6	30-0
Minimum radius: Main lines	in.	8.25	11.	16.5	22.	33.	44.
Other	in.	6.75	9.	13.5	18.	27.	36.
Multiply elevations by	in.	.4	.54	.73	1.	1.36	1.81
Parallel straight track spacing	in.	.79	1.09	1.45	2.	2.72	3.63
Curved track spacing, main lines	in.	1.38	1.9	2.54	3.5	4.76	6.34
Spacing of rulings	mm.	112.5	150.	225.	300.	450.	600.
Space vertically	m.	1.13	1.5	2.25	3.	4.5	6.
Space horizontally	m.	1.69	2.25	3.38	4.5	6.75	9.
Minimum radius: Main lines	mm.	206.	275.	413.	550.	825.	1100.
Other	mm.	169.	225.	338.	450.	675.	900.
Multiply elevations by	mm.	10.	14.	18.	25.	34.	45.
Parallel straight track spacing	mm.	20.	27.	36.	50.	68.	91.
Curved track spacing, main lines	mm.	35.	48.	63.	88.	119.	159.

was a plunge where you could soak in the great water. Glasses of spa water were kept fresh on tables in the lobby. It was said to cure more ailments than any other water taken twice.

The secret of the water was in the bog at the far side of the pond. Here a natural spring welled upward, then filtered through the decaying reeds to reach the pond. This gave it a natural carbonation, a pale tea color, and the flavor of roots. Much of its popularity was not due so much to its supposed curative properties as to its unique ability, as a mixer, to make cheap vodka taste like Scotland's own boggy brew.

A great wintertime specialty of the waterworks was to cut the ice from the pond in the old-fashioned way. The sawed blocks were hauled to the upper floor of the bottlehouse, then were cut and polished into precise 1″ ice cubes — the only effervescent ice cubes of their time and on the menus of better hotels only "in season."

The cubes were shipped in white refrigerator cars bearing the mermaid emblem and fancy lettering reading "Rowland Spa Icicle Cubes."

The interurban was a fairly crooked line with several short but rather steep hills to climb. In all other respects it was a first-class property. It had its own flatcar, several tank cars, and several refrigerator cars, but boxcars of other roads were used for the bottle goods. The pride of the line was in the two parlor cars that met all Grand Chunk trains in Trondheim to take guests to the hotel. These cars were a pale olive green with dark red trim and brass fittings, including a polished trolley pole. They had wide arched windows with ruby glass in their upper panels. The carpet was green and the seats were comfortable wicker armchairs. A white-turbaned Hindu porter handed you a glass of Rowland Water at the least provocation.

Each car had three tiffany lamps hanging from the ceiling with a leaded glass image of the mermaid carefully worked into the design. A big brass curving handbrake handle could be seen by the front window as the motorman pulled the car up to a stop — an assurance of the safety of the equipment.

Nearly always the cars were run in pairs. Sometimes the traffic required it but the real reason was that it was more impressive.

There was another car on the road. This was plainer, but well kept. It had a baggage compartment and coach seats behind. Every evening it made a run to the hotel to take the many chambermaids safely home. Its other important service was as a locomotive. It had heavy trucks with large motors and ordinarily could manage three boxcars or one tank car over the line. Things were different with wet leaves on the track. Then one of the parlor cars had to be summoned to shove from behind while the combine struggled in front to get one elephantlike tank car over the humps.

The reason the interurban line was so crooked takes us back to the first of the four eras of our story.

In the 1870's Trondheim was a village settled by people from the old country. The Grand Chunk Ry. had reached it and the future looked good. Rowland, farther south, had been bypassed by the railway, which made a deviation to reach Lewiston. There was not much at Rowland, anyway. A small sawmill had dammed the Mousemabroomtic River, creating the pond. This also created the bog which in turn created the strange spring water, but that was not appreciated for a while.

At first the farmers of the area were glad to have the railroad; then they began to forget its importance to them and grumble about the freight rates. Among the complainers was Knute Svenn of Rowland, a wealthy gentleman farmer whose mansion was on top of the mound where the Rowland Hotel was later built. Svenn got the idea of building a second railroad, to Trondheim, passing through Rowland, and he had a lot of support for his idea from neighboring farmers. They had learned about the economical way a 2-foot-gauge railroad had been built between Billerica and Bedford in Massachusetts.

Svenn went to the Maine state legislature and obtained a charter for the Casco Bay & Rumford RR. with the idea of running first from Trondheim to Portland, then extending north beyond Rumford. Stock certificates were printed and prospects looked good, but word came that the Billerica line had failed.

Most of the enthusiasm collapsed, but Svenn had a lot of Old World stubbornness and tried to go it alone. He had a plan he thought would be workable. He believed that the water from the spring had cured his gout and so should help others. He would build a 2-foot-gauge railroad from Rowland to connect with the Grand Chunk at Trondheim. Also, he would build an inn. The plan was to use the profits that should accrue in the first several years to extend the project.

Svenn put a down payment on one of the B&B locomotives and a car, bought enough of the rail to lay track, and got the line between Rowland — which he renamed Rowland Springs — and Trondheim into working order. Svenn did not have enough funds left to also build an inn. Instead, he converted his own home into a public house.

Springtime came and ads were placed in the Boston papers. This was in 1883.

Then came disaster. That summer it snowed in July, and no one vacationed at the new resort.

Svenn was bankrupt. He lost the farm to some neighbors who had lent him some support. The house, which no one wanted, lay idle, decayed, and eventually was struck by lightning and burned to the ground. The locomotive, car, and rail were used to build some of the better known 2-foot-gauge railroads of Maine. Only the crooked and steep roadbed remained as evidence of the project. This was used, in 1904, to build the interurban line; and that accounts for why the interurban itself was so crooked.

What happened to the interurban? That brings us to the third period of the histories of Trondheim and Rowland Springs.

WITH the end of World War I it became painfully evident that Bostonians were no longer charmed by Rowland Springs. They could drive farther north for their vacations. Both the interurban and the hotel were closed. The parlor cars were said to have been sold to a South American line, but I could find no trace of them. The combine body became a hotdog stand in Trondheim. Rails were never removed but the ties rotted beneath them.

For a while Rowland Spa Water was shipped by truck, but Prohibition had come, limiting demand. Then a spring freshet burst the dam and drained the pond. Now the spring was perfectly pure and so had no commercial value.

The great hotel building was soundly built, but nature took a toll of some of its wooden parts. The roof caved in over the grand staircase. Moss grew on the railings and water dripped onto the solid walnut planks of the floor. The lack of a road, although an original cause of the hotel's failure, now became a blessing. The nearest public road was a half mile away, too far for lazy vandals to walk to stone the many windows. Sometimes the older people of Trondheim would climb the hill behind their town and look far to the south to see the summer sunset reflected in the windows of the once grand building.

TODAY, less than 20 years after the fuel shortages came, we can again enjoy the offerings of Rowland Springs. This change came when some businessmen of Kennebunkport realized that there would again be a need for resorts one could reach without using an automobile. They remembered Rowland Springs and they found that the hotel building was mostly sound. They decided to re-create the resort, including a railroad to meet all trains at Trondheim. [The Eastern & Maritime Joint Canadien & American Railroad Authority had long since taken over the Grand Chunk, and passenger trains were again operating.]

New ties were slipped under the old interurban rails on the ex narrow-gauge roadbed. The worst of the curves and grades were reduced to more civil standards. At first a steam locomotive was used for all service on the new Rowland Springs RR., it having been obtained from a museum and reboilered. But traffic developed and the railroad now has two stainless steel self-powered cars. They are pooled with eight similar cars owned by the E&MJC&ARA for twice-daily through service from Boston to Rowland Springs and also to Bar Harbor.

The new stainless steel cars are the pride of the operation. The front car is a mail-baggage-buffet combine. The other has luxurious coach seats and a skytop tap lounge. The little mermaid is seen in bas-relief on the side of each car.

The roof was repaired on the hotel and a new dam was built. Chemists and naturalists found a way to re-create the famous Rowland Spa Water — a small amount of pollution had to be added to the pond deliberately, since less than natural pollution was otherwise found in American streams by that time.

Just as the project appeared to be ready to go, a calamity occurred that made it look like the Casco Bay & Rumford fiasco would be repeated. Not everyone had been in favor of the resort revival, including a certain county supervisor. He managed to have the state legislature pass a bill that ruled that no new railroad service can be established over public highway crossings unless the crossings are grade-separated. The Rowland Springs RR. had seven such crossings of public roads, all at grade. To finance them all would be impossible.

Here the Rowland Springs RR. lawyers did not give up. They went back into the history of the road and showed that the Casco Bay & Rumford had never been dissolved. They argued in the courts that it was fair and sensible to require railroad-highway crossings to be separated. They said this really should have been done from the beginning. The judges and everyone nodded. Then the lawyers went on and said that it was also fair and sensible that the first party to any railroad or highway site had priority; that it was unfair to expect the first builder to pay for a crossing that did it no service. The new Rowland Springs RR., operating on the right of way of the Casco Bay & Rumford, had inherited one grade crossing with the post road that existed before the original railroad. It is justifiable, they admitted, that the railroad should pay for the separation of that crossing. But, they continued, the other six crossings with public roads that were

built later were of no service to the railroad, in fact were a nuisance, and that the cost of separating them should be borne by the party or governmental body that built the offending highways.

This did not go well in the local county court, but the case went to higher courts and the highest ruling was in favor of the railroad. This famous case set the precedent for the fair play we now have in most states and provinces for allocating the expenses of grade crossing separations.

The railroad built its overpass over the post road. The county built three separations and closed the remaining roads.

Two of the railroad stations along the rebuilt railroad are shells made from the enameled steel panels of abandoned service stations, but these are rapidly being replaced with beautifully proportioned gingerbread structures in keeping with the historic past of the region. For railfan excursions, the steam locomotive pulls several old wooden cars. One of them, with an unknown history, came from South America; it has wide arched windows.

THE route for a model of the Rowland Springs RR. could be built as narrow-gauge, interurban, or short line; and it can be fitted into many room shapes. An L corner with the benchwork against the outer walls is suggested here. Track radii and length of trains and sidings will depend on space and equipment, but it would be out of character to make either too large.

The route is point to point with a loop at one of the terminals. A crossover at Bethel Junction permits lap running.

Most of the cars reaching Trondheim are switched to the Grand Chunk via the interchange track. They are lifted by hand at the end of this track and are stored on racks below the layout surface. Other cars are rerailed at the fiddle ramp. Even the self-powered cars for Boston leave the layout by this route.

Dashed black lines mark the minimum limits for the rear and one end of the layout, but it is better if several inches of scenery can be extended beyond, as shown in color. In HO and larger sizes, an access pit will be needed in the corner to reach nearby turnouts for maintenance.

One double-switched industry combination is suggested in the plan. Mica-bearing rock is mined and taken by mine-company-owned cars to the upper level of the processing plant by way of a spur at Rock Mill. After processing, the mica materials are dumped into railroad-owned cars from the lower level of this plant.

The main line has two intermediate stations with passing tracks. This makes dispatcher or timetable operation of trains practical, but it would then be helpful to add a second passing track at Warners so three-train meets could be made at at least one point along the line.

Sometimes it is not practical to represent all of the features of a prototype on a model layout. Here, for instance, the moat around the hotel has not been modeled, but there is a suggestion of the hedge maze.

Quonset & East Douglas Ry.

A short line serving a well-industrialized area

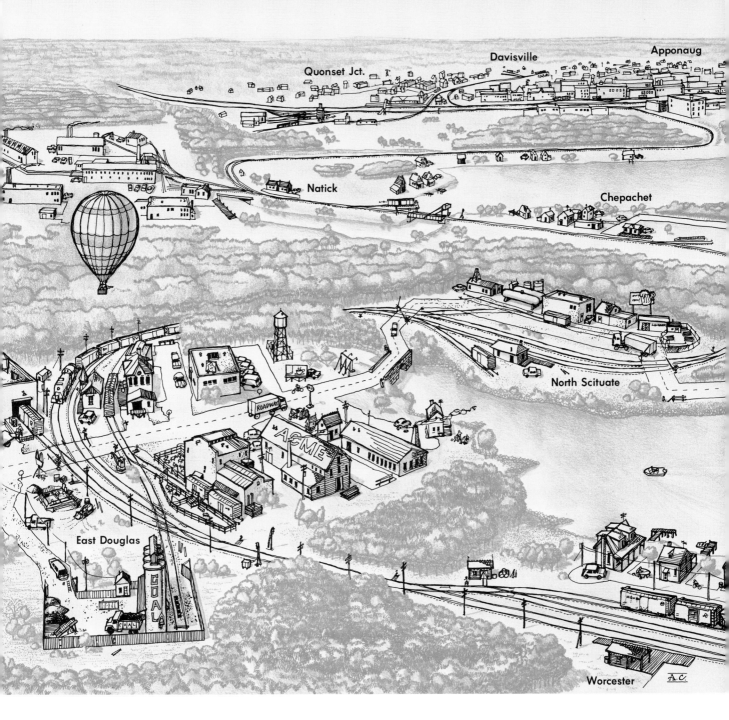

BY DON MITCHELL

"GO WEST, young man!" So said Horace Greeley more than 100 years ago. But there are many model railroaders who remain east of the Mississippi River, and therein lies the reason behind the Quonset & East Douglas Ry. Somewhere in Down East country there resides a model railroader with a penchant for his own layout and with about half a basement's worth of available space. The QED was planned to fit in this space, with appropriate allowances for such nonrailroad, but necessary, clutter as stairs, heaters, and the like.

The concept of the QED is that of a short line which branches off from a major through railroad in order to serve a well-industrialized area. The place names on the QED were chosen from real-life towns lying roughly between Providence, R. I., and Worcester, Mass. However real the place names, no intent is claimed for the QED as a logical candidate for building in the prototype. Neither investors nor civil engineers would be likely to be interested in a route which closely parallels the present-day Providence & Worcester, and

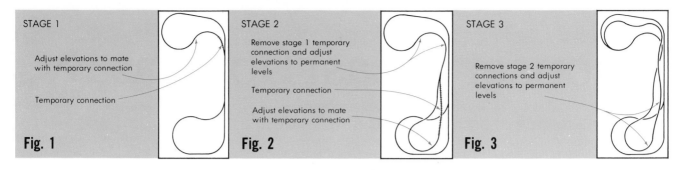

STAGE 1

Adjust elevations to mate
with temporary connection

Temporary connection

Fig. 1

STAGE 2

Remove stage 1 temporary
connection and adjust
elevations to permanent
levels

Temporary connection

Adjust elevations to mate
with temporary connection

Fig. 2

STAGE 3

Remove stage 2 temporary
connections and adjust
elevations to permanent
levels

Fig. 3

whose geographical profile consists of a descent as it proceeds inland away from the ocean.

Regardless of its failings as an imaginary real-life railroad, the QED makes a certain amount of sense as a layout plan for a model railroad. It has provisions for a reasonable out-and-back run, continuous running, and lots of switching at industries; and the logical sequence of operations would be quite convenient for the adoption of walkaround controls. Other features include the use of 24″-minimum-radius curves (in HO gauge), and track arranged so that the lowest level is nearest the edge of the layout in order to promote better scenic treatment and better operation. And, except for one corner of the layout, all turnouts are both visible and within 30″ of the operating aisle for ease in both construction and operation.

The hub of operations on the QED is Quonset Junction, probably the most visible feature because it is both the largest area and at the highest elevation. Here the QED interchanges with the main line of the New York, New Haven & Hartford RR. The cramped and inconveniently arranged QED yard exists in stark contrast to the well-maintained double-track main line of the New Haven. (Naturally we've elected to model an era when the NH was in its prime rather than its bankrupt and broken-down condition.)

While the New Haven main makes a majestic sweep across the topmost level in wide curves, the representation of NH trains and equipment is considerably less majestic. Since no place has been provided for the NH trains to go (or hide), a smallish peddler locomotive and its caboose are about the only NH equipment in visible action on the main. Their purpose is to service the industrial spurs leading directly off the NH line. If appropriate to the era modeled, further NH activity could be represented by an RDC run which terminated at Quonset Junction, or which even con-

tinued onto QED trackage as part of a joint run.

To prevent all that beautiful mainline track from lying fallow, our QED layout plan again deviates from the prototype by interweaving the branchline operation onto the NH rails. Switching the QED yard at Quonset Junction requires either the use of NH tracks or crossing them on the wye lead. Use of the wye for reversing the direction of equipment requires that the NH tracks be both used and crossed, while the dispatch of QED trains means joint use of the NH main between Quonset Junction and Apponaug.

The unlikeliness of these arrangements for use on the prototype is made to serve a purpose on the QED, however, as they provide visible justification for the interlocking tower extending upward from the corner of the NH/QED station at Quonset Junction. The joint use of this trackage could also be used as the setting for working interlocking signals on the model.

ALONG THE LINE

At Apponaug, the QED branches away from the NH and descends to the busy industrial town of Natick. The suggested industries in Natick provide a wide variety of logical routing destinations for individual cars. There is ample track capacity to handle these cars in this area, and the track arrangement poses enough problems to keep boredom from setting in during operating sessions.

Leaving Natick, the QED crosses a small through girder bascule bridge before diving under the NH main. The grade continues to descend as the QED passes through Chepachet, where the lone team track spur requires that cars be on the north end of the locomotive in order to be switched here. Chepachet is also the location of the connection for continuous running, which can be used to simulate an interchange point with another railroad.

The next town on the QED is North Scit-

uate, where the track reaches its lowest elevation. Here the industries have been somewhat squeezed to fit between the spur and the continuous cutoff track which ascends at the rear of the town. More space could have been made for these industries had not the monotony of tracks parallel to the table edge been purposely avoided.

The QED then disappears under Davisville for the run along the back wall to the reversing loop at East Douglas/Worcester. The hidden sidings, which represent Worcester, were included to increase operating possibilities, albeit at the cost of easy access to the turnouts and trackage involved.

The operating scheme for this end of the layout envisions that two trains will be held in the Worcester sidings at all times, one headed in each direction. As a third train arrives, it is alternately routed to the remaining empty siding via East Douglas or directly from North Scituate. Once this third train has been stopped on its holding siding, the other train headed in the same direction is released to continue. This little deception helps create the illusion that there is a considerable business for the QED in the unseen area of Worcester.

Some method will be required to indicate when the trains have cleared the hidden turnouts at Worcester. The light-sensitive detector circuit described by Peter J. Thorne in his book PRACTICAL ELECTRONIC PROJECTS FOR MODEL RAILROADERS [Kalmbach, $3.50] is one which would be well suited to this purpose.

A typical operation on the QED could commence with three trains in the East Douglas/Worcester area and one at Quonset Junction. A peddler freight would be started from each point, and while the peddlers are switching the en route industries the yard operator could be working the industries at Davisville and along the NH main. The cars from these industries would then be made into a train ready to depart Quonset Junction. As the two ped-

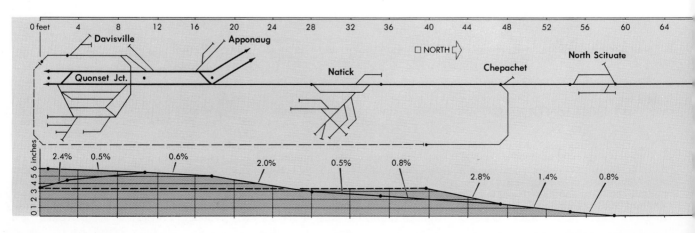

dlers on line pulled into the opposite ends of the QED from their starting points, two more peddlers would be dispatched on their way and the cycle would be started all over again.

If that isn't enough operation to keep the operators busy, passenger service could be added to intersperse with the freight operations. The previously mentioned RDC would be ideal for this because it could be fitted into many different back-and-forth patterns along both the NH and the QED tracks.

SOME ALTERNATIVES

For those modelers whose geographical preferences are more closely aligned with Greeley's advice, the QED can be converted into a western prototype by little more than substituting mines for the mills among the industries. Of course, some hills and cuts in place of the industrial buildings along the back wall would also contribute to a more suitable scenic setting.

"Narrow-minded" modelers will find that the sharper curves of their narrow-gauge prototypes would permit shrinking the overall dimensions of the QED by a quarter or a third and still preserve the basic plan. If the QED is shrunk or modeled in scales smaller than HO, some consideration must be given to rearranging the track in the Apponaug/Natick areas. Otherwise the covered access hatch would probably be reduced below a practical size. Elsewhere, overall reduction in dimensions will only improve access on the QED by making aisle-to-track reaches shorter.

In building the QED, construction should start at the lowest elevation and then should progress on to the higher elevations of track. Use of temporary connecting tracks at various stages (see figs. 1 and 2) would permit reasonable operation to be commenced soon after construction got under way. These temporary tracks would be removed and the elevation of the permanent tracks adjusted as the construction advances. In the next to last stage (see fig. 3), operation would utilize the continuous-run cutoff while the Quonset Junction wye and yards are being installed. In addition to the primary track sketched in figs. 1, 2, and 3, industrial spurs and passing sidings should be constructed before moving on to the next stage, as these tracks are one of the prime reasons for building the QED.

Whatever the advice Horace Greeley may have provided, the Quonset & East Douglas would seem to show that half a basement is better than none Down East. Q. E. D.!

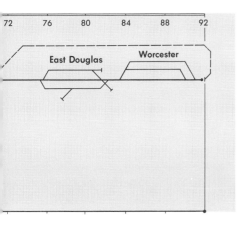

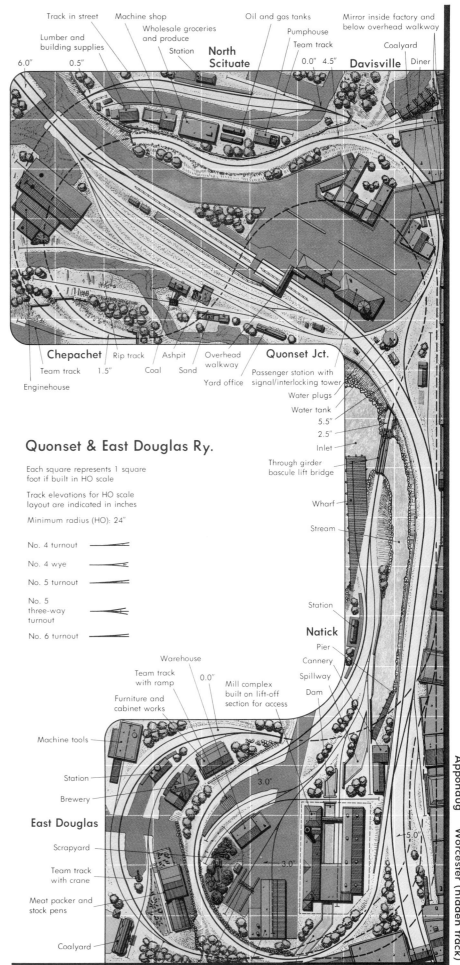

Quonset & East Douglas Ry.

Each square represents 1 square foot if built in HO scale

Track elevations for HO scale layout are indicated in inches

Minimum radius (HO): 24"

No. 4 turnout

No. 4 wye

No. 5 turnout

No. 5 three-way turnout

No. 6 turnout

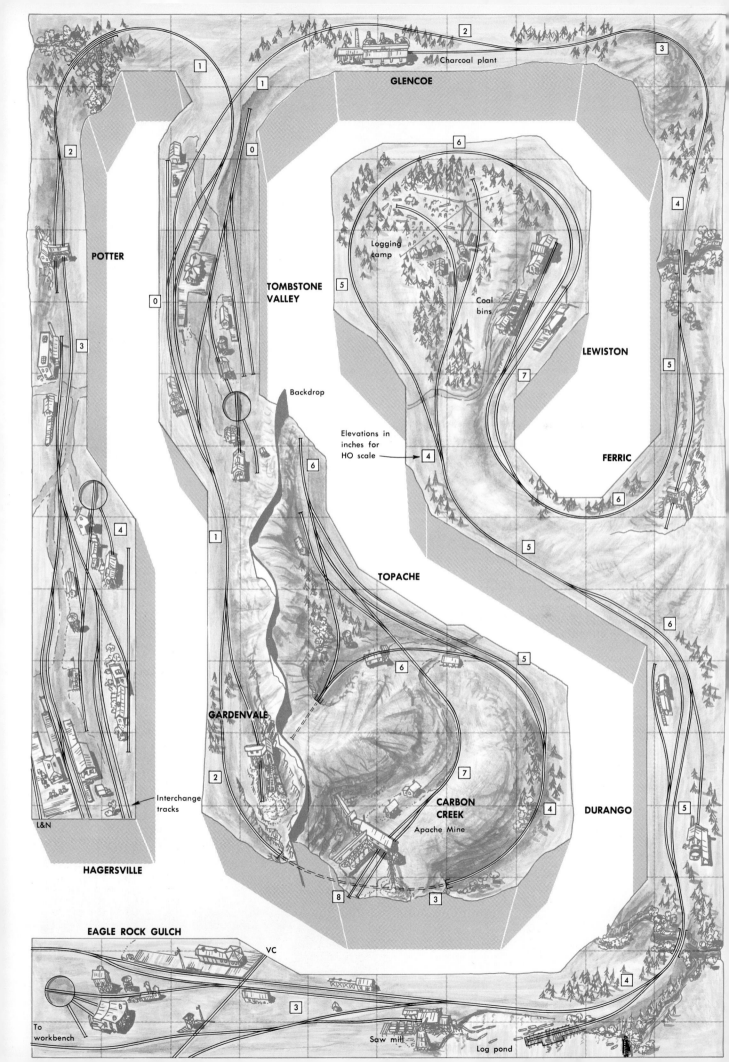

2

Charcoal plant

GLENCOE

1

1

3

0

2

POTTER

0

6

TOMBSTONE VALLEY

Logging camp

5

Coal bins

4

Backdrop

7

LEWISTON

3

Elevations in inches for HO scale

4

4

FERRIC

6

6

TOPACHE

5

4

6

5

1

6

GARDENVALE

6

5

2

7

CARBON CREEK

4

DURANGO

Apache Mine

Interchange tracks

8

3

5

L&N

HAGERSVILLE

EAGLE ROCK GULCH

VC

4

To workbench

3

Saw mill

Log pond

The trail of two railroads

Appalachian scenery and small-town operations are featured in a layout with two shortline companies both competing and complementing each other

BY MICHAEL WELCH

IN the heyday of railroading, many small railroads existed primarily to serve a particular industry or to transport a single product. Such railroads were often owned by large companies, and they had transfer facilities wherever they made connection with larger railroads.

The imaginary Apache Mining Company RR. and the Tombstone Valley & Eagle Rock Gulch RR. are two such small lines that interchange with each other and with secondary branches of two larger railroads. The AMC belongs to a coal mining company that owns one large mine and leases two smaller mines. AMC's base of operations is in Hagersville, where it interchanges with the L&N. At Tombstone Valley it interchanges with the TV&ERG. The Apache Mine is located up Carbon Creek near the rail's-end hamlet of Topache. This is the main revenue supplier of the line, but some coal also comes from the crusher at Gardenvale and a small mine at Potter.

The TV&ERG's base of operations is in Eagle Rock Gulch. It interchanges with the Virginia Central at this point. The lumber industry and an iron mine provide the major income for the TV&ERG.

The two railroads are set in the locale of the Appalachian Mountains near the Virginia-West Virginia border. Scenery is one of the most important elements of the layout. Since both railroads are short lines and the trackage is uncrowded, scenery can be used to heighten the effect of a wandering railroad, picking its way through the countryside to arrive at its destination with the least amount of difficulty and at a low construction cost. There are plenty of trees, to the point that at times trains on the TV&ERG get lost from sight. The effect can create the impression that the main line is much longer than it really is.

At Hagersville, three of the AMC's tracks extend to the edge of the benchwork, creating the illusion of continuing onward to become part of the L&N. Two

of these are the transfer tracks where the loads of coal are left and the empties are picked up. It would be quite possible to make this operation realistic by using dummy loads of coal for the hoppers and removing them after the cars have been spotted for pickup by the L&N. The AMC's engine facilities are located here. Due to the size of the railroad, it has only one engine. Two daily round trips are made to Topache, with the single engine performing all of the necessary switching duties en route.

The AMC picks up hoppers of coal and cars of sawed shoring timbers at Tombstone Valley. Ten small cars of iron ore are loaded daily at Apache. It also picks up an occasional load of tombstones from the local factory. Due to the lack of roads

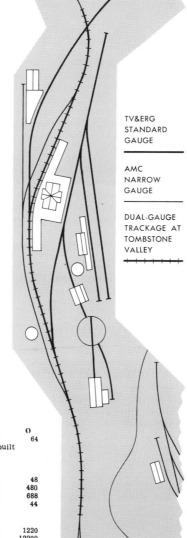

TV&ERG
STANDARD
GAUGE

AMC
NARROW
GAUGE

DUAL-GAUGE
TRACKAGE AT
TOMBSTONE
VALLEY

in this region the easiest method of crossing the mountain is to travel on the two railroads. There is a small amount of interline passenger service.

The TV&ERG delivers its lumber products to the transfer track in Eagle Rock Gulch and picks up general merchandise from the east coast. Much of this general merchandise continues on, via the AMC, to Hagersville. Engine facilities and the TV&ERG's carshops (also the AMC's) are located here. The sawmill of the Toothpick Timber Co. is located just outside of town. Both Durango and Lewiston are small towns that serve the people of their region and as such are mostly receiving towns for general merchandise.

Between Durango and Lewiston, the Toothpick Timber Co. has its major logging operations. The land is only partially logged off, and since this company is one of the pioneers in the field of reforestation, much of its logging region is covered by new growth. Lewiston has a unique industry in the form of a coalyard. It operates on a reverse principle to that of the usual coalyard. Small individual miners bring their wagonloads of coal to the yard. It is then massed together and shipped out by carloads.

Just outside Tombstone Valley at Glencoe is a small charcoal plant that uses slash and low-grade timber, and ships via both railroads. In Tombstone Valley, the TV&ERG has engine facilities and maintains the transfer facilities for the two railroads. The TV&ERG runs a single round trip daily and has as many special logging trains as are necessary.

These railroads might best be modeled to represent the predepression era, when relatively heavy traffic still made them a paying venture.

It would be a simple matter to make one of the railroads a narrow-gauge line: possibly the AMC. This would provide some interesting interchange facilities and dual-gauge trackwork at both Tombstone Valley and Hagersville. Another variation would be to increase the grade on the AMC from 2 percent to 3.5 percent between Tombstone Valley and Topache, thus making it necessary to double the hill or use a helper.

The arrangement of the aisles allows the engineer to follow the route of his train at all times. Walkaround control would be a cinch as long as the aisles were provided wide enough at spots to allow operators to pass each other. With the use of individual control panels mounted in the side of the benchwork, one could control his train without the nuisance of dragging cablework. Since it is possible to reach all parts of the layout, hand-thrown turnouts can be used, heightening the operating realism.

APACHE MINING COMPANY RR.
TOMBSTONE VALLEY & EAGLE ROCK GULCH RR.

SCALE MODELED	N	TT	HO	S	O
Drawing reduction 1:	16	24	32	48	64
Normal turnout size	Approx. no 6, all scales; scratchbuilt				
Maximum grade, main line	2 percent, all scales				
SIZES IN INCHES					
Spacing of rulings	12	18	24	36	48
Width of space	120	180	240	360	480
Length of space	172	258	344	516	688
Minimum radius	11	16.5	22	33	44
SIZES IN MILLIMETERS					
Spacing of rulings	305	457	610	914	1220
Width of space	3050	4575	6100	9150	12200
Length of space	4370	6555	8740	13110	17480
Minimum radius	280	420	560	840	1120

Class 1 for one man

The action is heavy and continuous, just like that at a prototype division point

BY E. S. SEELEY JR.

THE lover of class 1 trunkline railroading faces a special problem in designing a layout. How can one man possibly run a whole trunkline railroad all by himself? Obviously he can't — but he can handle a single part of such a railroad, no matter how heavily trafficked it may be. If he is willing to forego mainline running for the pleasures of yard switching and train servicing, he can easily fit a layout representing a portion of a trunk line into the kind of space most of us have available. The Great Central shows one way.

The area represents a medium-sized industrial center, the imaginary city of Dorchester. It is also division headquarters and an interchange point on the Great Central RR. We have modeled the GC's passenger station and storage tracks, freight classification yard, and engine terminal. We have been able to include the Dorchester Belt RR., a wholly owned GC subsidiary, as an operating bonus. The DBRR. runs through Dorchester's industrial district to an interchange with another trunk line, the Atlantic & Western, on the other side of the city. This gives us all we need to duplicate class 1 railroading in and around a typical industrial city.

There isn't any main line. Main lines demand a great deal of space if they are to be represented with any degree of reality. Unless the main line is to be the principal feature of a trunkline layout, it is best eliminated. On the Great Central we represent the main line with five hidden layover tracks connected to both ends of the division yards. These holding tracks take up no effective space, since they are located under the industrial district; yet they produce the equivalent traffic of two separate mainline divisions running for hundreds of miles in opposite directions from Dorchester.

The train movement sheet shows the volume of traffic in and around Dorchester in the course of a typical day. There are 25 trains, and each demands its own switching movements that vary each day. This traffic can be handled quite efficiently on the model layout by one man.

The layout's basic operating practices merit a closer look because they avoid a common but unprototypic situation found on many model layouts. Most of the rolling stock on the ordinary layout is found standing in the yards. Prototype road superintendents who know their job well would regard such a condition with horror. Their income depends on moving traffic, not letting it sit. Their motto is: "Empty yards and a full main."

On the Great Central model this is accomplished by starting each operating session with most of the rolling stock made up into four trains. These are out of sight on the layover tracks. Two are passenger trains; two are freights. The rest of our cars are divided more or less equally between the Atlantic & Western interchange yard, sidings along the Belt Line, and Dorchester division yards. This is a more realistic approximation of prototype car distribution. Now for the fun:

At specified intervals trains are brought into the division yards from the hidden layover tracks. They are serviced, classified, made into new trains, and sent on their way. The action is heavy and continuous, just like that at a prototype division point.

Despite the traffic volume the lone operator never has more than one train movement to handle at a time. If he wishes he can run by timetable and fast clock; but a layout like this is also a natural for "sequence operation." This means that you forget about synchronizing your movements to a clock. Time is merely taken in order. You regard each train movement as a separate step in a progressive chain.

For example: the 1 a.m. Belt Line way freight movement called for in the schedule takes place after the departure of no. 21. The operator can spend as much time with no. 21 as is needed. In sequence operation the passage of time is measured by the completion of railroad movements rather than by the progress of clock hands. Not only is scheduling easier but the operator can also take time out to answer questions, to rectify minor problems that are bound to occur, and to analyze and experiment with different kinds of switching moves. Sometimes he may just sit back and contemplate the fascinating harmony of the little world he presides over.

Regardless of what operating method he uses, the operator of this layout is handling a traffic volume that would do credit to a large club layout.

Kinds of traffic

The Dorchester yards see three general types of Great Central trains: freights that originate or terminate there, freights that run through, and through passenger trains. Freights can start or end their runs at Dorchester because it is a division point with interchange facilities.

On a prototype road a division point is nothing more than a bottleneck. Freight cars that have been moving nicely along main or branch lines must stop at a division point to be classified or reclassified as to destination and route before continuing their journeys. This kind of bottleneck is just as fundamental to traditional railroading as are the movements of long trains between two points hundreds of miles apart.

The freights that terminate at Dorchester from either direction arrive on track 5. Engines and cabooses are cut off; then the consist is classified according to destination and routing. Car destination can be determined by one of the card or thumbtack forwarding systems described in the past or it can be based on informal, spur-of-the-moment decisions. Track 6 is for classifying westbound through cars; track 7, for eastbound through cars. Track 8 is used for westbound way freights, track 9 for eastbound way freights, track 10 for cars bound for local destinations or the Atlantic & West-

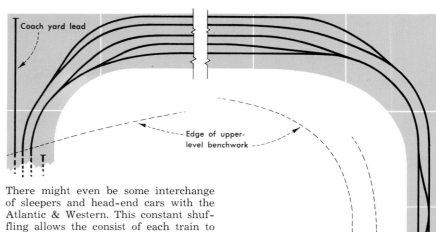

ern interchange. This gives the cars of any freight train four possible classification slots. When a classification track has filled, its cars are moved to the makeup track, track 5. There they are given an engine and caboose and sent on their way.

Many trunk roads operate "mainliners" — freights that run through a number of divisions before the cars are reclassified. The consist of such redball or time freights may be cars bound for the same destination, or cars bound for the same port, manufacturer, or distributor. In any case such trains are not reclassified (switched) but they do have to stop at division points for servicing and crew changes. On the Great Central nos. 21 and 22 are highball freights which continue from Dorchester after such a service stop on track 5. Since Dorchester is an important industrial center, such a train might have a cut of cars to drop or be added, thus varying the routine.

In operating the Great Central a string of cars may leave Dorchester as a through freight; this consist may return later as a way freight. This illustrates the principle on which the layout is run: once a train reaches the layover tracks it loses its identity, eventually becoming another train as called for by the operating schedule.

A heavy passenger schedule can be operated with only three strings of equipment. Each train stops at Dorchester to change crews and be serviced. The trains also pick up and drop diners, sleepers, parlor cars, coaches, and head-end cars.

There might even be some interchange of sleepers and head-end cars with the Atlantic & Western. This constant shuffling allows the consist of each train to reflect the traffic requirements of the time of day it stops at Dorchester — sleepers and head-end cars at night, coaches, parlor cars, and diners during the day.

We mustn't overlook operations on the Belt Line. Once each day the Belt Line transfer loco hauls cars from track 10 to the A&W interchange yard. On the return trip it brings cars routed via the Great Central. A way freight makes a round trip over the Belt Line each night. It switches the industrial sidings, Acme Fast Freight Co.'s terminal, and the adjacent team tracks.

The Great Central is by no means the only possible layout for the man who loves the glory and excitement of class 1 railroading. It simply indicates one way to model this kind of heavily trafficked railroading without the need for vast amounts of space and numerous operators.

LOWER-LEVEL BENCHWORK

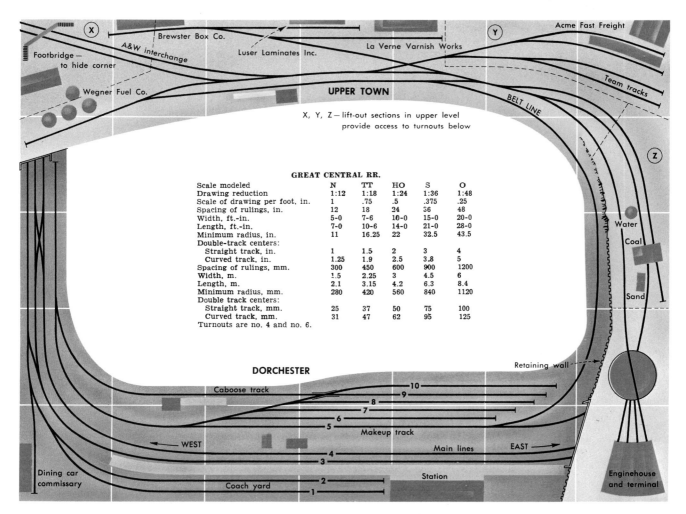

X, Y, Z — lift-out sections in upper level provide access to turnouts below

GREAT CENTRAL RR.

Scale modeled	N	TT	HO	S	O
Drawing reduction	1:12	1:18	1:24	1:36	1:48
Scale of drawing per foot, in.	1	.75	.5	.375	.25
Spacing of rulings, in.	12	18	24	36	48
Width, ft.-in.	5-0	7-6	10-0	15-0	20-0
Length, ft.-in.	7-0	10-6	14-0	21-0	28-0
Minimum radius, in.	11	16.25	22	32.5	43.5
Double-track centers:					
Straight track, in.	1	1.5	2	3	4
Curved track, in.	1.25	1.9	2.5	3.8	5
Spacing of rulings, mm.	300	450	600	900	1200
Width, m.	1.5	2.25	3	4.5	6
Length, m.	2.1	3.15	4.2	6.3	8.4
Minimum radius, mm.	280	420	560	840	1120
Double track centers:					
Straight track, mm.	25	37	50	75	100
Curved track, mm.	31	47	62	95	125

Turnouts are no. 4 and no. 6.

Sagatukett River RR. track plan

A layout for lots of switching with a modest amount of shelf space around the room

BY ROBERT SILAS

DRAWN BY ROBERT WEGNER

THE layout of the Sagatukett River RR. was inspired by the story of the West River RR. which I read in the book *36 Miles of Trouble* by Victor Morse. The prototype and my model project represent a shortline common carrier in New England. The model version connects the terminals of Jackpine and Equinox. From midpoint station Tinkle Creek, a branch extends to a third terminal at Corbel. The pike is designed for a maximum of switching operation with a minimum of trackwork. There are about 20 turnouts. Using handlaid track, I would build the three-way turnout at Jackpine as a stub type.

Industries along the line are of a general nature providing varied cross traffic between stations. A small logging camp is located on the Corbel branch. Logs are freighted from there to Jackpine, where they are dumped into the pond by a jill poke.

The trestle builder has plenty of opportunity to display his art. Don't build them too stoutly, though: a railroad like this should have spindly trestles. A boxcar or two floating in the river near the collapsed trestle, surrounded by a salvage crew, would make an interesting scene.

The storage track at Jackpine can serve both as a place for equipment between runs and as an imaginary interchange with foreign roads. Since storage is dear on a shelf layout of this kind, a little yard fiddling will help at this point. [A fiddle yard is a track or tracks where equipment is manually rearranged or as often exchanged for other equipment in order to increase the variety of rolling stock available for operations on a model railroad. Usually a fiddle yard is hidden, but not in this instance.]

Part of the fun of the SR RR. is in its limitations: The engineer may have a few choice words for the trackbuilders when he finds his train is too long to be run around at Corbel siding. Freight cars commonly get spotted on the turntable lead there. When the switch crewmen at Equinox figure out the easiest way to move a boxcar from the warehouse to the monument works, and to move the boxcar already at the monument works over to the freight house, and still have the engine pointed the right way to leave town, they can count on the arrival of the midday passenger train to gum up the works.

On some prototypes of such makeshift railroads — the West River RR., for example — derailments occurred almost with timetable accuracy. While I don't suggest building an automatic derailer,

I do suggest that rather than cussing at the locomotive the way I usually do, you use derailment as an excuse to run a work train. This train could consist of a boxcar of tools and a passenger car of volunteer helpers loaded at the nearest community. When the train arrives at the scene of the mishap, a little "big hook" action (meaning hand rerailing) is in order.

The layout, as drawn, will fit in a 10 x 15-foot room if you use curves of about 22" (560-mm.) radius. This is about the same whether you build it in HO, On2, or Sn3 size. Other room sizes for other model scales and gauges are indicated in the specification table — but note that the aisleway will be too narrow between Corbel and Equinox if you build with less than 22" radius, as in N or TT

scales or HOn3, etc. In such cases the room should be widened about 1 foot (300 mm.), and this much extra table should be inserted into the benchwork at the zones marked N1 and N2 in the main drawing.

Note that you can use the same track plan almost unchanged for narrow-gauge layouts of a larger scale. For example, a 22" radius can fit this layout into a 10 x 15-foot room in either HO standard, Sn3, or On2 gauge. But when using the larger scales for narrow gauge, track center separations will have to be increased over the HO version. Also, grades and elevations will have to be increased. The amount of increase is dependent upon the width and height of the narrow-gauge equipment, but a 50 percent increase is more than enough for 36"-gauge modeling and 80 percent is probably sufficient for On2, etc. The 2.7 percent grades then become 4.1 percent and 4.9 percent respectively.

MAXIMUM SWITCHING — MINIMUM SPACE

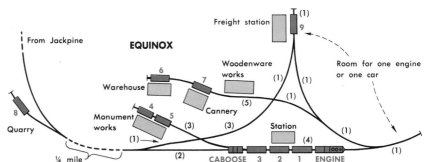

HERE'S a little problem on the Sagatukett River RR. layout that you might like to solve with the least number of moves: A train crew has arrived at Equinox and is receiving its switching instructions from the agent: see sketch of situation. Count as one move each time the engine starts. Uncoupling and reversing direction must be done stopped. Cars cannot be kicked, poled, nor rolled by hand or gravity.

The switch list shows that cars 4, 7, and 9 are to be picked up and eventually taken to Jackpine. Cars 1, 2, and 3 are for the warehouse, freight station, and woodenware works respectively. Car 8 has a load of rough stone to be switched

to the monument works. Car 5 has finished stone for the warehouse. Car 6 is an empty flat to go to the quarry. The pickups 4, 7, and 9 are to be taken with engine ahead, pointed properly, and caboose behind as the final move to Jackpine.

In case track capacity affects your solution, the number of cars that can be spotted in the clear on each part of the layout is shown in parentheses. One additional car can stand on any turnout or crossing not otherwise in use.

Since the caboose is fouling a switch at the beginning, the only practical first move is either to back the train or to uncouple the engine alone to move it around the wye. You go on from there.

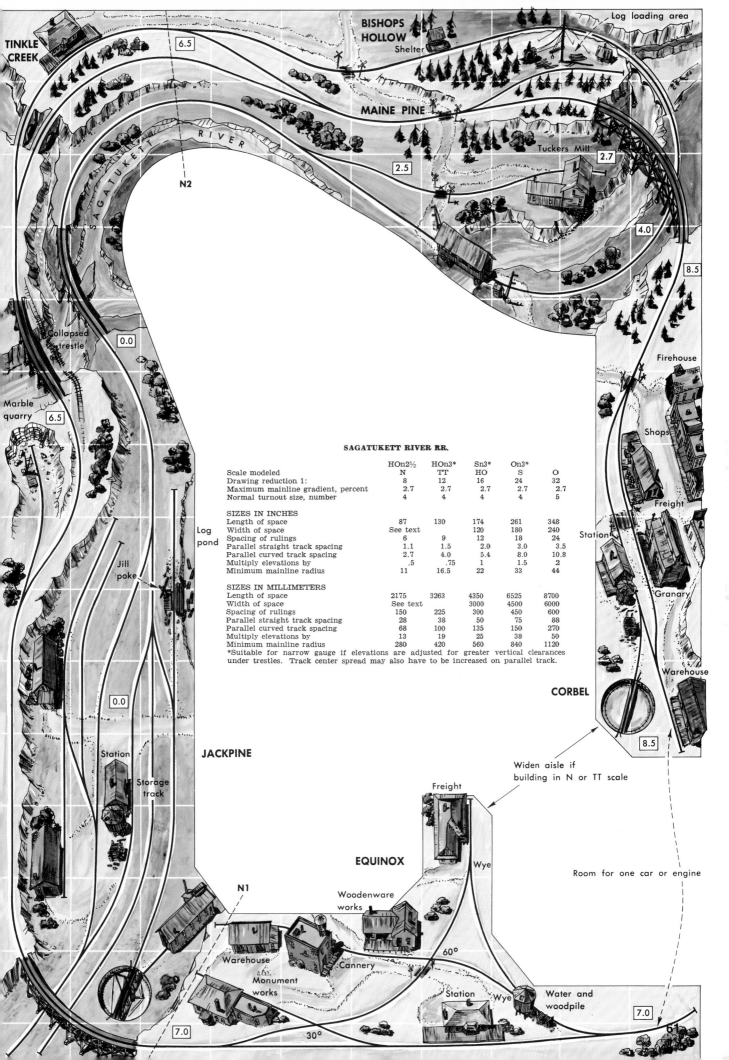

TINKLE CREEK · BISHOPS HOLLOW · Shelter · Log loading area · MAINE PINE · Tuckers Mill · Collapsed trestle · Marble quarry · Log pond · Jill poke · Firehouse · Shops · Freight · Station · Granary · Warehouse · CORBEL · JACKPINE · Station · Storage track · EQUINOX · Freight · Wye · Woodenware works · Warehouse · Cannery · Monument works · Station · Wye · Water and woodpile · Widen aisle if building in N or TT scale · Room for one car or engine

Elevation markers: 6.5 · 2.5 · 2.7 · 4.0 · 8.5 · 0.0 · 6.5 · 0.0 · 8.5 · 7.0 · 7.0 · 30° · 60° · N1 · N2 · 61

SAGATUKETT RIVER RR.

	HOn2½	HOn3*	Sn3*	On3*	
Scale modeled	N	TT	HO	S	O
Drawing reduction 1:	8	12	16	24	32
Maximum mainline gradient, percent	2.7	2.7	2.7	2.7	2.7
Normal turnout size, number	4	4	4	4	5
SIZES IN INCHES					
Length of space	87	130	174	261	348
Width of space	See text		120	180	240
Spacing of rulings	6	9	12	18	24
Parallel straight track spacing	1.1	1.5	2.0	3.0	3.5
Parallel curved track spacing	2.7	4.0	5.4	8.0	10.8
Multiply elevations by	.5	.75	1	1.5	2
Minimum mainline radius	11	16.5	22	33	44
SIZES IN MILLIMETERS					
Length of space	2175	3263	4350	6525	8700
Width of space	See text		3000	4500	6000
Spacing of rulings	150	225	300	450	600
Parallel straight track spacing	28	38	50	75	88
Parallel curved track spacing	68	100	135	150	270
Multiply elevations by	13	19	25	38	50
Minimum mainline radius	280	420	560	840	1120

*Suitable for narrow gauge if elevations are adjusted for greater vertical clearances under trestles. Track center spread may also have to be increased on parallel track.

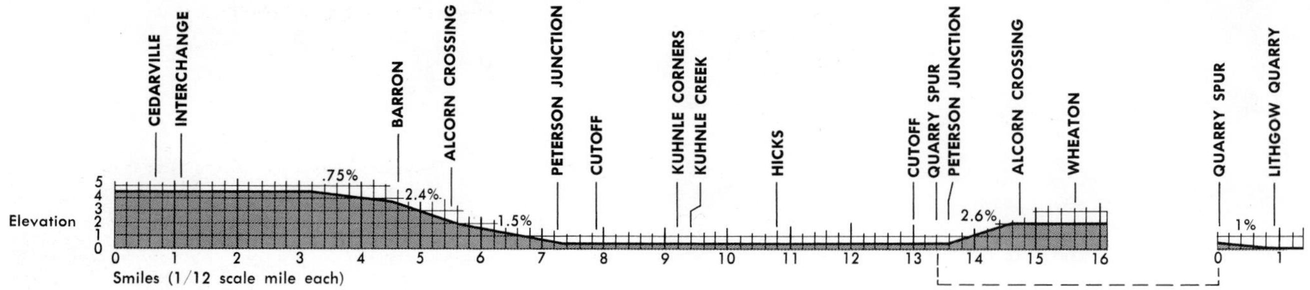

CEDARVILLE
INTERCHANGE
BARRON
ALCORN CROSSING
PETERSON JUNCTION
CUTOFF
KUHNLE CORNERS
KUHNLE CREEK
HICKS
CUTOFF
QUARRY SPUR
PETERSON JUNCTION
ALCORN CROSSING
WHEATON
QUARRY SPUR
LITHGOW QUARRY
.75%
2.4%
1.5%
2.6%
1%
Elevation
5 4 3 2 1 0
0 1 2 3 4 5 6 7 8 9 10 11 12 13 14 15 16
0 1
Smiles (1/12 scale mile each)

Multiply elevations by: ½" for N scale, ¾" for TT, 1" for HO, 1½" for S, 2" for O

The Interstate & Western

Track plan for a busy medium-size pike

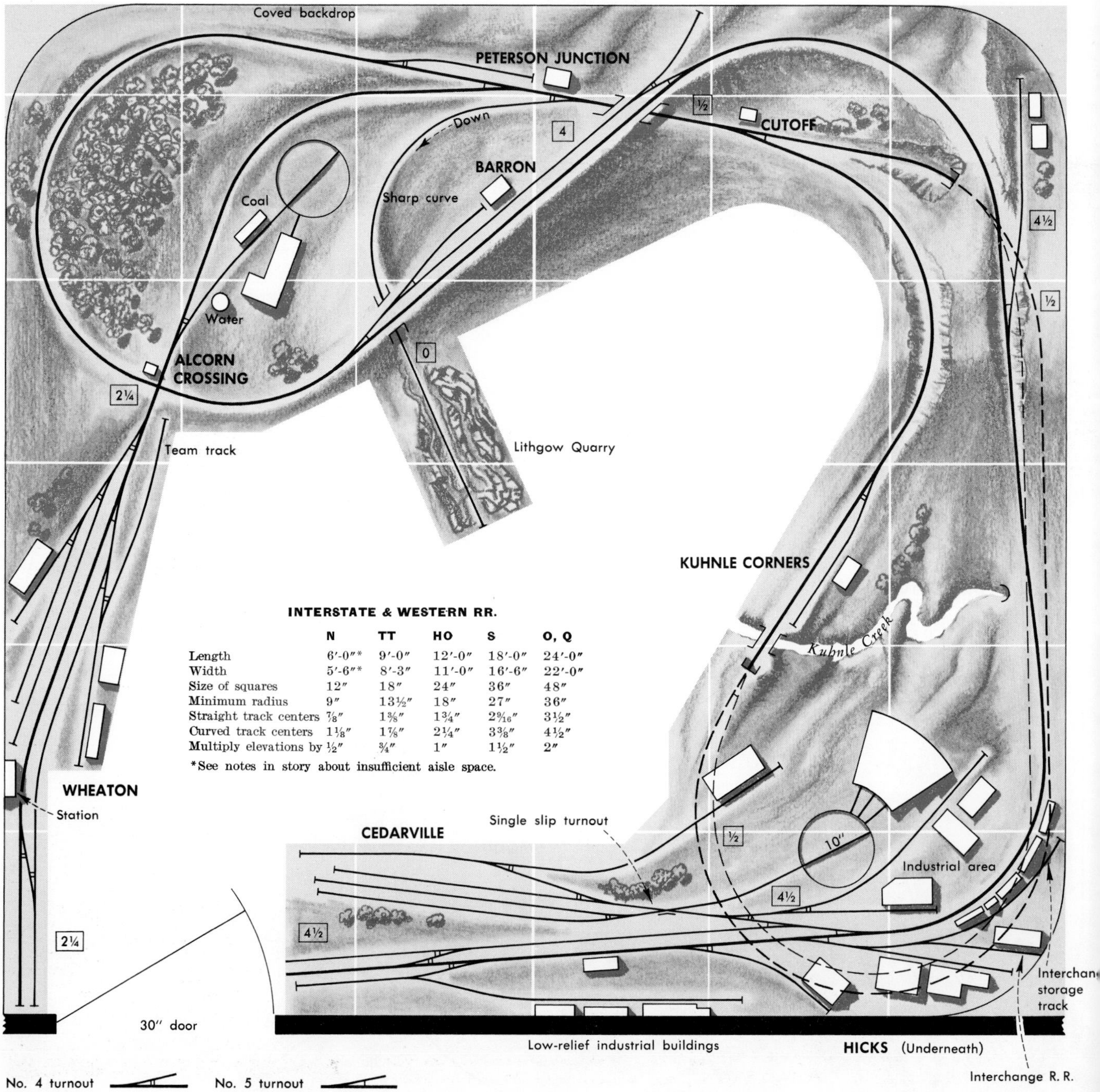

Coved backdrop
PETERSON JUNCTION
Down
BARRON
Sharp curve
Coal
Water
ALCORN CROSSING
Team track
Lithgow Quarry
KUHNLE CORNERS
Kuhnle Creek
WHEATON
Station
CEDARVILLE
Single slip turnout
Industrial area
10"
30" door
Low-relief industrial buildings
HICKS (Underneath)
Interchan
storage
track
Interchange R. R.
No. 4 turnout
No. 5 turnout
4
½
4½
½
0
2¼
½
4½
4½
2¼

INTERSTATE & WESTERN RR.

	N	TT	HO	S	O, Q
Length	6′-0″*	9′-0″	12′-0″	18′-0″	24′-0″
Width	5′-6″*	8′-3″	11′-0″	16′-6″	22′-0″
Size of squares	12″	18″	24″	36″	48″
Minimum radius	9″	13½″	18″	27″	36″
Straight track centers	⅞″	1⅜″	1¾″	2⁹⁄₁₆″	3½″
Curved track centers	1⅛″	1⅞″	2¼″	3⅜″	4½″
Multiply elevations by	½″	¾″	1″	1½″	2″

*See notes in story about insufficient aisle space.

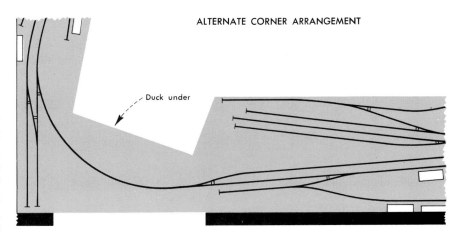

By Gordon Odegard

HERE is a layout which can be sce-nicked to suit the geographic and industrial interests of the builder. The I&W represents a common-carrier railroad that might be located in any part of the United States — rolling country, in the mountains, on the plains; timber country, mining country, farming country, or whatever you prefer. About 20 industrial sites and spurs are shown, and more could be added. These could be manufacturing plants, processing plants, farm cooperatives, in any combination to suit any area. Lithgow Quarry, for example, could be a mine or a lumber camp, or even — with a few more tracks — a very short branch line.

The main terminal is Cedarville, where the I&W interchanges with a foreign road. Pick your choice: ATSF, PRR, UP, GN, SAL, depending on whether you live west, east, north, or south. A curved spur hides a couple of interchange cars behind low-relief structures. [Low-relief structures are those that have their fronts or backs fully modeled but with the sides extending to a depth of only ½" or 1" or so, depending on the space available. They are often used by British modelers against a wall or for just this purpose: to hide tracks.]

There is a very unusual route pattern to the I&W main line, which loops to left and right at Cutoff and actually retraces part of the mainline trackage between Cutoff and Peterson Junction in the opposite direction to reach the "distant" terminal of Wheaton, some 1⅓ scale miles away — or 16 "smiles" if you want a more useful operating distance measurement.

Normal operation of the I&W is point to point: Cedarville to Wheaton, or Wheaton to Cedarville. However, if continuous running is desired, an alternate connection between Cedarville and Wheaton is shown.

The route pattern mentioned can best be seen by following a train as it leaves Cedarville. There is a comparatively long run to Barron, where one of the I&W's two passing sidings is located. Then the train crosses Alcorn Crossing and curves into Peterson Junction; just beyond, at Cutoff, it swings right through Kuhnle Corners and into a tunnel. Hicks, site of the I&W's second and longer passing siding, is actually hidden under Cedarville. From Hicks the hidden track emerges from a tunnel obscured from casual view by a deep cut and foliage, and the train approaches Cutoff again. It travels the main between Cutoff and Peterson Junction in the direction opposite to its first run, then swings left. Clattering over a level crossing that looks suspiciously like Alcorn Crossing seen from a different angle, it finishes its run at Wheaton

The Cutoff-Hicks reversing loop permits a tricky two-train operating maneuver. A westbound Cedarville-Wheaton

train, CW-2, travels the route described. Just after it crosses Alcorn, a Wheaton-Cedarville train, WC-1, leaves Wheaton eastbound. Both approach Peterson Junction at the same time, but CW-2 (superior by direction) precedes WC-1 over the track to Cutoff. Here CW-2 takes the right leg through Kuhnle Corners to Hicks while WC-1 dives straight ahead into the tunnel. The two trains meet at Hicks and continue. Now CW-2 will reappear from the tunnel and WC-1 through Kuhnle Corners as they approach Cutoff again. CW-2, still superior, leads WC-1 over the retraveled trackage, but at Peterson Junction CW-2 turns left into Wheaton while WC-1 continues ahead on its run to Cedarville.

Since Hicks passing siding is hidden, the sight of two trains each emerging from where the other disappeared on single track will really startle onlookers, in addition to creating a nice operating problem.

The layout was designed to fit against the walls of an 11 x 12-foot room, with the entrance door at a given place. Thus Wheaton had to be tucked in behind the door, with the framework notched to accommodate the open door.

L girders on either legs or wall brackets are suggested for the main supports. If there is a wall behind, brackets should be used for support under both yards.

A scenic background can be painted all the way around. If you curve it to form an 18"-radius cove at the corners, you will eliminate the problem of abrupt changes of direction.

The main line uses no. 5 turnouts, a size well suited to model railroading and

now available at least in HO. If you can't get them, use no. 4's — the industrial and yard turnouts are mainly no. 4 anyway. One special piece of trackwork is used at Cedarville — a no. 4 single slip switch connecting the turntable lead to other yard tracks. It's not absolutely essential, but it is interesting. Straight tracks are spaced a scale 13'-0" center to center; curved tracks are 16'-3" center to center.

The layout as drawn is adjusted for HO practices. Your room — and certainly your door — are likely to be different. You may be working in some other scale as well. Putting the layout in a larger space for the same scale is simple: just make the nearly straightaway parts of the trackage longer, keeping the areas of tight trackwork nearly the same as in the drawing.

Don't worry too much about locating every piece of track exactly where shown. Establish all curves of 90 degrees and more first, then all tight switchwork. Finally connect between them with whatever lengths of track are required.

In N scale you have to broaden the aisle space when you reduce the plan, or you won't be able to walk in. In any scale, make the aisles 24" wide for one man, 30" if you will have at most one or two visitors, 36" and wider for larger groups. Alternatively in N scale you could omit the center aisle entirely, covering the area with scenery and walking around the outside of the tablelike railroad. This may look like a smaller layout, but adding the aisle space necessary around at least three sides of a table-type layout will actually call for a larger, rather than a smaller, room to hold it.

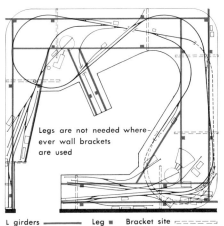

Legs are not needed wherever wall brackets are used

L girders ━━━━━ Leg ■ Bracket site ▭▭▭▭

ALTERNATE TURNTABLE LEAD

Regular turnouts used in place of slip switch

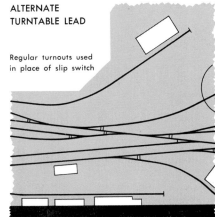

The road to enchantment

A track plan based on Santa Fe's
operations in the "Land of Enchantment"

BY DON MITCHELL

THE Atchison, Topeka & Santa Fe has attracted lots of attention ever since its beginning. Big: it touches the Great Lakes, the Gulf of Mexico, and the Pacific Ocean. Brawling: it fought Indians and General Palmer's forces from the Denver & Rio Grande as Santa Fe rails were pushed westward. Booming: it brought forth Harvey Girls to feed the rush of early travelers, deluxe name trains such as the Super Chief to accommodate latter-day passengers, and Super C freight speedsters to highball transcontinental cargo on passenger schedules. It's only natural that the Santa Fe has attracted many devoted fans among the modeling fraternity.

AN ATSF MODEL

The very qualities that make the Santa Fe attractive also make it a difficult railroad to model. Few are the modelers fortunate enough to have sufficient layout space available for adequately representing a prototype such as the ATSF. In the case at hand, the maximum territorial grant allowed by the Secretary of Household Affairs was limited to an area slightly smaller than 11 x 16 feet. It took a pretty hefty shoehorn to fit an HO scale model of Santa Fe proportions in this space, especially when the firm prerequisites specified that the minimum radius on the main line would be 30", that the aisles and tracks would be arranged for walkaround operation, and that there would be no duckunders or other skull knockers.

This latter specification precluded the use of an around-the-walls plan that might have permitted a more reasonable length of run for the main line. A lower than average ceiling (7'-0") and a taller than average modeler (6'-3") served to rule out an advanced multilevel plan, as any track high enough to walk under would be too close to the ceiling.

Within these constraints there are very few ways left in which tracks can be fitted into the available space. Some variation of a basic "waterwings" inevitably emerges in order to get a main line which suggests the ATSF in all its glory. And a mainline run of some form was definitely needed to provide operating track for the long-wheelbase steam locomotives which generated the 30"-minimum-radius requirement.

THE SHOEHORN DIVISION

The loop-to-loop plan which was eventually chosen was really squeezed into the space. As noted on the track plan, aisle widths are quite restricted in some places and the track has one critical S-curve area which resisted all efforts to straighten it out a bit more.

Passing sidings were added on the inside of each of the loops after considering and rejecting the idea of trying to fit some yard tracks into these areas. It may be some-what unusual to have a layout without a yard as such, but it is not at all illogical. Model yards can sometimes become little more than dead-storage tracks, so why devote space, turnouts, and controls to a non-operational function? It makes more sense in these cases to use the available space for operating trackwork. The passing sidings inside the mainline loops, although having radii less than 30", permit more trains to operate over the rather short main line. The sidings also have the advantage of being able to hold longer trains than could the dead-end tracks of a yard fitted into the same area. This seemed a reasonable

Overall room
dimensions:
11'-0" x 15'-9"

Fiddle yard and
test tracks

Workbench
under
test tracks

ATCHISON, TOPEKA &
SANTA FE — SHOEHORN DIVISION

trade-off against their inability to handle the long-wheelbase engines.

A spur or two can be tapped off the main line and run onto the workbench. These tracks can be used for testing, display, or even as a "fiddle yard." The "fiddle yard" is a delightful idea long enjoyed on many British layouts wherein an inconspicuous track away from the main scene of action is used to interchange equipment by a convenient but decidedly unprototypic method — hands!

Even with the fiddle yard included, our Shoehorn Division of the ATSF has limited operating potential. It is likely that even the most die-hard Santa Fe modelers would eventually tire of seeing trains chase themselves around an endless loop. Something more is definitely needed to keep up interest in the layout.

SCOUTING WESTWARD

The search for greater operating potential led westward along the main lines of the Santa Fe until reaching the state of New Mexico. Here the search crossed paths with some factual information gleaned from an excellent little book by David F. Myrick, entitled *New Mexico's Railroads*, which was published by the Colorado Railroad Museum in 1970.

New Mexico has many facets to attract potential model empire builders. Generally speaking, the territory can be characterized as being fairly rough and barren, with little vegetation other than scrub growth. There are many exceptions to this description, though, with specific scenic features ranging from desert to forest and from rugged mountains (such as the Raton Pass area with its tunnel and 3 percent approach grades) to the flatter irrigated farmlands along the Rio Grande and Pecos River valleys.

A bounty of potential industries suggest themselves to the modeler. Mineral traffic includes cinders, coal, copper, lead, zinc, potash, and uranium. Energy in the form of gas and oil was transcribed on bills of lading before the pipelines were completed to take this business away from the rails.

Lumber and livestock traffic originates from several areas in the state. Farm crops transported by rail include wheat, alfalfa, tomatoes, peaches, and other fruits. Even passengers could be considered an industry, since there once was a sizable rail tourist business associated with the Indian pueblos and the Carlsbad Caverns.

New Mexico also saw a pretty fair amount of narrow-gauge railroading during its time. Even at present, a segment of the once extensive 3-foot-gauge tracks of the Denver & Rio Grande Western is operated out of Chama as the Cumbres & Toltec Scenic Ry. The Farmington area of northwestern New Mexico was the scene of the last big freight boom over those same rails. Little 3-foot-gauge engines and cars manfully toted miles of pipe and other supplies into the gas and oil fields.

The state may also be the U. S. leader in transplanted narrow-gauge railroads. The 3-foot-gauge Death Valley RR. was brought from California to work the potash mines of the U. S. Borax & Chemical Co. near Carlsbad. This was first a steam operation and then was completely dieselized in 1956. A couple of geared locomotives from the storied 2-foot-gauge Gilpin Tram also were moved; they saw a brief later life in the hills of New Mexico on the Silver City, Pinos Altos & Mogollon RR.

Perhaps the ultimate prototype for a model industry native to New Mexico was discovered not from the pages of Myrick's

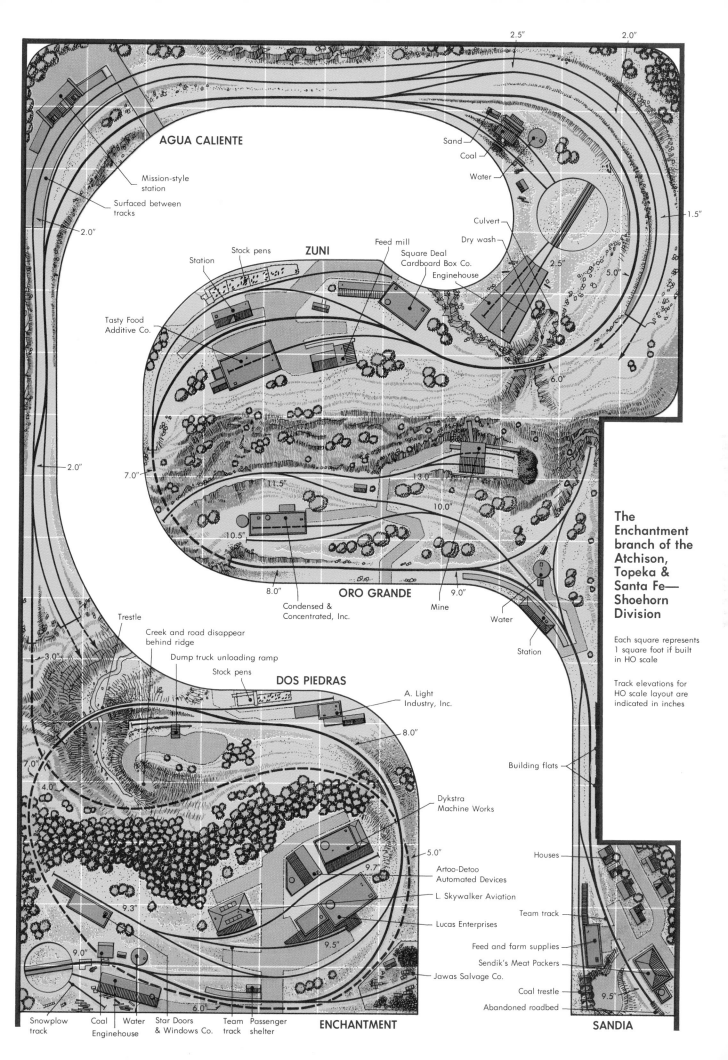

AGUA CALIENTE

Mission-style station

Surfaced between tracks

2.0"

2.5"

2.0"

1.5"

Sand

Coal

Water

Culvert

Dry wash

2.5"

5.0"

6.0"

Station

Stock pens

ZUNI

Feed mill

Square Deal
Cardboard Box Co.

Enginehouse

Tasty Food
Additive Co.

7.0"

11.5"

13.0"

10.0"

10.5"

8.0"

ORO GRANDE

9.0"

Mine

Water

Station

Condensed &
Concentrated, Inc.

Building flats

The
Enchantment
branch of the
Atchison,
Topeka &
Santa Fe—
Shoehorn
Division

Each square represents
1 square foot if built
in HO scale

Track elevations for
HO scale layout are
indicated in inches

Trestle

Creek and road disappear
behind ridge

Dump truck unloading ramp

Stock pens

DOS PIEDRAS

A. Light
Industry, Inc.

8.0"

3.0"

7.0"

4.0"

Dykstra
Machine Works

5.0"

9.7"

Artoo-Detoo
Automated Devices

9.3"

L. Skywalker Aviation

Lucas Enterprises

9.5"

Jawas Salvage Co.

Houses

Team track

Feed and farm supplies

Sendik's Meat Packers

Coal trestle

Abandoned roadbed

9.0"

Snowplow
track

Coal
Enginehouse

Water

Star Doors
& Windows Co.

Team
track

Passenger
shelter

6.0"

ENCHANTMENT

9.5"

SANDIA

book but while passing through the state on a cross-country drive some years ago. We spotted some intriguing railroad cars on a spur some distance from the road but could not positively identify the car type. Detouring to take a closer look, we discovered a building that was the answer to something which has perplexed model railroaders for quite some time — a loading station for those helium tank cars!

A BRANCH LINE

It soon became obvious that the "Land of Enchantment" was aptly named as a source of modeling inspiration. It was equally evident that there wasn't much chance of representing any specific section of the Santa Fe with even the broadest grant of modeler's license. A caricature of the ATSF in New Mexico was the most that could be hoped for.

Some preliminary sketching and calculating showed that branches could be tapped off the main line of the Shoehorn Division and run into the area occupied by the loops. A branch was added running from Sandia to Enchantment. This joins and crosses the main line in the valley where Agua Caliente is located.

A reasonably substantial station building is located at Agua Caliente in order to accommodate the flux of travelers visiting the hot springs which give the location its name. The station building, in turn, provides visual justification for the stops made by the important through passenger trains.

A turntable and a two-stall enginehouse have been located in close quarters at the east end of Agua Caliente under the guise that they are needed by the existence of a 2 percent helper grade in both directions which crests here. In actuality, helpers are not needed for the relatively short grades, but a place to display and store long-wheelbase engines is needed. With only the outer loop tracks on the main line meeting the 30"-radius criterion, there is a limit to the number of these engines that can be on the line at any one time.

Eastward from Agua Caliente, the branch ascends a 4 percent grade on an embankment which rapidly rises to screen off the mainline tracks from view as they

curve around the back corner of the layout room. The branch runs through Zuni, Oro Grande, and Sandia in rapid order, with each location having industrial spurs to generate traffic and switching action. A wye located between Oro Grande and Sandia provides turning facilities for any motive power which can traverse the 24"-minimum-radius curves used on the branch.

Use of such a fairly liberal radius is in consonance with the steep grades built into the branch. These grades, which include the previously mentioned 4 percent as well as 6 percent on the switchback to Aerie Mine, demand sturdy motive power; and the curvature was selected accordingly.

In the other direction out of Agua Caliente, the branch dives into a tunnel almost as soon as it diverges from the main line. Once out of sight, the track twists around until it emerges near Dos Piedras. The unseen convolutions are a necessary part of the walkaround scheme, which requires mating the movements of the operator and the train.

Enchantment is the home base for the branch engine and is replete with turntable, one-stall enginehouse, and minimal servicing facilities. A runaround track and several industrial spurs complete the trackwork at this location.

SCENERY

Scenic possibilities along the branch line are adequate to allow a suggestion of the hillier parts of New Mexico. Depiction of the flatter and desert parts of the state is more difficult, so this type of terrain has been limited to Agua Caliente. The narrow shelf here is almost entirely filled with tracks, so most of the scenic import will have to be provided by the backdrop. Little room is left for three-dimensional effects after allowing for wide-enough aisles, so only the station building itself is shown as being fully modeled.

In order to take advantage of what scenic opportunities there are, the layout has been visually organized into a series of separate focal points. These focal points are located so that the view of one focal point from another is either cut off by a view block or restricted by the wide angle between them. Upon entering the layout room, for example, Enchantment is immediately to the viewer's left, while Sandia is almost straight ahead and on the far side of an aisle. Viewing both requires a swing of almost 90 degrees to catch all the details. A high ridge topped with a view block separates Enchantment from Dos Piedras and the rest of the layout on that side of the room. The only way to see Enchantment and Dos Piedras at the same time is to stand in the aisle with your back to Sandia, and the ridge and view block still forces a head swing of 45 to 60 degrees to see the full extent of both areas.

Similar separations exist for the remainder of the layout. There is a 90-degree swing between Sandia and Oro Grande; 180 degrees between Oro Grande and Dos Piedras; another ridge and view block combination between Oro Grande and Zuni; 90 degrees between Zuni and the turntable area; 90 degrees between the turntable and Agua Caliente; and 180 degrees between Agua Caliente and Zuni.

These scenic focal points are also the operating focal points, as the track has been

laid out so that most of the switching movements are made in these same locations. Thus, the movements of the trains tend to reinforce the visual separation of the various areas. There is no place where the whole railroad can be seen at one time.

OPERATION

Operating possibilities abound, mostly centered around the branch interchange with the main line at Agua Caliente. Mainline trains can roar past, but more often they stop to switch cars to and from the branch. Freight traffic predominates, but it is not uncommon for the branch to see an occasional pullman movement — another benefit of the 24"-radius curves chosen for the branch. The pullman movements might even occur on a scheduled basis, depending on the era modeled.

Other operations at Agua Caliente could include helper movements utilizing the turntable facilities and even an infrequent changeout of mainline power. Meets can occur between various combinations of mainline and branch trains, with one mainline train sometimes overtaking another. This is no problem for westbound trains, but eastbound overtaking movements will involve the use of the shorter passing siding which is nominally part of the branch.

Branch movements through Agua Caliente include local peddler freights which interchange cars with mainline trains of all descriptions. A little drama can be injected by creating a sense of restrained urgency as the branch engine bustles about to add cars of perishables to hotshot trains of solid reefers speeding the sensitive cargoes to distant markets.

On a more prosaic level, passenger traffic for the branch can be accommodated by trains of one or two coaches which make across-the-platform connections with the mainline limiteds. These same trains could handle the pullman movements that occur. Poorer times might see the coach tagged onto the end of the peddler for mixed-train service.

All of these operations taking place on the minimal trackwork at Agua Caliente would put even an experienced operator in hot water if they occurred in rapid succession. For that reason, an alternate track arrangement has been provided for those of you who want to increase the operational flexibility for those times when more than one operator is present. While this alternate plan will support more train movements and ease operating problems, it is not without some costs. Tracks are even more crowded onto the narrow ledge, and complexity has been introduced in the form of a double slip switch and a crossover built to fit between the two mainline tracks as they curve behind the turntable area.

Reasonably long mainline trains of about 20 40-foot cars can be accommodated by the passing sidings on the mainline loops and at Agua Caliente, so the layout has the ability to suggest such prototype movements as the aforementioned passenger limiteds and solid reefer hotshots. The six loop tracks plus the two main lines through Agua Caliente would permit as many as seven trains to be on the main at one time, but movement would be on a strictly stop-and-go basis as each train successively moved into the empty section of track. A much more satisfying operation will result from using only four or five

ALTERNATE TRACK ARRANGEMENT AT AGUA CALIENTE

Not to scale

Double slip switch

Curved turnouts built to fit

trains on the main line. This will allow some trains to run through Agua Caliente without stopping.

CONTROL SCHEME

One of the purposes of a walkaround design is to let the operators accompany their trains as they move along the track. This sort of scheme has several advantages from the control standpoint. The operators are always on the scene where they can manually operate the turnouts.

This advantage has been maximized on our plan by placing all visible turnouts within 24″ of the table edge, with most of these turnouts being within only 12″ or less of the operator. However, the 10 turnouts associated with the loop and fiddle tracks will require some sort of remotely operated mechanisms. Another useful addition to these tracks would be an automatic stopping section to prevent the trains from fouling the turnouts as they are brought to an unseen stop on the hidden loop tracks.

Walkaround speed and direction controls take many forms, often being mounted in small boxes which are connected to the layout by a tether. These controls allow the operator to stay right with his train at all times — a very nice feature. A better choice for a layout with restricted aisle widths in some places would be the control post version of walkaround control.* Because these are installed at fixed locations, they would reduce random movements by the operators which might clog the aisles. Since the controls could be operated with one hand while turnouts were thrown with the other hand, operators would still have a range of 4 to 5 feet on either side of the control post locations. These locations should coincide with the focal points previously mentioned. Extra controls will be needed at Agua Caliente to handle the greater number of movements at that point, including control of mainline operation on the two loops.

CLOSING REMARKS

It may not meet the fondest expectations of fervent Santa Fe modelers to end up with only 20 running feet of double track to represent mainline operations of that farflung class 1 railroad, yet the hidden loops provide the capacity to hold more trains than other schemes for the same area. This permits the diversity and frequency of rail traffic past one point — Agua Caliente — to easily suggest the busiest of ATSF lines.

Others, charmed by the many faces of New Mexico, might wish for more scenic variety than has been captured in the Shoehorn Division/Enchantment Branch plan as it stands. The lumbering area served by the Southern Pacific line to Cloudcroft comes to mind as another source of inspiration. A quick forestation program, coupled with a change of industries to sawmills and the like, could effectively change the appearance of the Oro Grande area without having to change a bit of track.

The combination of Atchison, Topeka & Santa Fe rails with New Mexico topography is certainly an intriguing one. Perhaps the combined features will prove captivating enough to cause a start on the Road to Enchantment.

*One such circuit was described in the January 1975 issue of MODEL RAILROADER. Using this circuit, no significant extra costs are incurred by having several control posts connected to the same throttle.

LITTLETON & BOX SPRINGS RAILWAY

Plan by Jan Meyer

THIS track plan is much like the one Jan Meyer of Darien, Conn., used, but we have redrawn it with some additions. Jan used Märklin track and was able to build it (without the industrial spurs) in a 7 x 10-foot space in HO. A photo of Jan's version appears above. Jan says: "If there is any resemblance to other layouts that have been published in MODEL RAILROADER, there should be. I have been a reader since 1940 or so."

One thing that helped cram more track into the plan was the use of three slip switches. Another was the use of turnouts with rather sharp curves through them. Were you to revise the layout to use more conventional curves and turnouts, it would take even more space than we have used for our redrawing.

While the track pattern is largely a display type — the trains go around and around — a good deal of way switching is possible. A sort of out-and-back, point-to-point operation is also possible by starting counterclockwise from Littleton to Box Springs, then making one more lap through both stations before taking the bridge over Great River to return to take another lap or to return directly to Littleton.

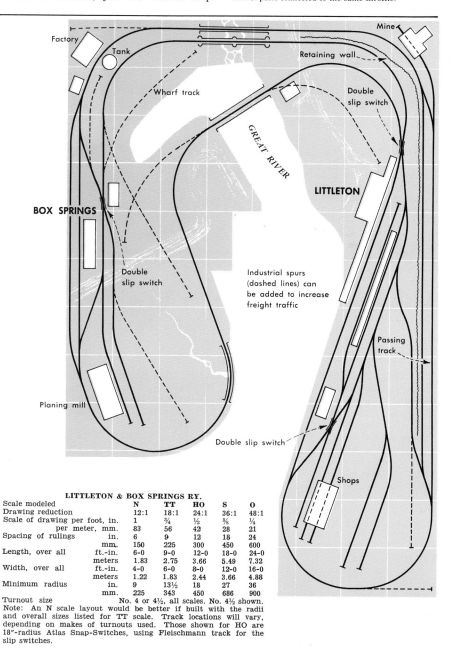

LITTLETON & BOX SPRINGS RY.

Scale modeled	N	TT	HO	S	O
Drawing reduction	12:1	18:1	24:1	36:1	48:1
Scale of drawing per foot, in.	1	¾	½	⅜	¼
per meter, mm.	83	56	42	28	21
Spacing of rulings in.	6	9	12	18	24
mm.	150	225	300	450	600
Length, over all ft.-in.	6-0	9-0	12-0	18-0	24-0
meters	1.83	2.75	3.66	5.49	7.32
Width, over all ft.-in.	4-0	6-0	8-0	12-0	16-0
meters	1.22	1.83	2.44	3.66	4.88
Minimum radius in.	9	13½	18	27	36
mm.	225	343	450	686	900

Turnout size   No. 4 or 4½, all scales. No. 4½ shown.
Note: An N scale layout would be better if built with the radii and overall sizes listed for TT scale. Track locations will vary, depending on makes of turnouts used. Those shown for HO are 18″-radius Atlas Snap-Switches, using Fleischmann track for the slip switches.

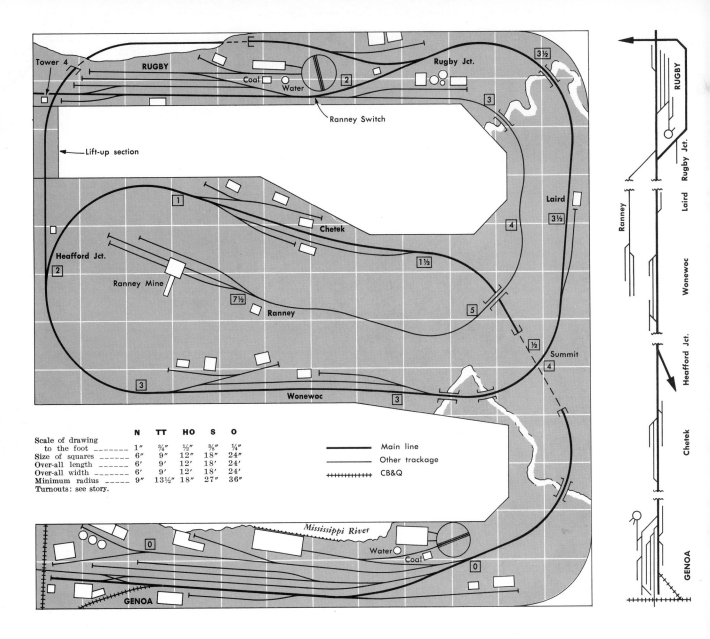

Scale of drawing	N	TT	HO	S	O
to the foot _____	1″	¾″	½″	⅜″	¼″
Size of squares _____	6″	9″	12″	18″	24″
Over-all length _____	6′	9′	12′	18′	24′
Over-all width _____	6′	9′	12′	18′	24′
Minimum radius _____	9″	13½″	18″	27″	36″

Turnouts: see story.

———————— Main line
———————— Other trackage
++++++++++ CB&Q

Genoa & Eastern: a river-country pike

By Gordon Odegard

THE Genoa & Eastern Ry. is the imaginary prototype for this layout featuring river terminal activity on the Mississippi, and running up deep valleys to the rolling hill country of western Wisconsin. This is a country that has always interested me, and while this particular plan may or may not be used for my next home railroad, it carries the general spirit that intrigues me. Exploratory trips to such river towns as Hannibal, Dubuque, Savanna, Prairie du Chien, and Winona provided inspiration and prototypes for Genoa, the main terminal of the G&E. (There actually is a Genoa on the CB&Q along the river.)

From the riverbanks, the main line climbs to Summit, passing several sidings on the way. From here it descends slightly to Rugby. Almost in Rugby is Ranney Switch. From here a branch line winds to a lead mine at Ranney. (A lumber camp or coal mine are also possibilities.) At Rugby Junction, on the outskirts of Rugby, a cutoff ducks into a concealed tunnel opening, passes behind the backdrop, and reappears as a foreign line crossing the G&E at Tower 4. The August 1957 MR had a "Closeup" feature of the East Dubuque (Ill.) station of the IC showing a similar track arrangement. This can be referred to for model and scenic ideas. This cutoff provides for continuous operation on an oval plan for testing or extended runs, but basically the railroad is a point-to-point plan.

The layout has space for at least 35 industries including an interchange track at Genoa. Every station has a team track: the larger towns should have a gantry or pillar crane. In operating, advantage can be taken of the fact that many industries require the service of more than one type of car. For instance, the lead mine needs mainly ore cars, but also requires hoppers of coal (or tank cars of oil) to supply fuel for the machinery, boxcars carrying parts or supplies, and occasionally a flatcar carrying an extra-large spare part or a new piece of machinery.

The main line has conventional curves, and a maximum 3 percent grade from Wonewoc to Summit. The Ranney branch has sharp curves and a 3½ percent grade.

No. 5 turnouts, now available commercially in some gauges (with code 70 rail in HO) are suggested for all mainline turnouts. No. 4 turnouts are used at Genoa industrial spur and engine terminal lead, Chetek and Wonewoc industrial spurs, Rugby industrial spur and engine lead, and all Ranney Mine turnouts.

This is a lot of railroad to build and maintain, but the plan permits gradual construction and elaboration. The aisleways are fine for walkaround control if you provide a liftout section of track at Tower 4.

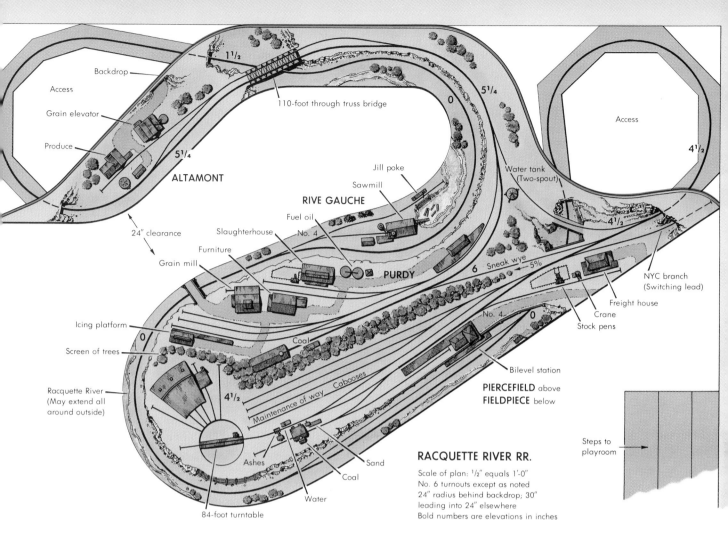

Backdrop

Access

Grain elevator

Produce

1½

110-foot through truss bridge

5¼

0

5¼

Access

4½

ALTAMONT

5¼

24" clearance

Jill poke

Sawmill

RIVE GAUCHE

Water tank
(Two-spout)

4½

Slaughterhouse

Furniture

Grain mill

Fuel oil

No. 4

PURDY

6

Sneak wye

5%

NYC branch
(Switching lead)

Freight house

Crane

Stock pens

Icing platform

0

No. 4

0

Bilevel station

Screen of trees

Coal

Racquette River
(May extend all
around outside)

4½

PIERCEFIELD above
FIELDPIECE below

Maintenance of way

Cabooses

Ashes

Sand

Coal

Water

84-foot turntable

RACQUETTE RIVER RR.

Scale of plan: ½" equals 1'-0"
No. 6 turnouts except as noted
24" radius behind backdrop; 30"
leading into 24" elsewhere
Bold numbers are elevations in inches

Steps to
playroom

The Racquette River RR.

A free-form layout designed for walkaround control

BY LEONARD BLUMENSCHINE

THE Racquette River RR. is a good-sized free-form layout that features walk-around control to get the maximum utilization of space in a room measuring only 10 x 16 feet. A run from one end of the line to the other requires the operator to walk about 60 feet, counting changes of direction and overlapping some aisle areas.

To follow a train around the layout, one might begin at the Piercefield yard. As the train leaves the Piercefield service area, one walks to the first tunnel to wait while it turns back behind the scenic backdrop. When the train emerges on the lower level, one picks up a different feeling as it passes Fieldpiece. A walk along the long cliff or stone retaining wall (or combination of both) brings the train to the Rive Gauche sawmill.

Soon the train ducks under a through truss bridge and into a second tunnel. It climbs through a hidden loop to Altamont. Farming goes on here, and the train pauses to pick up some fresh produce or a load of grain — leaving an empty or two in the process — before rattling through the bridge and ascending the last turn into Purdy.

Specific industries or traffic sources are indicated at Piercefield, Rive Gauche, Altamont, and Purdy, but almost anything small-time will go. The idea was to lay out a general-purpose shortline railroad, the kind that used to provide freight and passenger service in the lower Adirondacks. The period can be anywhere from the turn of the century to the 1940's. Piercefield, with its fair-sized yard, engine facilities, and passenger station, is meant to be the principal connection with the world at large. That's why the switching lead, which vanishes into a tunnel entrance, is labeled as a branch of the New York Central. It provides the excuse to bring in traffic for the system. An ambitious modeler with a lot of extra cars could pull the plan farther from the wall, extend the NYC branch around the back of the hidden loop, and add a hidden layover yard reachable from the access space.

Although this layout features point-to-point operation, the old idea of "turn 'em loose and let 'em run" can be done by ignoring Purdy or Piercefield and taking the short continuous-run connection. A three-coach Racquette Rambler can be running for many miles while a freight is being made up at Piercefield. Then, when the Purdy peddler run pulls out, it has to make a meet or two with the varnish at the Fieldpiece and Altamont passing sidings.

Purdy is only 1½" higher in elevation than Piercefield. This was done purposely to allow for a short continuous-run connection saving extra track clutter. A screen of trees will help separate the two terminals even more, especially if the whole layout is built somewhere between elbow and shoulder height. Most of all, this not-too-great elevation difference lets one work-in a "sneak wye" from Purdy to the Piercefield main line. A stiff 5 per cent drop from Purdy, combined with the continuous-run connection, allows one to turn engines at Purdy for the trip back. One of the real kicks in plan-making is to come across bonuses like this, little extras or happy accidents that add to flexibility and operating fun without taking up more space or needlessly complicating the plan.

Scenery is one thing that can be treated according to taste — heavy or light, like spice in a favorite dish. The left bank of the river can be modeled all the way around the main framework from Fieldpiece to the sawmill. A long, curving backdrop could be anything from sky paint to an Adirondack landscape, or one could eliminate it and erect some impressive mountains in its place. As it is, the backdrop seems to "un-square" the layout as well as hide the two tight turnbacks of 22" radius. The visible radii all start out at 30" and work down to 24". They may not be curves with true easements but they come pretty close.

Tupper Lake & Faust Junction Ry.

Track plan features include the "golf links" principle and the accidental crossover

BY LEONARD BLUMENSCHINE

MY HO scale Tupper Lake & Faust Junction Ry. has existed in many forms over the past 20 years: as a 12-foot take-apart "suitcase railroad" aboard an aircraft carrier [December 1953 MR], as an over-the-bed pothandle yard with wyed loop raised and lowered by ropes and pulleys, and for the last dozen years on dozens of sheets of drawing paper.

I find drawing track plans is a peck of fun, but it can also be devilishly frustrating. How many times have you curled in one more curve in a plan for a 4 x 8 layout, or squeezed in another pair of sidings on a shelf extravaganza — all in search of something original and visually exciting — and finished with nothing but graphite garbage? Or even worse, if your pride is as flinty as a 7H pencil, discovered later that Messrs. Westcott and Armstrong did something similar, and far better, years ago. Originality is the name of the track-planning game when you really play it, or when it gets to play on you. Qualify that and call it practical originality, the practical referring to all manner of personal things such as available space, equipment, money, skills, and your own brass-hat notion of the kind of railroad you'd like to build.

Perhaps with this plan I've hit a fresh idea button, one that might give you some fun the next time you start sketching. I call it the "golf links" principle. Before you start seeing rails bridging sand traps, I'd better define the term. Long ago, when the Scots decided to do something in the heather besides hunt grouse, they built what they called a golf links. All modern golf courses are descended from this Scottish brain wave, but I'm told the original at Saint Andrews sported one essential difference. Instead of each fair-

way having its own green, as is the case today, several fairways were linked to a common green, approaching from different directions, spokes-in-a-wheel fashion. That's the principle I've used in designing the TL&FJ. The layout has two "fairway terminals," Tupper Lake and Faust Junction. Start from either terminal, follow the main line (ignoring the crossover at Big Wolf for the moment), and when you wind up at the other terminal you'll find yourself putting your Mikado on a common turntable, a 16-incher that links both terminals, even though the terminals are distinct from each other in character and function and are located more than 2 scale miles apart.

What makes this smidgen of originality good for the TL&FJ? That's where the practical part comes in. Some of the dictates that governed the progress of pencil over templates were these: provide a good long walkaround point-to-point main line; go easy on resulting benchwork and scenery requirements; equip it for one-man control; and accomplish this in a space 10 feet deep and 13 feet long plus a little extra space at one corner tucked behind one of the basement columns: see plan.

Here's how the common turntable idea absorbed those dictates and helped shape the design. By keeping the terminals necessarily close together it created an interesting-looking island and walking space for operating purposes. By eliminating the need for two turning facilities (either a second turntable or a space-eating wye), it simplified and compacted the whole design but left a maximum of space for main line. Also, and perhaps most important to a dedicated plan fan, it led to something aesthetically pleasing as well as practical: a graphic design that looked like it was going somewhere and doing it

gracefully. In fact, that common turntable gave the feeling of penciling around a bull's-eye or being drawn to a magnetic center — a strange sensation indeed.

At first, the road was planned purely point to point, about 140 feet of folded and twisted main line. It was only when I was laying the sawmill siding at Big Wolf that I discovered that the addition of one simple crossover would provide for continuous lap running as well. Whether a train makes one lap or repeatedly uses the "accidental crossover," it is always headed for the other end of the line, and it never has to pass directly through its destination or origination point along the way while building up mileage. That wrinkle tickles me no end.

The accidental crossover creates a sort of dogbone pattern wrapped around the space and folded upon itself. In all, the lap is about 90 feet long — a scale mile and a half. Say you're feeling expansive one evening. You pull the Adirondack Midday Flyer, a venerable Varney Ten-Wheeler with an Ambroid consist of combine and two 60-foot coaches, out of Tupper Lake, heading east. You stop at Glory Hole, Doebury Switch, and Big Wolf, threading the Arab Mountains on the way, three times in and three times out, rising 76 feet (10.5"), then falling. You're 2 scale miles out and facing the crossover. Normally, you'd continue on the descending main line the last third of a mile into Faust Junction, but instead you take the crossover and roll around another lap. When you finally do pull into Faust Junction, you have traveled close to 4 scale miles — not bad for a medium-sized layout.

At Faust Junction you turn your engine on the same turntable it rolled from when it left the Tupper Lake enginehouse.

Freight operations should consist of 8- to 10-car trains. Loads left at Faust Junction by the New York Central (the imaginary junction is, of course, the accidental crossover) are taken to Tupper Lake industries, which in turn ship out canned goods, meats, and machinery. Most of the industries are also designed around flow patterns: sawmill to Ovalwood Dish Co. and Darrell's Box Factory, grain elevator to Allen's Mill, stock pens to slaughterhouse, etc.

Romantically speaking, it's never earlier than 1920 nor later than 1935 on the TL&FJ; and the Adirondack scenery, gentle old hills peppered with rock faces, is perpetually summer-green; and the air is heavy with pine scent.

TUPPER LAKE & FAUST JUNCTION RY.

Scale modeled		Z	N	TT	HO	S	O
Size of squares	in.	4.50	6.00	9.00	12.00	18.00	24.00
Length of space	ft.-in.	7-2	8-11	12-4	15-9	23-8	31-6
Depth of space	ft.-in.	6-3	7-0	8-6	10-0	15-0	20-0
Radius, turnback curves	in.	8.25	11.00	16.50	22.00	33.00	44.00
Radius, behind Glory Hole and lowest turnback	in.	9.00	12.00	18.00	24.00	36.00	48.00
Radius, Adirondack Switch	in.	10.13	13.50	20.25	27.00	40.50	54.00
Radius, other corners and at Glory Hole	in.	11.25	15.00	22.50	30.00	45.00	60.00
Parallel straight track spacing	in.	.71	.98	1.31	1.80	2.45	3.26
Spacing on broad curves	in.	1.00	1.36	1.81	2.50	3.40	4.53
Multiply elevations by	in.	.40	.54	.73	1.00	1.36	1.81
Turntable pit diameter	in.	6.33	8.70	11.60	16.00	21.75	29.00
Size of squares	mm.	112.50	150.00	225.00	300.00	450.00	600.00
Length of space	m.	2.15	2.66	3.69	4.73	7.09	9.45
Depth of space	m.	1.88	2.10	2.55	3.00	4.50	6.00
Radius, turnback curves	mm.	206.00	275.00	413.00	550.00	825.00	1100.00
Radius, behind Glory Hole and lowest turnback	mm.	225.00	300.00	450.00	600.00	900.00	1200.00
Radius, Adirondack Switch	mm.	253.00	338.00	506.00	675.00	1013.00	1350.00
Radius, other corners and at Glory Hole	mm.	281.00	375.00	563.00	750.00	1125.00	1500.00
Parallel straight track spacing	mm.	18.00	24.00	33.00	45.00	61.00	82.00
Spacing on broad curves	mm.	25.00	34.00	45.00	63.00	85.00	113.00
Multiply elevations by	mm.	10.00	14.00	18.00	25.00	34.00	45.00
Turntable pit diameter	mm.	158.00	218.00	290.00	400.00	544.00	725.00

TUPPER LAKE & FAUST JUNCTION RY.

"Golf links" principle: both terminals share a common turntable

Wall

ADIRONDACK SWITCH

GLORY HOLE

6.5

3.5

0

3.5

9.5

10.5

6.5

ACCIDENTAL CROSSOVER

1.8

2.2

Gas meter

Franklin County Machine Works

Ice platform

Nettie Oil Co.

Passenger yard: six 60-foot cars

Caboose and maintenance of way

Passenger station

Freight yard: 20 cars

← EASTBOUND

TUPPER LAKE

FAUST JUNCTION

WESTBOUND →

Darrell's Box Factory

Ellison Meat Packers

Meig's Canning Co.

Coal conveyor

Turntable with larger turning wheel beneath

Stone retaining wall

Duckunder entry

Washrack

Ashes

Coal

Sand

Oil

Water

Stock pens

Freight house

Car repair

0

9.5

BIG WOLF

Sawmill

1.5

Allen's Mill feed and coal

0

6.5

Ovalwood Dish Co.

Arab Mountain Tunnels

6.5

3.5

Concrete arch

Backdrop

Column

10.5

9.5

DOEBURY SWITCH

Grain elevator

Access

Wall

0

9.5

71

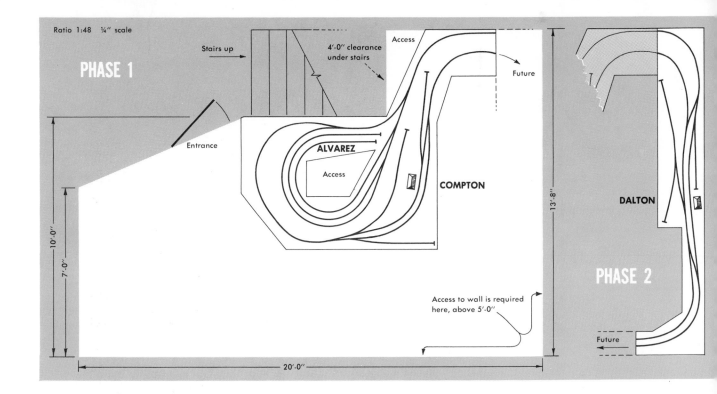

Ratio 1:48 ¼" scale

PHASE 1

Stairs up

4'-0" clearance under stairs

Access

Future

Entrance

ALVAREZ
Access

COMPTON

13'-8"

DALTON

PHASE 2

10'-0"

7'-0"

Access to wall is required here, above 5'-0"

Future

20'-0"

A walk-in layout in phases

Plan permits early operation but a longtime building program if desired

BY EDWARD A. VONDRAK

THREE years ago we moved into a new house, and I marked off the space for my Quanta RR. in our wide-open, unfinished basement. I have done much finishing these past 3 years, including putting in a couple of walls. The railroad room and its track plan are now ready. This is the story of the track plan.

Because the Q is my hobby, I work on it only whenever I have time and whenever I feel like it. Progress is fairly constant but slow. This calls for a track plan which can be built in several successive sections. Operation should be possible from the beginning. Other guidelines were these: all track should be within arm's reach; there should be a minimum number of access hatches; I want no steep grades; the main line's route should be fairly realistic — not a contorted bowl of spaghetti.

These requirements led to a walk-in plan. The design was strongly influenced by my reading John Armstrong's book TRACK PLANNING FOR REALISTIC OPERATION. In fact, the plan has been designed to allow, ultimately, expansion to a double-decker layout, again a la John Armstrong. The name of my railroad is taken from the field of physics, not from the CB&Q as many modelers might assume. The town names on the Q are all names of scientists, arranged alphabetically. These reflect my profession as a physics and math professor.

Phase 1 is now under construction. The main line is not realistic at this stage, but operation is possible in switchback fashion between the Alvarez yard and Compton.

Phase 2 introduces the third station: Dalton. Now operation improves a bit. One can operate on a kind of teardrop out-and-back route, Alvarez-Dalton-Compton-Alvarez (or the other way around), or as point to point, Alvarez-Dalton-Compton, then return to Alvarez by the same route.

The tedious construction of a large yard has been left for phase 3 rather than being included in the initial construction, where it might become a discouraging job. The main line now looks much better, and operation has improved considerably. Continuous running is available, if desired: west from Franklin yard, out the switch lead which is tied to the spur at Dalton, west over the south Dalton track to Compton, around past Alvarez, east over the north Dalton track, onto the passenger track at Franklin and then the northernmost Franklin spur against the wall, around the loop near the Franklin engine terminal, and back into Franklin yard from the east. This route is not for serious operation, but it provides for continuous performance with little attention for testing and when relatives just want to see the trains run.

For serious operation, the Franklin switch lead, where it is marked with a series of beads on the track plan, is considered to be unconnected from Dalton. This connection to Dalton can be obscured by high weeds and other vegetation, or

perhaps by a lineside building placed over the track. Also, the return loop near the Franklin switch lead is considered as merely industrial spurs. Scenery can be developed to imply this.

Operation can now be a partial out and back, Franklin-Dalton-Compton-Alvarez-Dalton-Franklin, or point to point, Franklin-Dalton-Alvarez loop, with a branch to Compton from Dalton.

During phase 3 the main yard at Franklin is installed; also, a full-height view-blocking backdrop is erected in the phase 1 area, completely concealing Alvarez. This becomes a hidden return loop with concealed storage tracks.

The railroad is fairly complete in phase 3, but if one yearns for expansion we add phase 4. In phase 3, Alvarez, Compton, Dalton, and Franklin are all on the same level or tier, with track elevation at about 42" from the floor. This is a bit lower than I would prefer, but it allows expansion to the upper tier. The editor points out that you could build at a higher level originally, then shorten the legs and lower the wall brackets if the railroad needs lowering at this stage. He says he has lowered his own layout twice this way.

For phase 4 we put up another view-blocking backdrop to conceal a helical stack of five 24"-radius turns within the Franklin loop. This helix, rising at a 2.5 percent grade, raises the main line to Gilbert, 60" above the floor and 18" directly above the Franklin yard. Phase 4 is quite a job, but from Gilbert it is a fairly simple expansion to add, in phase 5, the town of

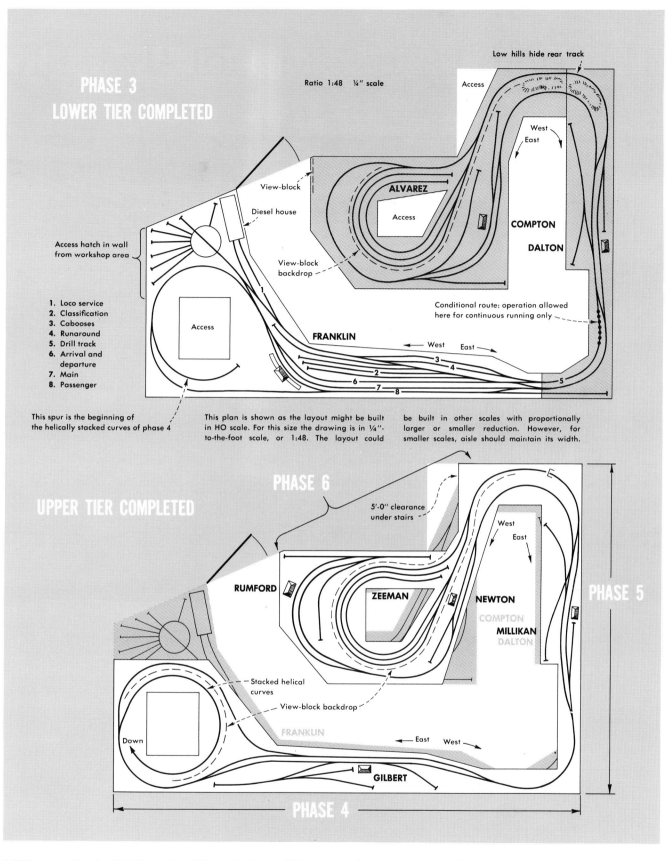

PHASE 3
LOWER TIER COMPLETED

Ratio 1:48   ¼" scale

Low hills hide rear track

Access

West
East

View-block

Diesel house

ALVAREZ

Access

COMPTON

DALTON

Access hatch in wall
from workshop area

View-block
backdrop

Conditional route: operation allowed
here for continuous running only

1. Loco service
2. Classification
3. Cabooses
4. Runaround
5. Drill track
6. Arrival and
   departure
7. Main
8. Passenger

Access

FRANKLIN

West   East

3
4
2
6
7
8

5

This spur is the beginning of
the helically stacked curves of phase 4

This plan is shown as the layout might be built
in HO scale. For this size the drawing is in ¼"-
to-the-foot scale, or 1:48. The layout could

be built in other scales with proportionally
larger or smaller reduction. However, for
smaller scales, aisle should maintain its width.

PHASE 6

5'-0" clearance
under stairs

UPPER TIER COMPLETED

RUMFORD

ZEEMAN

NEWTON

PHASE 5

COMPTON

MILLIKAN

DALTON

West
East

Stacked helical
curves

View-block backdrop

FRANKLIN

Down

East   West

GILBERT

PHASE 4

Millikan, on a level with Gilbert. Franklin
now becomes a midline division point.

Phase 6 will be another major job.
Above Alvarez we add a concealed return
loop and storage tracks at Zeeman, plus
a branch from Millikan to Newton and
Rumford. Operation over the entire layout
is now point to point with return loops
available at both terminals. Compton,
Newton, and Rumford are on branch lines.

Grades could be put in wherever desired,
provided that sufficient vertical clearances
are maintained between tiers.

For people who just want to see the
trains run it is possible to have continuous
running on the lower tier as described
earlier, and to have loop-to-loop running
on the upper tier between the hidden Zeeman loop and the loop at the west end of
Gilbert. This feature also makes it pos-

sible for a single operator to let a train
run by itself on one tier while switching
a way freight on the other.

A guesstimated work schedule might
have phase 3 completed in perhaps 10
years. Why rush? I'll be operating long
before then. After phase 3, it's anybody's
guess; I might never add the second tier
—but then again, I can. The possibility
is built into the plan from the beginning.

The Moth Lake & Mount Ahab RR.

A walk-in HO scale layout to fit an 11 x 18-foot room

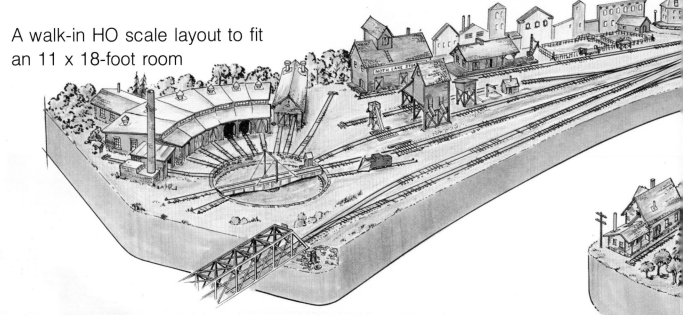

THE MOTH LAKE & MOUNT AHAB is a free-lanced Adirondack Mountains railroad having its last fling in the 1930s before interstate highways and out-of-sight costs finally turn it into abandoned trackage. A touch of the virgin spruce and hemlock logging that gave the line its start around 1880 remains, and there is still enough general freight business, despite the Depression, to call for six- to eight-car trains. Adventurers eager for the bass fishing and camping around Big Bear and

BY LEONARD BLUMENSCHINE

Mount Ahab still transfer from the New York Central at Moth Lake in large enough numbers to make a combine and a coach or two daily a necessity.

Steam is the thing and this railroad has plenty of it. Though Ten-Wheelers and Consolidations provide most of the motive power, there's room for a ringer like a 2-6-6-2 in the roundhouse, on the turntable, or on the main line. This big fellow

could prance off with just about everything the road owns and make the punishing climb from Big Bear to Mount Ahab as if the grade weren't a steep and turning three percent. When the external combustion Paul Bunyan isn't cutting the hill down to size, the smaller 4-6-0s and 2-8-0s leaving Moth Lake could pick up a helper at Big Bear to make the mountaintop reasonably intact and on schedule.

The ML&MtA is a walk-in, walkaround layout with features intended to give it a

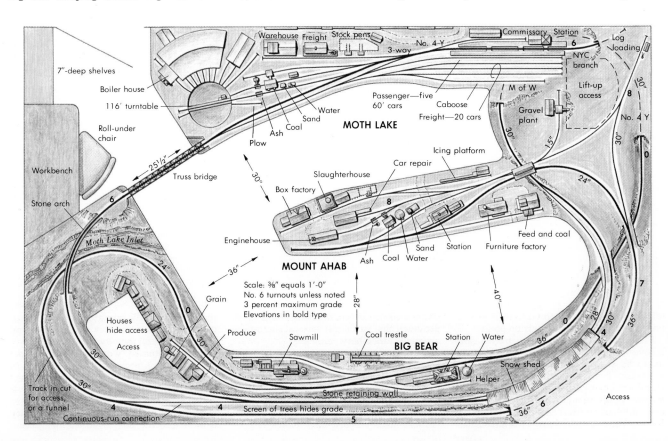

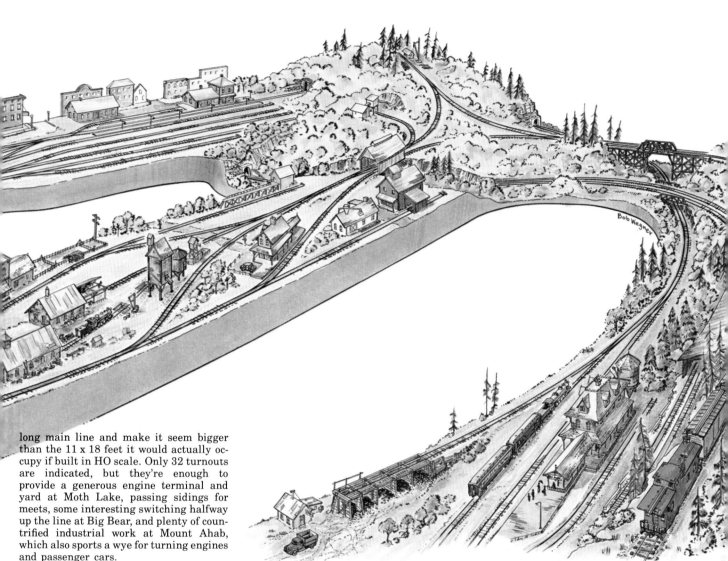

long main line and make it seem bigger than the 11 x 18 feet it would actually occupy if built in HO scale. Only 32 turnouts are indicated, but they're enough to provide a generous engine terminal and yard at Moth Lake, passing sidings for meets, some interesting switching halfway up the line at Big Bear, and plenty of countrified industrial work at Mount Ahab, which also sports a wye for turning engines and passenger cars.

The mainline core is that old favorite of track planners, a folded and twisted dogbone. Continuous running is made possible by a connection behind the town of Big Bear. Without this 3-foot stretch of straight track, the railroad would be point-to-point only, and the run between the terminals would be about 1.3 scale miles.

The continuous run connection gives the operator the option of adding on miles — the dogbone loop is just a foot or so under a scale mile long — without having to pass through either terminal in the process. You can spot cars or make up trains at Moth Lake or Mount Ahab for as long as you wish and still have the *Adirondack Mountaineer* or a peddler freight wearing down the main line without running over you every few minutes.

Although there's room for two operators, the ML&MtA was designed as a solo show. In the bargain, some pretty nice scenery for the chief engineer, brakeman, and tourist guide is encountered along the way.

Leaving Moth Lake, you cross over to wooded, hilly country on a graceful bridge at least 230 scale feet long. It's strictly a one-track affair and what you want to make it: truss, cantilever, or steel arch.

Spanning empty space so all alone and high above the floor — pardon, water — just may produce some curious feelings in the pit of your stomach. Now, you might think the bridge spans the distance between benchwork sections to provide an easy, duck-under entrance to the operating heart of the railroad. What it really does is

physically isolate Moth Lake from the rest of the line and help create the impression of "reaching somewhere" whenever it's crossed at very slow speed.

The first stop after leaving Moth Lake, a scale mile away, is Big Bear, arrived at after cindery plunges through a snowshed and a turnback tunnel. At Big Bear, the lowest point on the line but still back in the hills, some switching is done if you're operating a peddler, and a waiting helper can be picked up from behind the station. It's a steady climb to Mount Ahab after leaving Big Bear, or you can break it up by taking the continuous run connection for a few laps.

Once Mount Ahab is reached, your Moth Lake locomotive is run in for some refreshment while a local switcher busies itself with whatever cars you brought along. The helper, if you needed one, can deadhead tender-first back down the hill to Big Bear while your own engine is turning on the wye and getting ready to return to Moth Lake with more freight or passengers.

As I mentioned, logging prompted the start of this (and many a real) backwoods railroad. If post-Civil War and pre-1900 cars and engines are your interest, you can still build the main line as laid out and be fairly prototypical. Since the daredevil builders of those early railroads were usually in one heck of a hurry to get to where the timber was, they bothered with few cuts, fills, and frills and followed the terrain as much as possible.

The principal alterations you should make to represent an earlier period include making the long steel bridge a rickety wooden trestle resting on a strip of scenery and making the roundhouse and turntable at Moth Lake smaller. Mount Ahab would be devoted mostly to noisy saw mills, at least two of them, and every building there would have a boom town or tent city look. Big Bear could be the site of additional log-handling activity and Moth Lake could be the brick and mortar metropolis where finished lumber would be taken for manufacturing and where cars would be interchanged for more distant destinations.

The ML&MtA was designed to line the walls and poke into the middle of a spare room that was formerly a screened porch. Closing in such a space is a common home improvement these days in a climate where an open porch is usable less than half the year and moving to a bigger house is a bankbook-breaker. Some space was reserved for a workbench and storage shelves, but not much. It could be occupied instead by a narrow gauge logging or mining line connecting with the bigger railroad at Big Bear.

The main thing is to have fun with an interesting, buildable track plan no matter what era's rolling stock you like to run or what kind of country you enjoy running it through. Why, even the most modern diesels hauling 80-foot hi-cubes would look terrific teetering close to eye level up on those mountain sides!

DESIGNS FOR INTERURBAN LAYOUTS

Lap and terminal scheme provides variety of runs for various sorts of equipment

The interurban electric railway developed in the early years of this century from America's desire for greater mobility between cities and between city and country. Transportation was hampered by the lack of good roads, which made horse-and-buggy trips difficult; steam railroad local service was often marginal; the automobile was still an undependable horseless carriage.

By the time of World War I a number of interurban networks had developed around large cities and in the more populous regions, only to disintegrate in the next two decades because they were not fitted to compete with paved highways and the automobile. In 1961 the last remaining line in the Southwest, a remnant of the great and far-flung Pacific Electric system, abandoned passenger service and tore down its overhead wire — and the interurban era came to an end.

Famous interurban names still exist. In the Midwest the South Shore Line still operates, but more as a freight railroad and a suburban rapid-transit line than as a typical interurban. In the East, the Philadelphia & Western is strictly a suburban line, and it has lost the cars of the Lehigh Valley Transit, a true interurban which once used P&W tracks as an entrance to Philadelphia.

Other remnants of once-large systems remain but are not used in the interurban manner. For example, a remnant of the Milwaukee Electric still remains under

wire at East Troy, Wis., where a box motor hauls freight cars from that town to the nearby Soo Line interchange. Still others remain but have been converted to dieselized freight operation, such as the Illinois Terminal.

Interurban lines in the East, the Midwest, and the Far West had their own regional characteristics. Eastern lines tended to be true "between city" lines;

midwestern interurbans joined comparatively distant cities and served the farmlands in between; in the Far West the interurban more closely resembled an electrified railroad short line with carload freight operation not usually found in the East or Midwest.

In the following feature, E. S. Seeley Jr. presents three layouts based on these regional differences.

BY E. S. SEELEY JR.

THE design of any interurban model railroad layout must reflect the fact that passenger traffic is a very large part of the operating picture; and to be a true interurban we must provide a main line that simulates long runs. Unless we have access to a room about the size of a college gymnasium, I consider the closed-lap main line as our best bet. Arranging the lap around the walls of a room helps stretch the run even farther than if built on a central table. It also gives us the walls for a background where varied settings can be represented. Terminals branching off the lap of track can represent different cities or towns to provide the kind of point-to-point running that paves the way for prototype operation. More car destinations can be operated simply by adding more terminals. In making a run, an interurban car leaves one terminal and circles the lap (perhaps under some form of automatic control)

for as long as the brass hat wishes, then runs into the terminal designated as the end of that particular car's route.

Let's examine three sample layouts to see how this principle can be applied to three different types of interurban operation.

Public Service Traction Co.

Here is an eastern-type layout for the traction modeler whose eyes light up at the mention of the Eastern Massachusetts Street Ry., the Connecticut Co., or New Jersey Public Service. It offers a fine setting for deck-roofed Brill cars grinding along city streets, hitting an unaccustomed 30 m.p.h. on the shoulder of the county pike, and returning at day's end to a big multistall carbarn for a quick wash and running-gear inspection.

The PSTC is a multiple-route system designed so the routes can be combined in different schemes typical of the region. For example: The major routes of the Connecticut Co. followed an end-to-end

pattern, starting from the New York state line and running along the shore to New Haven, then heading north to Hartford and the Massachusetts state line. Routes of the Eastern Massachusetts Ry. crisscrossed the area they served; routes of the New Jersey Public Service fanned out in different directions from the main Newark terminal. With the proper variation in station names, each pattern can be simulated on the PSTC as illustrated, when the brass hat desires a change. A study of the layout will reveal many interesting and varied possibilities.

In planning route patterns, note that the barn lead on Mill St., and both sides of the lap of track around the park — opposite Newark terminal — can be used as terminals along with the more obvious turnback facilities at Newark, Caldwell, Elizabeth, Paterson, and Englewood. Imaginative pairings of terminals will create a lot of operational variety to keep the layout from ever becoming dull. A small box motor terminal has been included at

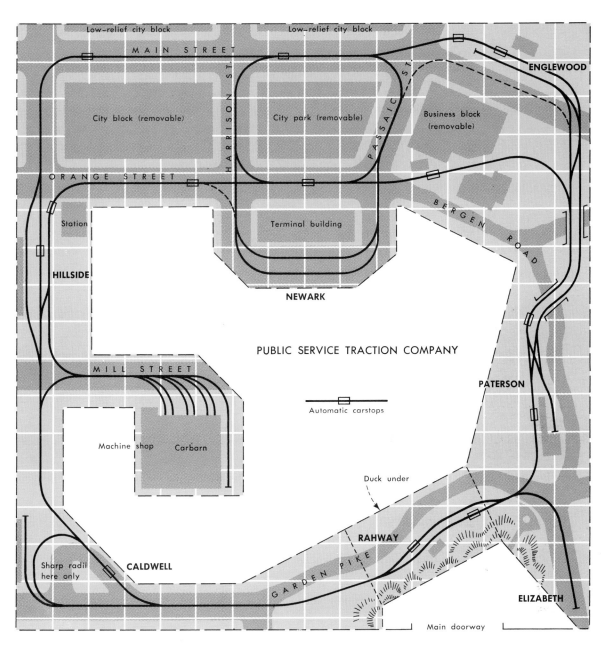

Public Service Traction Company

Scale modeled		N	TT	HO	S	O
Drawing reduction	1:	16	24	32	48	64
Scale of drawing per foot	in.	¾	½	⅜	¼	3/16
per meter	mm.	63	42	32	21	16
Spacing of rulings	in.	6	9	12	18	24
	mm.	150	225	300	450	600
Width	ft.-in.	8-0*	12-0	16-0	24-0	32-0
	m.	2.45*	3.68	4.90	7.36	9.80
Length	ft.-in.	8-2*	12-3	16-4	24-6	32-8
	m.	2.50*	3.75	5.00	7.50	10.0
Mainline radius†	in.	6	9	12	18	24
	mm.	150	225	300	450	600
Track center spacing‡	in.	9	1.3	1.67	2.25	3.3
(straight track only)	mm.	23	33	43	57	84

*Does not allow adequate aisle width near Caldwell and Hillside.
†Loop at Caldwell has 20 percent shorter radius: 10″ in HO, etc.
‡May not allow some steam-road equipment to pass.

Hillside so package freight or express service can be run.

Northern Indiana Light & Power Co.

The Northern Indiana is typical of midwestern interurbans that once laced Indiana, Ohio, Michigan, and Illinois. Two routes run in opposite directions from the city of Bloomington: the longest terminates at Fort Marion, seat of the next county, while the shorter line runs through farmland to the small but important agricultural town of Peru. Suburban service is also operated on the Fort Marion line between downtown Bloom-

ington and the powerhouse just outside the city.

We have a big interurban terminal in Bloomington, freight houses in each terminal city, and even a steam railroad connection. (Maybe the Northern Indiana is lucky enough to have an interchange agreement with this steam road; if so, watch out for that 48-foot curve on the main line in downtown Fort Marion. More typically the connection would be limited to moving hopper cars of coal to the powerhouse.)

Mergers were a common practice in the interurban's golden age, so we're on safe

ground in assuming the NI's two routes began life as independent companies. Let's call them the Bloomington, Fort Marion & Western and the Bloomington Eastern just to keep things straight. Cars on the suburban run to the powerhouse might be lettered for the Bloomington Traction Co. for greater variety. This offers the brass hat some choice in lettering his cars and in the kind of service operated. He can model the period before the merger by lettering his smaller cars for the BE and his larger cars for the BFM&W. Each group of cars would be restricted to runs between the appropriate cities, but perhaps as an indication that merger is just around the corner, one BFM&W car might operate as a through limited between Fort Marion, Bloomington, and Peru.

Or consider that the merger has just taken place but not all cars have been relettered for the new company. What a grand mixture of colors and names could move through downtown Bloomington! There would be new, heavy cars lettered NORTHERN INDIANA; older cars lettered BFM&W and others BE; plus a few city cars still lettered BLOOMINGTON TRACTION. If

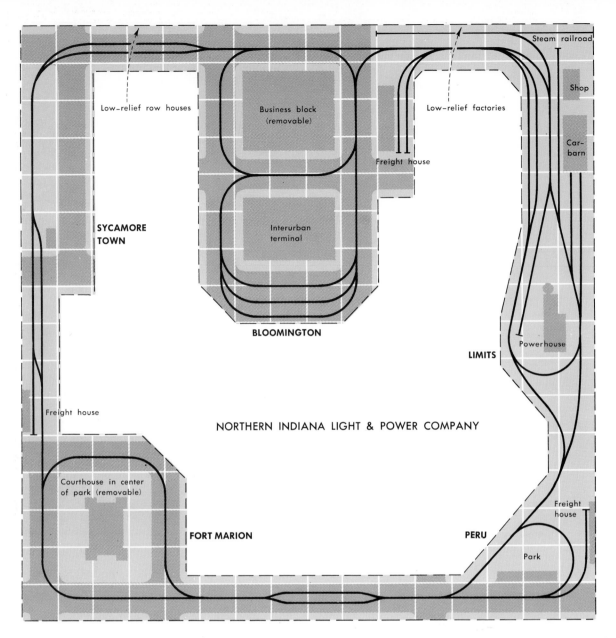

Low-relief row houses

Business block (removable)

Freight house

Steam railroad

Shop

SYCAMORE TOWN

Interurban terminal

Low-relief factories

Car-barn

BLOOMINGTON

LIMITS

Powerhouse

Freight house

NORTHERN INDIANA LIGHT & POWER COMPANY

Courthouse in center of park (removable)

Freight house

FORT MARION

PERU

Freight house

Park

NORTHERN INDIANA LIGHT & POWER CO.

Scale modeled		N	TT	HO	S	O
Drawing reduction	1:	16	24	32	48	64
Scale of drawing per foot	in.	¾	½	⅜	¼	³⁄₁₆
per meter	mm.	63	42	32	21	16
Spacing of rulings	in.	6	9	12	18	24
	mm.	150	225	300	450	600
Width and length	ft.-in.	8-0*	12-0	16-0	24-0	32-0
	m.	2.45*	3.68	4.90	7.36	9.80
Mainline radius	in.	6	9	12	18	24
	mm.	150	225	300	450	600
Track center spacing	in.	1.0	1.3	1.8	2.5	3.25
(straight track only)	mm.	25	33	46	64	83

*Aisles need widening at Sycamore and Limits if built in N scale.
This will make N scale layout 10 feet (3 meters) long.

each company has its own style of equipment and color scheme, we have a prototypic justification for the variety many interurban modelers like to see on their layouts.

South Bay Electric Ry.

Heavy freight drags behind steeplecab growlers, steam road carload interchange, multiunit commuter and school trains, wharf trackage serving ocean steamers and coastal schooners, a big ferry terminal and express shed — these are some of the features that mark South Bay Electric as a far western interurban. It is ideal for the interurban modeler who wants to add freight operation.

The fictional prototype of South Bay Electric starts at Coronado, a port city across the bay from a major west coast metropolis. From the Coronado ferry slip it skirts the edge of the bay for several miles, passing through industrial districts and commuter towns. Then it runs inland along a river valley to the important railway junction at Palomar. There is also a branch that runs from the Coronado ferry terminal along the ocean shore to North Beach.

The SBE was probably built by a class 1 steam road as an alternate freight route between Palomar and the big city (with car floats used to move cars across the bay); but electrification meant fast and

frequent passenger service too, which resulted in the rapid growth of the commuter towns and industries along SBE's main line. The North Beach branch originally may have been an ancient steam short line that was made part of the SBE and electrified to serve popular resort towns along the ocean. With readily available transportation, Coronado's own port facilities were developed. This resulted in more business and additional revenue.

The kind of passenger service operated on the main line depends on how long we imagine the route to be — 50 miles or more, perhaps? Then we can run our own version of Sacramento Northern's Comet complete with parlor-observation cars. A main line of 20 or 30 miles would mean shorter but more-frequent trains like those Pacific Electric once ran on its lines to Long Beach, San Pedro, Santa Ana, and Pasadena. It's up to the modeler. With enough rolling stock he can vary his mainline schedules from day to day.

Service on the North Beach branch would normally be operated by single cars, probably of lighter design than mainline stock, running at frequent intervals. On this line, however, there could be multicar specials transporting city

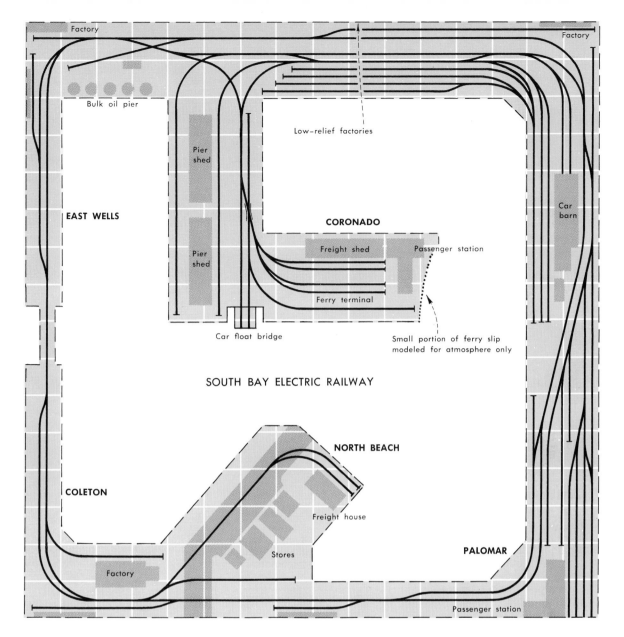

Factory   Factory

Bulk oil pier

Low-relief factories

Pier shed

Pier shed

EAST WELLS

Car barn

CORONADO

Freight shed   Passenger station

Ferry terminal

Car float bridge

Small portion of ferry slip modeled for atmosphere only

SOUTH BAY ELECTRIC RAILWAY

NORTH BEACH

COLETON

Freight house

Stores

PALOMAR

Factory

Passenger station

SOUTH BAY ELECTRIC RY.		N	TT	HO	S	O
Scale modeled		N	TT	HO	S	O
Drawing reduction	1:	16	24	32	48	64
Scale of drawing per foot	in.	¾	½	⅜	¼	3⁄16
per meter	mm.	63	42	32	21	16
Spacing of rulings	in.	6	9	12	18	24
	mm.	150	225	300	450	600
Width and length	ft.-in.	8-0*	12-0	16-0	24-0	32-0
	m.	2.45*	3.68	4.90	7.36	9.80
Mainline radius	in.	7.5	12	15	24	30
	mm.	190	300	380	600	760
Track center spacing	in.	1.0	1.3	1.8	2.5	3.25
(straight track only)	mm.	25	33	46	64	83

*Aisles need widening generally if built in N scale. This will make N scale layout 10 feet (3 meters) in width and length.

crowds to the beaches on Sundays and holidays.

Rush-hour commuter schedules can be included on both lines, along with morning and midafternoon school trains.

Freight operations can be as extensive as on any steam or diesel layout. We have long drags between the Palomar interchange yard and the Coronado carferry floats, way freights in both directions to serve mainline industries and freight houses, and ferryloads of cars from across the bay destined for ships moored at Coronado's docks. Both freight yards would be busy places indeed on the SBE layout. Don't forget box motor service on the North Beach branch (and on the main

line if you wish), not to mention possible daily RPO runs.

Once a year, on the weekend after Thanksgiving Day, the world-renowned Neptune Parade is staged at Coleton, followed by the great football game in the Fish Bowl nearby. Then every piece of passenger equipment on the system is pressed into service; and it takes a good bit of planning and patience for the dispatcher to get the equipment into and out of Coleton in time for the events, and then to take people home. Try that one on your layout! It is, of course, based on the actual operations of Pacific Electric when it once served the Pasadena New Year's Day events each year.

One last comment

Despite the comparative wealth of ready-to-run HO equipment and the fine array of parts and kits in ¼″ scale, interurban model railroading still remains a scratchbuilder's stronghold. This is especially true where trackwork and overhead wire construction are concerned. Some scratchbuilding practice certainly is desirable before undertaking any interurban layout as complex as the three described.

For this reason the novice interurban modeler should first get his feet wet with a small steam or diesel layout utilizing sectional track components and a few pieces of dependable, low-cost ready-to-run equipment. After some operating experience he can experiment with one or two ready-to-run interurban cars, most of which can be run on a two-rail system. Then he can try hanging some overhead wire, building special trackwork, and perhaps scratchbuilding a few of his own cars. The knowledge gained from such an expandable trial-and-error layout will pay important dividends later, when he begins work on a more complicated interurban layout based on a real or fictional prototype.

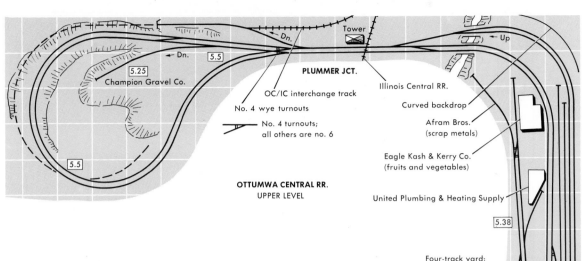

Champion Gravel Co.

5.25

5.5

5.5

Dn.

Dn.

Tower

OTTUMWA CENTRAL RR.
UPPER LEVEL

OC/IC interchange track

No. 4 wye turnouts

No. 4 turnouts;
all others are no. 6

PLUMMER JCT.

Illinois Central RR.

Curved backdrop

Afram Bros.
(scrap metals)

Eagle Kash & Kerry Co.
(fruits and vegetables)

United Plumbing & Heating Supply

5.38

Four-track yard:
13-foot centers

Station spur

OTTUMWA

Chas. Weinhagen
(box mfr.)

Station

E. W. Schmeling & Sons
(coal and coke dealer)

Yard office and outbuildings

Storage tracks: 13-foot centers

Oil unloading facility

Oil storage facility
(Mid Continent Oil Corp.)

Interlocking tower RA
(OTTUMWA JCT.)

Wigdahl Bros.
(electrical machinery
and supplies)

Diesel fuel
storage

Team
track

Dn.

Diesel service

Diesel
house

Mendota Mfg. & Transfer Co.
(agricultural implements)

5.25

5.75

Up

Ottumwa Central RR.

Plan of a railroad that can be operated by one, two, or even more engineers

BY GORDON ODEGARD

THE OTTUMWA CENTRAL is a variation of an N scale layout I'm constructing for myself. It is a general-haulage railroad that simulates the general traffic found on many prototype railroads and utilizes freight cars of all types. The track design is loop to loop with a connecting track between the two reverse loops to create diverse routings. The exposed main line is on one level, with the yard and spur tracks set slightly below. The only two grades are at the extremities leading to the holding yard beneath the main level. All mainline curves have easements to provide a smooth transition from the straight tracks into the curves.

I designed this layout for one- or two-man (or woman, or one of each) operation, but it could occupy the efforts of at least four people: one working the yard, one or two mainline engineers, a way freight engineer, and a towerman at Plummer Junction. The focal point is Ottumwa, where there is a small yard, several industries, engine facilities, and an interchange track. The interchange could be handled as a connection with a foreign line that the OC has trackage rights on, or it could be handled as another route of the OC. The diesel facilities include a two-stall enginehouse and servicing facilities with fuel storage tanks. The area could easily be modified for steam locomotives, including a turntable.

Two of the yard tracks join the main line at both ends, but they are accessible to mainline trains only from Plummer Junction. One of the mainline tracks going over the crossing serves as a switching lead without interfering with mainline train movements. Most yard switching is done at this end of the yard.

There is a wide variety of industries at Ottumwa. All names and industries on the OC are taken from a 1943 Milwaukee Road *Official Freight Shipper's Guide and Directory*. My favorite is the fruit and vegetable shipper. Modelers are often kidded about the silly names used on model railroads, but we have nothing on the prototype. How about the Eagle Kash & Kerry Co.! This was (and still may be) an actual company located at Moline, Ill. This industry has a pair of tracks in its yard, one of which can be used as a team track in addition to serving as a run-around for switching operations. There is plenty of room for more industrial tracks, so you may want to change some of my suggestions to fit your tastes.

Plummer Junction can be a busy place with a crossing and a dummy interchange with a foreign road, plus a simulated branch line of the OC which actually connects with the hidden return loop at that end. The interchange track is a most versatile spur. Any type of car can be left or picked up there. An interesting feature would be to actually interlock Plummer Junction with either an electric or a mechanical device, and then install proper signals to match. The branch line runs into a tunnel near the backdrop. Its portal is concealed from view by steep rock cuts on both the main line and the branch line.

The hidden station, Holcomb, has two storage tracks and a main line. Complete trains can be held here and periodically enter the scene to keep the action lively at Ottumwa and Plummer Junction. More tracks can be added to store additional equipment or hold more trains. Model railroads tend to have a low ratio of mainline trackage compared to yards, and on the average layout a moving train will arrive at a station more often than necessary. If trains are sent to a hidden holding track for a specified time, operators of way freights and yard engines will have sufficient time to complete their tasks, even if the layout is very small.

For motive power, I'd suggest using a pair of diesel switchers and up to four dual-service freight locomotives. An eight- or nine-car passenger train with a suitable pair of passenger road diesels will also help provide more action. The OC is primarily a freight line, but the passing of an occasional passenger train will add to the overall effect.

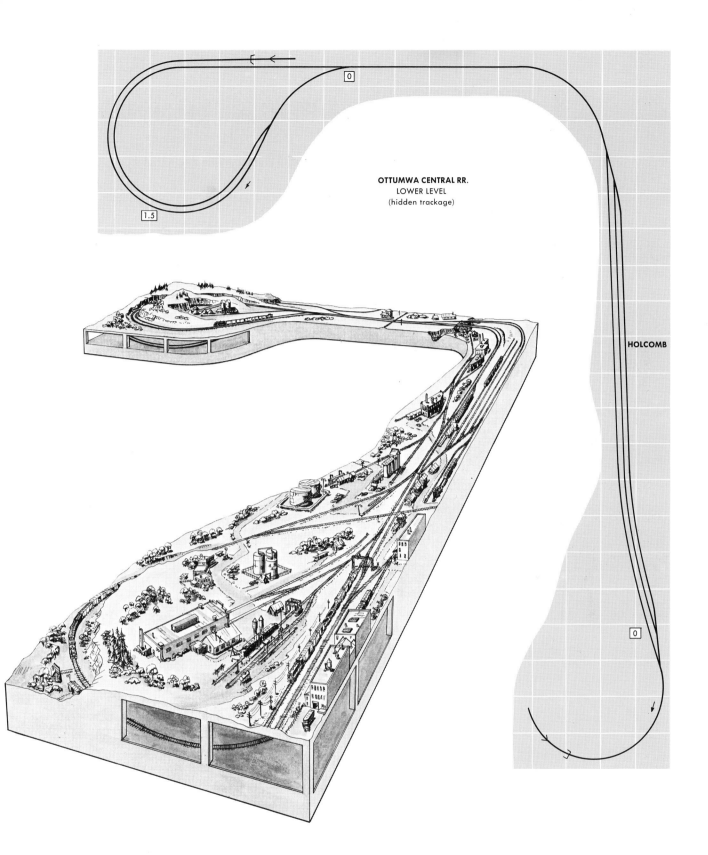

OTTUMWA CENTRAL RR.
LOWER LEVEL
(hidden trackage)

HOLCOMB

		Z	N	TT	HO	S	O
OTTUMWA CENTRAL RR.							
Scale modeled							
Spacing of rulings	in.	4.5	6.0	9.0	12.0	18.0	24.0
Space vertically	ft.-in.	7-6	10-0	15-0	20-0	30-0	40-0
Space horizontally	ft.-in.	6-2	8-3	12-5	16-6	24-9	33-0
Minimum radius	in.	9.0	12.0	18.0	24.0	36.0	48.0
Multiply elevations by		.38	.50	.75	1.00	1.50	2.00
Parallel straight track spacing	in.	.71	.98	1.31	1.80	2.45	3.26
Curved track spacing	in.	.99	1.36	1.81	2.50	3.40	4.53
Spacing of rulings	mm.	112.5	150	225	300	450	600
Space vertically	m.	2.25	3.00	4.50	6.00	9.00	12.00
Space horizontally	m.	1.86	2.48	3.71	4.95	7.43	9.90
Minimum radius	mm.	225.	300.	450.	600.	900.	1200.
Multiply elevations by		9.	13.	19.	25.	38.	50.
Parallel straight track spacing	mm.	18.	24.	33.	45.	61.	82.
Curved track spacing	mm.	25.	34.	45.	63.	85.	113.

LF&S RR. track plan

Adapted from the original design of Christof Lindenstruth

THE Lake Forest & Scagattville RR. system represents a medium-sized railroad serving an industrial area. It also passes over a large mountain range, forming a bridge between two class 1 railroads.

The line began in the last century, when North America was being crisscrossed by enterprising new railroad companies. A group of local gentlemen foresaw the need for a railroad to handle the needs of Lake Forest's businesses. The new rail line was built up the Lake Forest valley to a town called Fort Peterson. The area prospered, more stock was sold, and this in turn allowed for further expansion to the end of the original line at Rutherford. But the discovery of coal on the other side of the mountain range led to further extension of the line, across a generally snow-covered pass, to the town of Scagattville. By connecting with the main line of another road there, the LF&S RR. became a bridge route, with increased traffic as a result.

Lake Forest is the operating headquarters of the LF&S RR. system. The major locomotive servicing facility is located there. It includes a turntable and a six-stall roundhouse. Fuel, water, and a car washing facility make up the balance of the railroad property.

Scagattville is just the opposite. A small freight house, a depot, and a car repair shed are the main LF&S RR. facilities. The reason for this primitive atmosphere is that the LF&S RR. uses the connecting line's nearby locomotive service facility for repairs if needed; otherwise, the engine is simply turned and sent back. A rough shed type of enginehouse gets things out of the weather. Two additional tracks, opposite the enginehouse, hold snowplows for the winter battles to keep the line open.

Helper engines are required on all trains, in either direction, between Fort Peterson and Rutherford. A water tank is located near the short spur that holds the helper engine until the train passes.

The snowshed near Rutherford must be kept in good order because of the high snowfall found in this area.

Bottomwater Junction serves as the terminal of a steeply graded branch line as well as an interchange point with the LF&S RR. A Shay engine is used to move cars up the 10 percent grades to the mine at the summit, high in the mountains.

Freight traffic is moved between more than 40 industries arranged in "production chains." By grouping the industries in a chain of separate but interrelated industries, an interesting traffic pattern is developed. For example, logs are loaded and shipped to the lumber mill; the lumber is shipped to a furniture factory; the finished furniture is then sent either to a local warehouse or to one of the connecting lines. Other similar chains can be developed with meat, produce, ore, and many other items which must be processed a number of times.

The long siding that drops down to the riverbank at Rutherford serves a rock crusher that has a cable line picking up material from the opposite bank.

In the 1880's the LF&S RR. operated two daily passenger trains which carried a combine and a coach. This pattern was carried on until passenger service was abandoned in the early 1950's.

Current operations are on a freight-only basis, using a fleet of aging first-generation diesels. Some of the older factories and the local coal mining operations have closed, but the discovery of oil near Fort Peterson has rejuvenated the declining traffic situation. Several tank car trains are shipped out of the Fort Peterson area every day.

The track plan is shown as it appears in HO scale. A few modifications are needed if it is used in other scales. For use in smaller scales, the aisles will have to be enlarged to a 24" minimum by adding to the benchwork as shown in the sketches. For larger scales, some extra access hatches may have to be positioned so as to be able to reach some distant areas of the track.

Construction can be done in stages which will allow operation of the completed sections while the next stage is being built. Start with one yard and then build toward the other. A temporary "fiddle" siding and turntable can be attached to the end of the current stage so trains can be turned around.

LAKE FOREST

LAKE FOREST & SCAGATTVILLE RR.

Scale modeled		Z	N	TT	HO	S	O
Spacing of rulings	in.	4.5	6.0	9.0	12.0	18.0	24.0
Space vertically	ft.-in.	10-3	12-4	16-6	20-8	31-0	41-4
Space horizontally	ft.-in.	11-1	12-9	16-2	19-6	29-3	39-0
Minimum radius	in.	.9.00	12.00	18.00	24.00	36.00	48.00
Multiply elevations by	in.	.40	.54	.73	1.00	1.36	1.81
Parallel straight track spacing	in.	.71	.98	1.31	1.80	2.45	3.26
Curved track separation at Fort Peterson	in.	.99	1.36	1.81	2.50	3.40	4.53
Spacing of rulings	mm.	112.5	150.0	225.0	300.0	450.0	600.0
Space vertically	m.	3.08	3.70	4.95	6.20	9.30	12.40
Space horizontally	m.	3.32	3.83	4.84	5.85	8.78	11.70
Minimum radius	mm.	225.	300.	450.	600.	900.	1200.
Multiply elevations by	mm.	10.	14.	18.	25.	34.	45.
Parallel straight track spacing	mm.	18.	24.	33.	45.	61.	82.
Curved track separation at Fort Peterson	mm.	25.	34.	45.	63.	85.	113.

The overall sizes shown in the specifications table allow for a minimum of 24" aisleways.
With 1:220 Z, 1:160 N, and 1:120 TT scales this will require adding amounts or multiples of
15", 12", and 9" respectively along the dashed lines that cross the plan in six places.

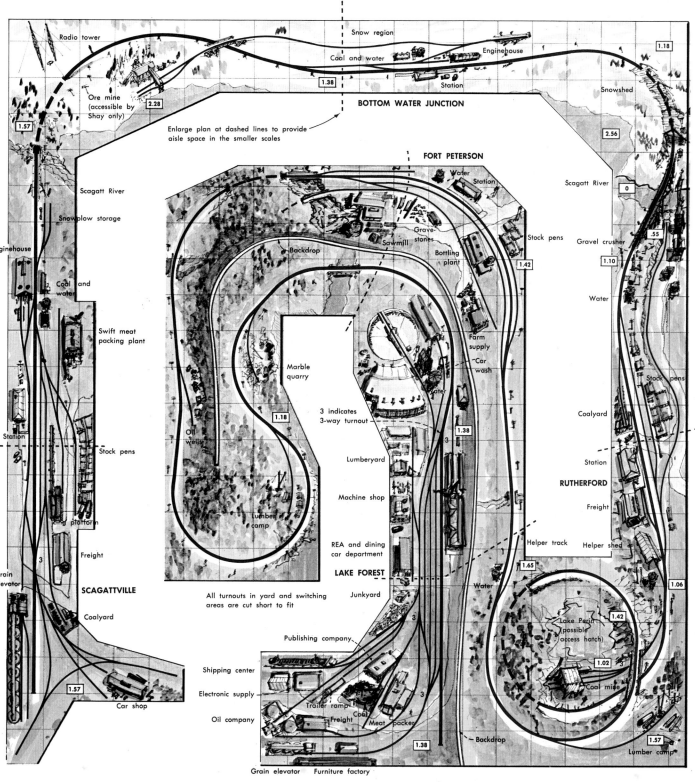

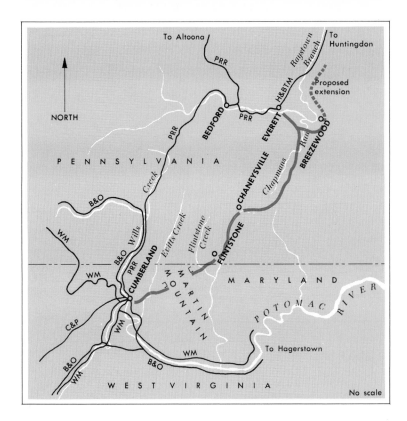

The South Penn never ran a train but maybe this pike will. Way switching is emphasized

BY DEANE MELLANDER

Cumberlan

I BELIEVE the best basis for planning a model railroad is to simulate an actual geographic area. I like to choose a location and route so that if a prototype actually had been built it would have offered useful transportation service to the area.

A case in point is the imagineered Cumberland & Susquehanna RR. I wanted a short line that would serve the territory lying east of the Allegheny Mountains beginning at Cumberland, Md. Here four railroads — Baltimore & Ohio, Western Maryland, a PRR branch, and Cumberland & Pennsylvania — offer interchange. The other terminal should be a place offering interchange for through shipments. After studying the area in an atlas, I decided on Everett, Pa., as the northern terminal. It was once served by the Huntingdon & Broad Top Mountain RR. and indirectly by Pennsy's Altoona-Bedford-Cumberland branch.

I planned the imaginary C&S to pierce through the ridge of Martin Mountain in the vicinity of Flintstone, then continue northeast to Everett through the valley cut by Chapmans Run. Since this is coal country, I decided there must be at least one large mine to generate on-line traffic in that commodity. I assumed that the valley below Chaneysville was primarily

agricultural with some light manufacturing. I went to work on the design with these things in mind.

Since the model was to be in N scale, the plan was designed with this scale in mind, using broad curves and a lot of relatively uncluttered trackage. I also used very broad curves where normally straight track might be expected. It has always seemed to me that a scale model train on broad curves more closely resembles the prototype than when it is on absolutely straight track. I also think broad curves tend to make the layout seem larger.

As designed the main line of the C&S is 40 feet long, or approximately 1.5 N scale miles. It can, of course, be built to any other scale. You may find it desirable to revise the aisle and trackwork widths in such cases.

I decided to place the two terminals adjacent to each other for three reasons. First, most of the complicated trackage is located in these areas, close together. This makes not only for ease of initial construction but also of maintenance. Second, the entire end of that peninsula of trackwork could be treated as a city, one which might have two separate railroad terminals. Third, by considering the double track that joins Cumberland to Everett directly as interchange trackage,

a switcher at either terminal can shove outgoing cars onto the interchange for pickup at the other end as incoming traffic. This connection, of course, provides lap running.

Provision is made for industrial and way-freight switching to industries located near all stations. The Flintstone Mine is the major shipper on the Cumberland & Susquehanna.

In common with many short lines, the C&S started to build toward the ultimate goal — the Susquehanna River — hence the railroad's name. It never finished the line. As part of the suggested scenic treatment, the dotted line leaving Chaneysville and disappearing under the bridge is a suggestion for an abandoned railroad grade. This was the way the builders of the C&S hoped to continue northward to the Susquehanna.

The Breezewood branch reaches several industries at that town. It was built as a temporary line to serve the town until the extension was built. For this reason the C&S never did build a station building at Breezewood.

For the C&S I visualize small motive power and vintage equipment. Consolidations (2-8-0's) would be the prime freight power with possibly a Ten-Wheeler (4-6-0) for dual service. Some other passenger service might be handled by gaselectric cars, with an aging 4-4-0 as standby power. Passengers would be carried in open-platform cars. Passenger traffic would call for two morning trains, one in each direction, and a similar evening operation. Sometimes these might carry extra miners' coaches to be dropped at Flintstone.

Cumberland & Susquehanna's freight cars would mostly be wood-sheathed, archbar-truck cars but would include steel hopper cars for the coal traffic. Except for coal, cars used in interchange would all be from foreign roads because archbar trucks are barred in interchange.

Operation would include nonstop freights carrying interchange bridge traffic between Cumberland and Everett, one in each direction. A daily peddler freight (or mixed train) in each direction would make the setouts and pickups at industries. The mine has a switcher to shunt cars between the loading tipple and the storage sidings. When business is especially heavy the mine at Flintstone sends solid trains of coal in each direction to the interchanges. In these times, at the beginning of each shift a miners' train carries workers from and to towns along the line.

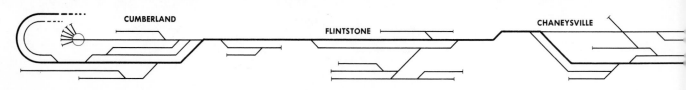

& Susquehanna RR.

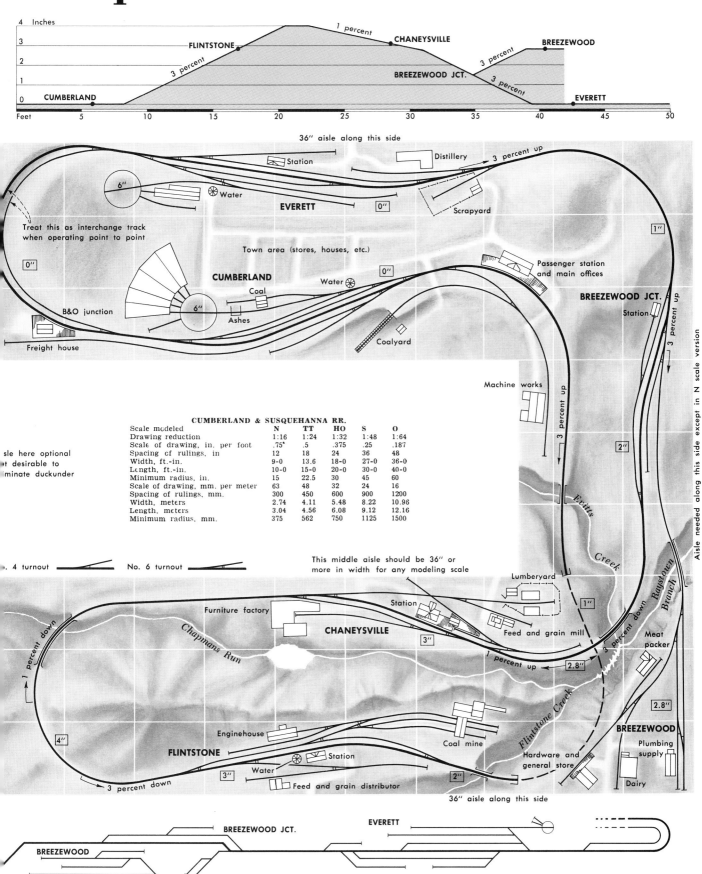

CUMBERLAND & SUSQUEHANNA RR.				
Scale modeled	N	TT	HO	S	O
Drawing reduction	1:16	1:24	1:32	1:48	1:64
Scale of drawing, in. per foot	.75*	.5	.375	.25	.187
Spacing of rulings, in.	12	18	24	36	48
Width, ft.-in.	9-0	13.6	18-0	27-0	36-0
Length, ft.-in.	10-0	15-0	20-0	30-0	40-0
Minimum radius, in.	15	22.5	30	45	60
Scale of drawing, mm. per meter	63	48	32	24	16
Spacing of rulings, mm.	300	450	600	900	1200
Width, meters	2.74	4.11	5.48	8.22	10.96
Length, meters	3.04	4.56	6.08	9.12	12.16
Minimum radius, mm.	375	562	750	1125	1500

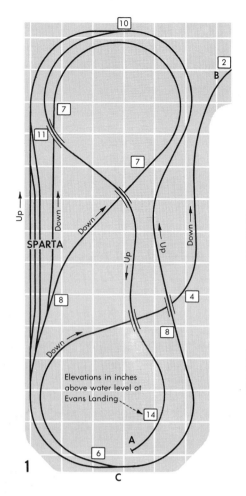

1

SPARTA

Elevations in inches
above water level at
Evans Landing

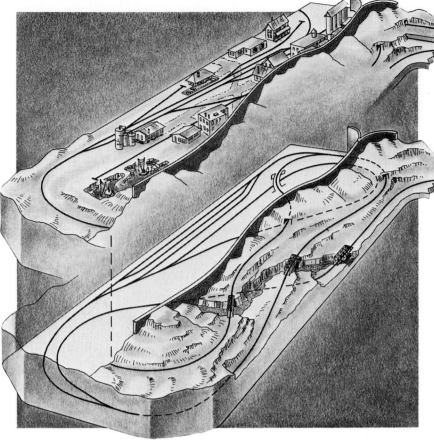

2

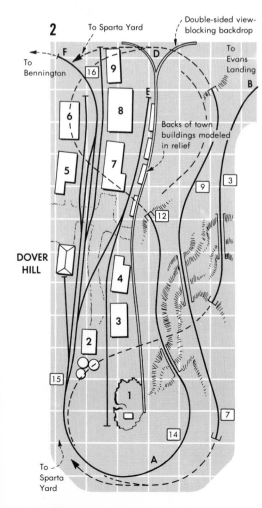

To Sparta Yard

Double-sided view-
blocking backdrop

To
Bennington

To
Evans
Landing

Backs of town
buildings modeled
in relief

DOVER
HILL

To
Sparta
Yard

Dover Hill Western

Here's a track plan designed for early operation,
with progressive stages for expansion as you wish

BY ED VONDRAK
SKETCHES BY ROBERT WEGNER

I WAS fascinated by Dr. Robert Rothe's story "Railroads in the mountains" in the October 1974 issue of MODEL RAILROADER. Studying those looping track arrangements, I started brainstorming. The Dover Hill Western RR. is the result.

My favorite way to build a railroad is in progressive stages, but planned for early operation. I worked out a track plan that begins in a simple enough way, on a peninsular bench, then expands to the walls of the room. In later stages the route takes to stacked benchwork, one shelf above the other, to gain mileage and elevation. Few modelers would want to build my entire plan, but it is designed so that you can stop extending it at whatever point the layout suits you or whenever it reaches your capability of maintaining it.

While the railroad can be built in various scales, the drawings are in HO version. To adapt it to other scales you must remember that aisles and clearances for your hands between shelves depend on the size of people rather than the trains. This layout requires a room about 15½ x 22½ feet, with an 8-foot ceiling, no windows or wall obstructions, and only one strategically placed entry door—which preferably opens outward.

Curves, in an HO version, have a minimum radius of 24". Turnouts are no. 6 in any scale, as are the maximum grades of 2.5 percent. However, these dimensions could be changed somewhat without seriously affecting the plan. You might want to use somewhat broader radii on the main line (but watch some of the clearances), and tighter radii on industrial spurs and branch lines.

If you should build the entire system, you will eventually have three shelves stacked against the right wall, two against the left, and a double-deck peninsular shelf in the center of the room. This also has a hidden track in its lowest level under the visible track.

One thing to watch is the vertical clearance between shelves. I've made some full-size mockups with cardboard, and have learned that the minimum workable clearance between the top of one shelf and the underside of the next is about 14″ or 15″, which means that you have to plan for a minimum of about 18″ between the tracks on stacked shelves. This depends on how thin you build the benchwork of the upper shelf. In deep shelves this minimum vertical clearance would be the same for all model scales. Therefore, it could affect the ruling grades drastically.

Nearly all of the layout can be supported by brackets built out from the walls. The peninsular sections will need two legs running from the upper shelf through the lower shelf to the floor. In an HO or larger version, a leg will also be needed under all three shelf levels (somewhere near the tier on the right-side lower level in fig. 3).

Diagonal braces to the wall will be needed under all upper shelves, as well as under the lower shelves. This will reduce lower-shelf clearance at these points, so the location should be planned with scenery in mind.

Step 1

The layout begins as an oval with a small double-ended yard at Sparta, a return loop, and two branches off the main line: see fig. 1. One branch reaches point A; the other descends to point B. We could operate this railroad as point to point from A to B, with continuous running on the lap used to extend the length of the trip.

The unusual things about this initial track pattern are (1) Sparta Yard is built on a fairly steep grade, and (2) the yard turnouts are not in the usual diagonal ladder arrangement. The reasons for these irregularities will become apparent later.

It doesn't take very long to get this stage of the layout into operation. Don't put any scenery in at Sparta, because it will soon become partly hidden under other scenery.

Step 2

From point A on the original plan, fig. 1, complete a semicircle on an up-grade to the town of Dover Hill, built directly above Sparta Yard. Put in a view-blocking backdrop through the middle of the bench.

The placement of the turnouts at Sparta now becomes logical. They are accessible through small doors cut in the front panel of the bench, directly under Dover Hill. The turnout at point C is similarly accessible, but access to the turnout at point D will have to be from underneath the table.

Operation now can be out and back or point to point from Dover Hill, with a branch to point B. The long grade leading directly from point A to point B on the right side of the backdrop was adapted from Canadian Pacific's spiral tunnel pattern shown in fig. 5 of Rothe's article. I was going to duplicate his track pattern, but then decided to in-

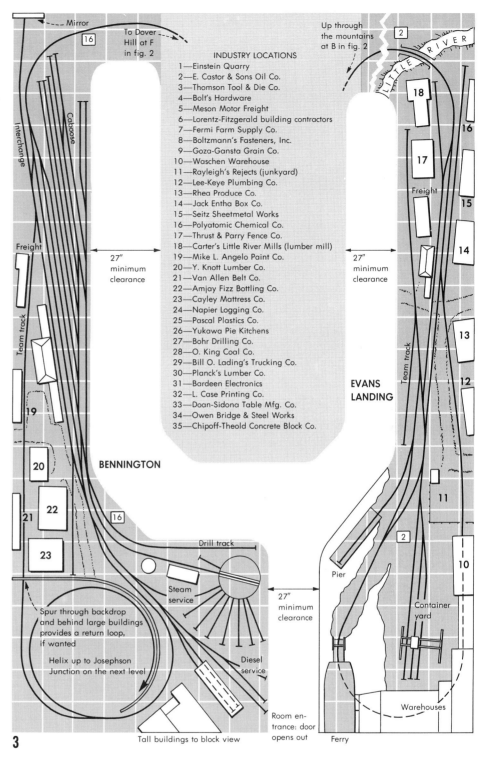

INDUSTRY LOCATIONS
1—Einstein Quarry
2—E. Castor & Sons Oil Co.
3—Thomson Tool & Die Co.
4—Bolt's Hardware
5—Meson Motor Freight
6—Lorentz-Fitzgerald building contractors
7—Fermi Farm Supply Co.
8—Boltzmann's Fasteners, Inc.
9—Goza-Gansta Grain Co.
10—Waschen Warehouse
11—Rayleigh's Rejects (junkyard)
12—Lee-Keye Plumbing Co.
13—Rhea Produce Co.
14—Jack Entha Box Co.
15—Seitz Sheetmetal Works
16—Polyatomic Chemical Co.
17—Thrust & Parry Fence Co.
18—Carter's Little River Mills (lumber mill)
19—Mike L. Angelo Paint Co.
20—Y. Knott Lumber Co.
21—Van Allen Belt Co.
22—Amjay Fizz Bottling Co.
23—Cayley Mattress Co.
24—Napier Logging Co.
25—Pascal Plastics Co.
26—Yukawa Pie Kitchens
27—Bohr Drilling Co.
28—O. King Coal Co.
29—Bill O. Lading's Trucking Co.
30—Planck's Lumber Co.
31—Bardeen Electronics
32—L. Case Printing Co.
33—Doan-Sidona Table Mfg. Co.
34—Owen Bridge & Steel Works
35—Chipoff-Theold Concrete Block Co.

clude the continuous lap in the Dover Hill Western track plan.

In planning scenery between A and B you could simulate the CP prototype or experiment with something original.

The track in Dover Hill could be modified to suit your tastes, but I wouldn't put a big yard there unless you don't plan to expand any farther.

Step 3

Now you have a choice: fig. 3. For a big yard and locomotive servicing facilities, expand to the left from Dover Hill via point F to Bennington. If a seaport intrigues you, expand to the right from point B to Evans Landing. Evans Landing is fairly low, at 2″ above datum on

the HO version. This is 38″ from the floor. This low level is one of the compromises I made to get a lot of railroad into the room.

Much of the track at Evans Landing, including the neat way to conceal the return loop via the ferry boat, was patterned after the wharf area of MR's KR&D project layout of 1972. At Bennington I arranged the track so as to keep most of the turnouts near the front edge of the table, for ease in construction and maintenance. With some tricky carpentry the turnouts in the diesel servicing area could be made accessible through a small removable hatch in the view-block backdrop. Note that the front part of the return loop at Bennington

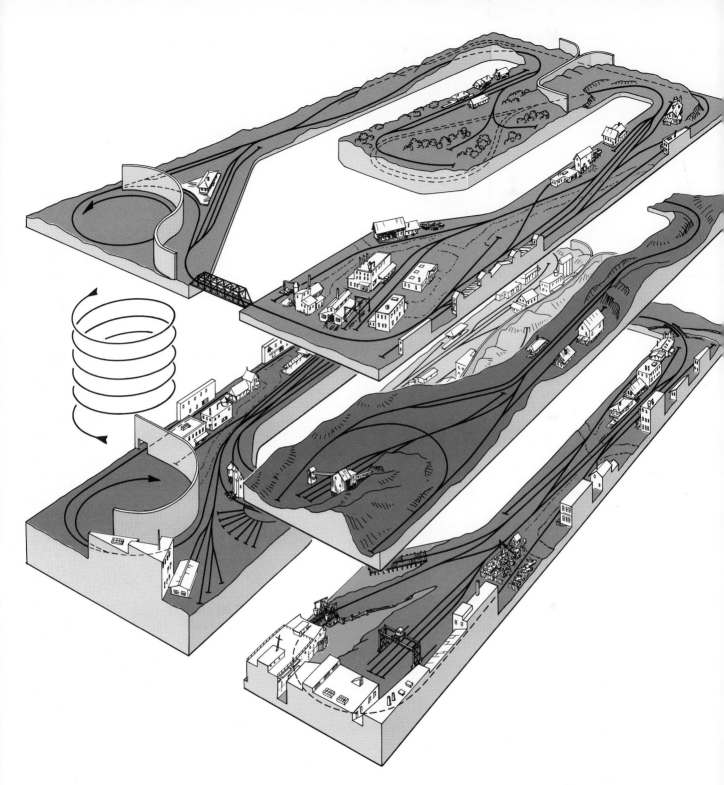

should be modeled as a well-kept main line; the loop portion at the rear of the table should appear to be a rundown industrial spur. Large buildings should be placed to block any view of the tracks going behind the backdrop.

Step 4

Now you build whichever part you didn't built in step 3. When Bennington and Evans Landing are finished, you have a railroad that provides for plenty of operation, especially for way freights.

Step 5

From point E, behind the industrial buildings at Dover Hill, the branch line

goes through the backdrop, emerging roughly above point B of the step 1 plan. This branch line to Greendale, fig. 4, is built on a shelf directly above Evans Landing. Above point B, the edge of the Greendale shelf blends into the side of the mountain. This technique has been used before in MR, and is also illustrated in John Armstrong's book TRACK PLAN-NING FOR REALISTIC OPERATION.

Greendale, a mining town, is on a separate shelf and is not related to Evans Landing, beneath it. Thus, the scenery should be quite different.

Step 6

Within the return loop at Bennington there is provision for a six-turn helix

(24″ radius on about 2.5 percent grade) to reach the uppermost shelfwork. The track there emerges from behind a backdrop at Josephson Junction, fig. 5, at a height of a little over 6 feet from the floor — a bit less than 2 feet from the 8-foot ceiling. People might question putting a shelf 18″ or 24″ from the ceiling, but I think the gain in railroad length is worth the price of climbing a stool or platform to see it. (But don't install radiant electric ceiling heat in the train room!)

At Josephson Junction on the uppermost shelf, a line to the town of Bristow branches to the left. Bristow is the site of the Napier Logging Co.

Going to the right at Josephson Junc-

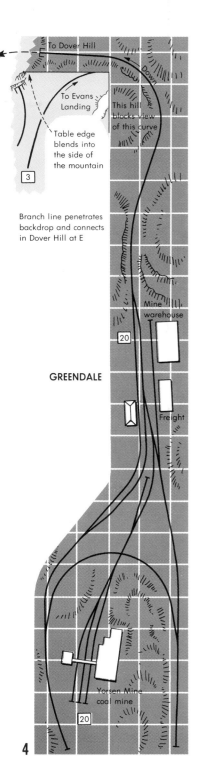

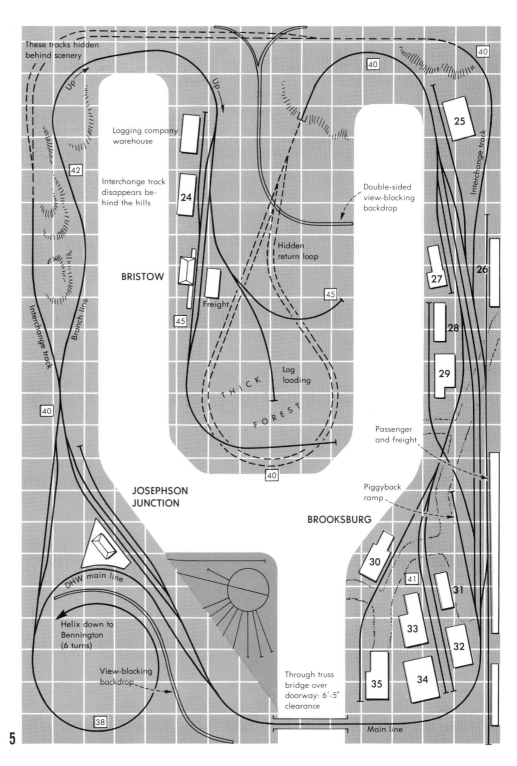

To Dover Hill

To Evans Landing

Table edge blends into the side of the mountain

3

Branch line penetrates backdrop and connects in Dover Hill at E

Down

This hill blocks view of this curve

Mine warehouse

20

GREENDALE

Freight

Yorsen Mine coal mine

20

4

These tracks hidden behind scenery

Up

Up

40

40

42

Logging company warehouse

Interchange track disappears behind the hills

24

25

Double-sided view-blocking backdrop

Interchange track

BRISTOW

45

Freight

45

Hidden return loop

27

26

28

Interchange track

Branch line

THICK FOREST

Log loading

29

Passenger and freight

40

40

JOSEPHSON JUNCTION

BROOKSBURG

Piggyback ramp

DHW main line

Helix down to Bennington (6 turns)

30

41

31

View-blocking backdrop

33

32

Through truss bridge over doorway: 6'-5" clearance

35

34

38

Main line

5

tion, the main line crosses over the doorway into the room to reach Brooksburg. At this crossing point, a 1"-thick board is located under the truss bridge to protect it. To prevent tall people from bumping it, the board is painted with red and white stripes and bears blinking lights. I provided more than minimum clearance between the upper shelves in order to clear the doorway.

The town of Brooksburg has 10 industries, a piggyback ramp, a team track, an interchange track, and a freight terminal. From Brooksburg the main line goes around a curve and disappears into a tunnel that conceals concentric return-loop and storage tracks. I added a hidden track on the

uppermost tier, between the logging branch and the far end of Brooksburg, to provide a continuous-run lap at this top level.

It seems appropriate at this point to talk about the placement of industries. In general, industries that ship goods to one another should be placed as far apart as possible, or at least in different towns. Also, you should try to use industries that can send shipments to many other locations. For example, on the Dover Hill Western, Boltzmann Fasteners, Inc., can ship items to perhaps half of the other industries on the layout. Also very important in this respect is the inclusion of team tracks, interchange tracks, and the wharf and

ferry spurs. Almost any type of rolling stock can be spotted at these tracks.

Your final, and perhaps most creative, step is naming your towns and industries. Most of the town names on the DHW were chosen from an Indiana state map because they struck my fancy. However, any resemblance between the sites of the prototype towns and this track plan are coincidental. I wasn't trying to duplicate a prototype. You can use prototype names or create your own. Ideas can come from any number of sources, but for a starter you could consider friends' names, alliterative words, or puns. The only limits at this point are how far you let your imagination wander.

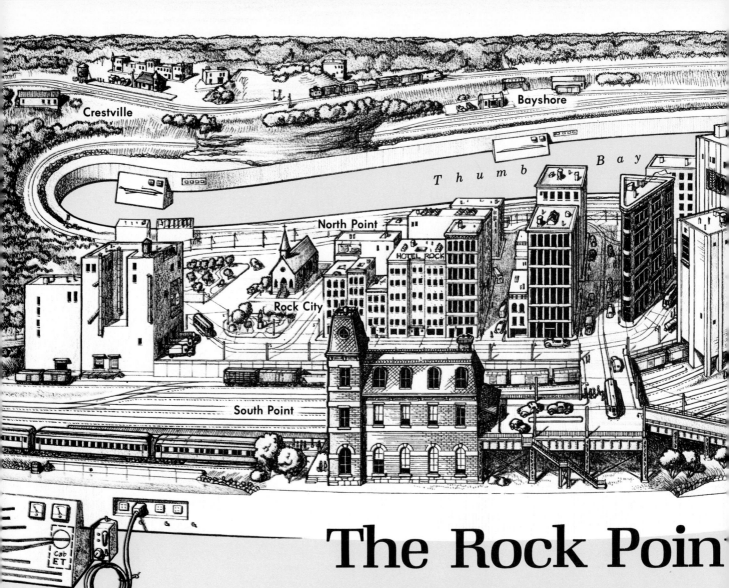

Crestville

Bayshore

North Point

HOTEL ROCK

Rock City

South Point

Cab ET

Thumb Bay

The Rock Poin

A point-to-point railroad with a comm

BY ROBERT J. LUTz

I WANTED to design as large a layout as possible that would fit in one half of the basement of a typical Cape Cod house while still providing a modest-size finished family room and the usual laundry, furnace, and workshop room. The result of my efforts was the Rock Point & Coast RR. The floor plan shows a typical Cape Cod basement arrangement. A partition wall is built as an open staircase with built-in storage area under the stairs. The room is finished with paneling and finished ceiling.

The laundry area contains the furnace, water heater, washer and dryer, storage closets, and a workbench.

The railroad room is entered through a sliding pocket door next to the furnace. This room occupies approximately one half of the total basement. The room dimensions are typical for this style of house.

LAYOUT DESIGN

The Rock Point & Coast RR. is a pure point-to-point railroad. It runs twice around the perimeter of the room and has a main line approximately 160 feet long. Access to the layout is through a lift-out section which spans the door opening.

The focal point of the railroad is the engine terminal on the end of the peninsula in the middle of the room. The engine terminal serves both ends of the railroad, eliminating the need for duplicate engine facilities as required on typical point-to-point railroads. This layout design feature cuts engine terminal maintenance in half and allows more space for the balance of the railroad. There are two access aisles having a minimum width of 27" on each side of the peninsula. All tracks, and in particular the turnouts, are within a 30" arm's-length reach.

The peninsula can be built using the L-girder method of construction, which lends itself well to free-form layout shapes. The portion of the railroad around the walls can be wall-mounted. I suggest using ladder frame construction and supporting it by knee brackets from the wall.

The Bay Head & Western is an independent short line with a main line about 46 feet long. It could be modeled as a branch line of the larger road, although I chose to make it a separate road for more variety in road names and interchange traffic on the layout.

The short line runs along the south wall, turns northward, and continues through the dividing wall into the family room. The

portion in the family room is built as a bookshelf railroad and is approximately 15 feet long. The construction of this portion is taken from my two-part article "Bookshelf railroads," published in the January and February 1977 issues of MR.

The bookshelf section of the BH&W can be operated from within the family room. This feature permits you to put in an occasional appearance with the family. This portion of the layout can also be operated remotely from the railroad room. The hinged picture on the partition wall serves as a viewing port.

The layout is designed primarily for HO scale, but the concept can be used for other scales. For HO scale the minimum-radius curves are 27". If you are building in N scale I suggest you maintain the 27"-radius curves but modify the parallel track center spacing to N scale standard practice. This will give broad, sweeping curves and greater scenic expanses between the main lines. This is a deviation from the usual practice of reducing the overall layout size for N scale and should add considerably to the illusion of long distance.

This is a large railroad with plenty of space, and we can afford to be a little extravagant. Use no. 8 turnouts as the lead switches at both ends of all mainline pass-

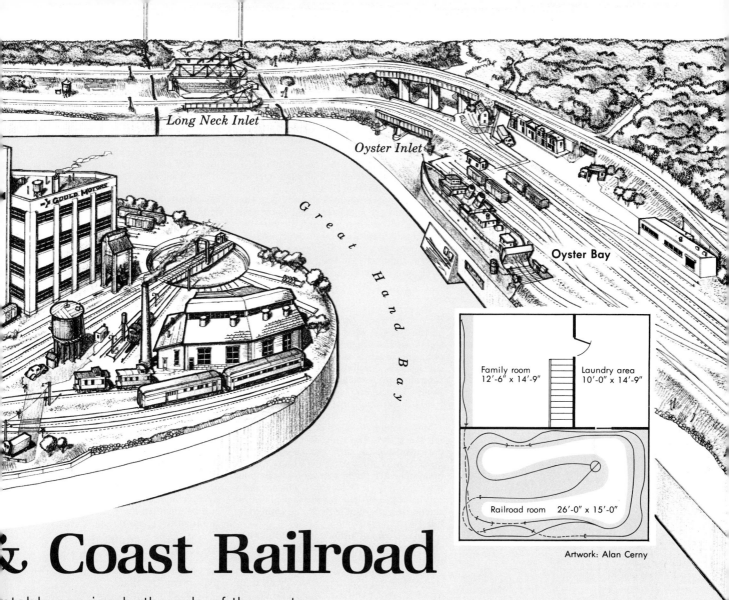

Long Neck Inlet

Oyster Inlet

Great Hand Bay

Oyster Bay

Family room
12'-6" x 14'-9"

Laundry area
10'-0" x 14'-9"

Railroad room   26'-0" x 15'-0"

Artwork: Alan Cerny

& Coast Railroad

ntable serving both ends of the system

ing sidings. Trains look more like the prototype running through these longer turnouts, particularly the long passenger cars. Use no. 6 turnouts in the yards and throughout on the BH&W. No. 4 turnouts can be used for some industrial sites as long as the tangent portion lies on the main line.

GEOGRAPHY AND HISTORY

Rock Point is a large rocky peninsula running eastward from the mainland out into the middle of Great Hand Bay. Two smaller bays are on both sides of the peninsula: Thumb Bay to the north and Index Bay to the south.

Located on the peninsula is Rock City, which was formerly the twin towns of North Point and South Point. The railroad was originally constructed to run from North Point around the end of Thumb Bay to serve the shoreline communities to the east. The railroad was originally the North Point & Bay Shore.

The railroad bored and blasted the rock cliff at North Point and filled-in the edge of the bay to create a shelf upon which a modest yard and passenger terminal was built. The engine terminal was built on the lowland at the east end of the peninsula.

The town of North Point was built on top

of the cliff, and the original wood frame passenger station still stands on the edge of the cliff, with an overpass and stairway down to the platform tracks. The yard tracks are all long, sweeping curves squeezed between the cliff wall and the bay shore.

North Point prospered, and in a few years expanded southward across the peninsula toward the shore of Index Bay. The exposed low rock profile of the southern side was soft and crumbling, so a stone block retaining wall was built and backfilled with rock from the mainland. This permitted the expanding town to be built all at one elevation and on a firmer footing.

The residents on the south side decided they wanted their own town, so a referendum was held. The proposition passed and the town of South Point came into being. South Point grew rapidly and prospered too. The political leaders of the time and several wealthy merchants decided the town needed its own railroad.

The Peninsula & East Coast Ry. was organized to run from South Point around the end of Index Bay and serve the new towns lying on the ridges above the bays. The organizers were determined to build better facilities than those of the North Point & Bay Shore over in North Point.

A conventional yard with straight parallel tracks was built between the stone retaining wall and the shore of Index Bay. The passenger station and platform were built right on the shore of the bay. The station was a three-story red brick building and access to it was over a steel viaduct. The viaduct spanned the yard tracks from the retaining wall and ended at the second-floor level of the station. The viaduct was built a little too low, so there is a close clearance over trains.

The organizers' plans for the yard were a little too grandiose, and there was no space left for an engine terminal. The road was forced to resort to a long-term lease arrangement with the North Point & Bay Shore for access to and use of its engine terminal. Thus came about the present common engine terminal.

While both towns continued to enjoy prosperity, there was a constant dispute over the boundaryline between them. The citizens of both towns became fed up with political hassling and insisted on a referendum to make the town one. The referendum passed and the two towns became one, which was named Rock City. The two previous names were retained only to identify the two railroad stations.

Several years later a recession hit the

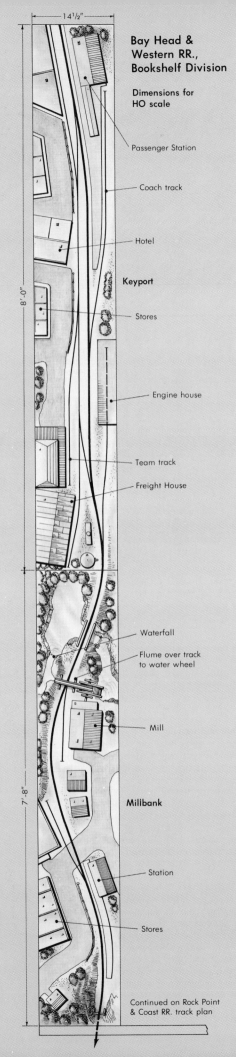

Bay Head & Western RR., Bookshelf Division

Dimensions for HO scale

14½"

Passenger Station

Coach track

Hotel

8'-0"

Keyport

Stores

Engine house

Team track

Freight House

Waterfall

Flume over track to water wheel

Mill

7'-8"

Millbank

Station

Stores

Continued on Rock Point & Coast RR. track plan

area, and to financially survive, both railroads merged into one company: the present Rock Point & Coast RR. The two former end terminals at Bay Head and Crestville were eliminated and these two points were tied together to form one continuous railroad.

The Bay Head & Western is a small independently owned and operated short line which was built to serve a modest coal mine at Ridgeway on the mainland. It maintains both freight and passenger interchange with the RP&C at Bay Head. The mine operation at Ridgeway was successful and the road expanded northward to Millbank and Keyport, and it serves several small industries in these two towns. Coal from the mine at Ridgeway is used by several industries on the RP&C as well as by the engine terminal at Rock City.

FACILITIES AND CAPACITIES

There are a total of 36 industrial sites on the two railroads: 22 on the RP&C and 14 on the BH&W. Most of the industries are small, with sidings that hold only one or two cars. Much of the freight traffic is on-line service, one industry serving another. Interchange service takes place at Bay Head with the Bay Head & Western. Additional interchange also takes place at Oyster Bay with the car ferry.

Most model railroaders have more rolling stock than the railroad can accommodate, and the car ferry serves as a convenient means of rotating the excess cars. A hand-operated fiddle yard is located under the tablework at Oyster Bay. The car ferry can be taken off the layout and placed at the fiddle yard, and cars can be rotated by hand.

The capacity of all industrial sidings and yard tracks is well over 100 cars. To provide reasonable space for car movements and train makeup, use about 70 percent of the total on line at any given time. The balance of the cars should be kept in the car ferry/fiddle yard and to form an interchange car pool. After all, the prototype railroads never have every track fully occupied.

For passenger service there is a total storage capacity for 21 80-foot cars. The two main coach yards each holds six cars. The station stub tracks at the two terminals hold three cars. The stub track at Bay Head holds two cars and the one at Keyport holds three cars. Don't be tempted to fill every available space. That is a lot of passenger cars, and you will never have on-time departures with the yards that packed with cars. I suggest a maximum of 12 cars. A good assortment of cars would be: two combination baggage-coaches, five day coaches, two parlor cars, one club diner, one full diner, and one observation-lounge car. The only sleeper service intended was one through car, North Point to Keyport via interchange at Bay Head with the BH&W.

The Bay Head & Western owns two 65-foot coaches and a small gas-electric car for light midday service.

Some foreign-road passenger cars could be operated by interchange via the car ferry, which can carry four 80-foot cars. Keep these cars in the fiddle yard and operate them on a fast turnaround to avoid jamming the yards.

Passenger train operation is really not much different than freight train opera-

tion. All that is needed is a logical reason for people going someplace, and then a train can be made up to suit the purpose or destination.

THE ROCK CITY TRANSIT CO.

I have included a small traction system for those who would like to try their hand at some trolleywork. This is a functional little system rather than a trolley car chasing itself around a loop in center city.

The Rock City Transit Co. operates two single-truck Birneys, referred to by the local citizens as "the Rock City Ramblers." This is not a reference to a rock musical group, but to the rambling gait of a four-wheel Birney on not-too-well-maintained track. The track plan provides for four possible routes with two in operation.

One car runs from the small carbarn down Bay View Rd., and serves the residential area. The car stops at North Point station, then swings up through Main St. and across the viaduct to South Point station. It serves as a crosstown shuttle between the two railroad stations.

The other car serves the two industrial areas. It starts at the west end, then runs down Railroad Ave. and into the major industrial area at the east end. It turns past the post office, North Point station, up through Church St., around Church Sq., and back to the west end. Both cars could make alternate trips on the other two routes if desired.

The curves on the line are tight, so four-wheel Birneys are about all that could be operated. The single-truck trolleys made by Tyco and AHM could also be used. They can be modified quite readily to eliminate the toylike appearance.

SCENERY

Most of the scenery can be built using either hardshell terrain or screen wire and plaster construction.

Rock City is intended to be built as a visual divider between the two yards. The center of the city is a few inches in elevation above the tracks. The business area of stores, hotels, and office buildings should be of various heights: three-, four-, or five-story buildings. Vary the adjacent building heights so they don't have a uniform block-like appearance. A row of apartments or town houses can be located along Railroad Ave. overlooking South Point yards. The two hotels should be the prominent buildings. Make them five or six stories high. The large industrial buildings at the east end of the city are at track level with entrances at street level. They, too, should be multistory and of different heights. They don't all have to have a multitude of windows; some moving and storage warehouses have almost blank walls. Some buildings should have water tanks on the roofs; others should have sawtooth skylights. The center city area lends itself to being completely built on a Masonite panel on a light frame which can be dropped in place between the stone retaining wall and the rock cliff. The industrial buildings can be set down at track level and nested tightly against the raised city panel.

I have omitted specifying most industries by type, as most modelers prefer to use their own imagination. The overall effect should be that of a large city but without overpowering the railroad.

Consider lighting for the city's buildings

and streets. Fiber-optic lighting would be very effective. It provides low-key lights, and many buildings can be illuminated from one source.

OPERATIONS

Both railroads are designed for walk-around cab control, and suggested locations for local plug-in panels are shown on the layout plan. The main line is pretty much self-explanatory. Rather than describe a typical run over the line, I will cover some of the major points.

Passenger service is intended to be through trains, both locals and expresses from North Point to South Point in both directions. All trains leaving North Point are eastbound and those leaving South Point are westbound. Morning and evening commuter service operates from North Point to Bay Head in both directions, using two-car trains pulled by tank locomotives such as Jersey Central 4-6-4T or Boston & Albany 4-6-6T. There is no commuter service out of South Point.

There are several through parlor car runs a day between North Point, South Point, and Keyport on the BH&W. There is also one night sleeper run daily between Keyport and North Point. Interchange on these runs takes place at Bay Head.

The pride of the BH&W, The Ridge Runner, operates as a through train from Keyport to North Point and return. The two BH&W coaches are run with a parlor car from Keyport to Bay Head, where an

RP&C locomotive takes over the train for the run to North Point. The turnaround must be quick, as the BH&W coaches must get back to their home road.

Freight service on the RP&C is operated in both directions as local way freights. The way freights are not permitted to switch cars in the carferry yard at Oyster Bay and may only set out or pick up cars in blocks at that point.

A yard switcher is permanently assigned to work the car ferry and yard. It may also operate on the east and west mains at Oyster Bay but only to serve the industries located there.

The main line of the RP&C is double-tracked from the approach curve to Oyster Bay through to the west end of Bay Head station.

The long tunnel between Bay Head and Crestville is double-tracked with the lead switches located just outside the two tunnel portals. This track arrangement eliminates the bothersome maintenance nuisance of turnouts hidden under the scenery. The double track can also be used as a passing siding. The longest train operated should be less than the length of this tunnel, as it is used as a holdover point. Both eastbound and westbound trains are to be run into the tunnel and brought to a stop. The engineer then unplugs his cab controller, walks around to the opposite access aisle, and plugs the controller in at the local panel. Then he starts the train and brings it out of the tunnel on the other side.

The time delay introduced by this operation adds to the overall running time of all trains.

To add some complications to car movements, I have purposely omitted any car interchange tracks between North Point and South Point yards. An occasional hopper or tank car might move from one yard to the other, by way of the turntable, after use in the engine terminal. This should be the limit of interchange traffic between the two yards.

The BH&W operates two diesel locomotives, one passenger and one freight. Freight trains north of Ridgeway are limited to a maximum six-car length because the main and passing siding at the Keyport terminal have a capacity of only six 50-foot freight cars each. These two tracks at Keyport will also accommodate three 80-foot passenger cars with just enough room to allow a locomotive to run around the train. The station stub track will also hold three passenger cars.

The tunnel between Ridgeway and Millbank is long enough to hold a six-car train and is to be used as a holdover point while relocating the cab controller from one panel to another.

This is a large and extensive railroad, so go at its construction slowly. Build the two terminals, then the main line with only the passing sidings and interchanges. Then add the industrial sidings as you see fit and as traffic demands, which is pretty much the way the prototype does it.

Rock Point & Coast RR.

Continued in family room, see detail plan on opposite page

Each square represents 1 square foot if built in HO scale

Track elevations for HO scale layout are indicated in inches

5.0"
Entrance door
2.0"
Liftout section
Long Neck Inlet
0.0"
Oyster Inlet

Walkaround throttle plugs and layout panels
Mail track
Post Office
Main St.
Freight yard
Coach tracks

Bayshore
Bay
North Point
Church St.
Rock City

Crestville
0.0"
4.0"
T h u m b

Panel for remote operation in family room
Car barn
Bay View Road
Drill lead
1.0"

Oyster Bay
1.0"

Ridgeway
Great Hand Bay
4.0"
2.0"

0.0"
Diesel service track
Coach yard
Ramp
Railroad Ave.
Caboose track

Drill lead
1.0"
7.0"
Index Bay
Coal mine
Church Square
South Point
Coach or diner drop track
Engine terminal
Carferry drill lead

Hamilton
Coal yard and trestle
4.0"
Bay Head & Western RR.
Bay Head
Freight interchange
Coach track
0.0"
3.0"
Franklin

6.0"
2.0"

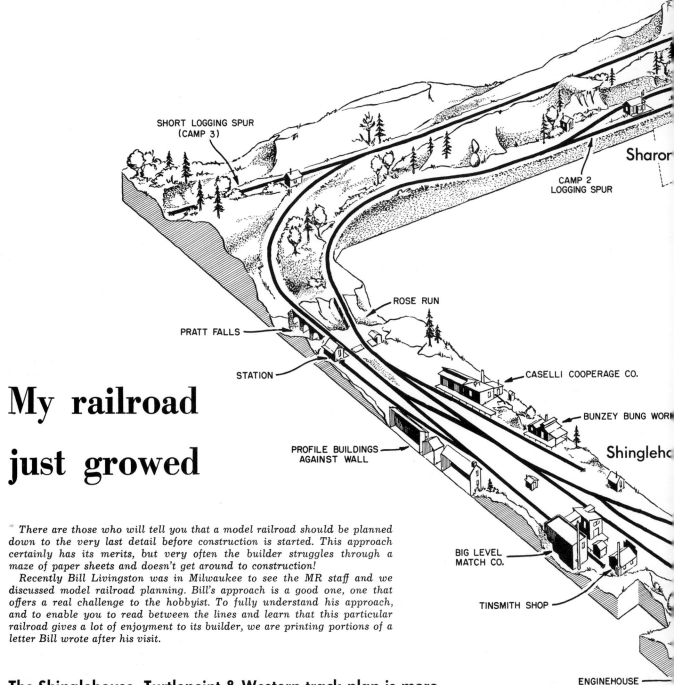

SHORT LOGGING SPUR (CAMP 3)

Sharor

CAMP 2 LOGGING SPUR

ROSE RUN

PRATT FALLS

STATION

CASELLI COOPERAGE CO.

BUNZEY BUNG WOR

Shingleho

PROFILE BUILDINGS AGAINST WALL

BIG LEVEL MATCH CO.

TINSMITH SHOP

ENGINEHOUSE

My railroad just growed

There are those who will tell you that a model railroad should be planned down to the very last detail before construction is started. This approach certainly has its merits, but very often the builder struggles through a maze of paper sheets and doesn't get around to construction!

Recently Bill Livingston was in Milwaukee to see the MR staff and we discussed model railroad planning. Bill's approach is a good one, one that offers a real challenge to the hobbyist. To fully understand his approach, and to enable you to read between the lines and learn that this particular railroad gives a lot of enjoyment to its builder, we are printing portions of a letter Bill wrote after his visit.

The Shinglehouse, Turtlepoint & Western track plan is more of a track non-plan but it's fun to operate all the same

By Bill Livingston

I seem to recall, when I was in Milwaukee I told you that I had never drawn a scale plan of my pike — which is true. But I do have the drawing [shown] that, although it is not drawn to exact scale, is a fairly accurate, albeit crude, representation of the Venango Valley Coal & Lumber Co.'s trackage and facilities.

Can't rightly say whether it's a plan which anyone else could use to build from, but then I lay no claim to its being a gem of a track plan anyway. As I mentioned to you, this pike literally "jest growed." The area at Shinglehouse came first (in HOn3, in 1953, by the way).

Then another leg, the Sharon Junction portion, was added. Construction stopped there for a while, since the second leg terminated at a cabinet built into the cellar wall, until I decided to add the Big Level area on top of the cabinet and build a long grade up to it.

The Big Level portion eventually grew until it occupied a shelf over my workbench (the workbench is directly under the Tionesta Turpentine Works on the plan), and a fourth addition carried the trackage around the corner at Millport in the form of a sort of a reversing loop. Then 3 years or so ago, when the motif

changed from mining to logging, I tore out the reversing loop and added the two tracks to complete the two ovals.

Town names have changed over the years, along with trackage, and up until about 1955 the pike was all narrow-gauge. At one time the trackage from the Sharon Junction area to where Millport is now located was operated by steeple-cab freight locomotives under wire. No passenger interurbans or trolleys were ever used, however. The present layout plan seems slated to remain stable for a while — too much fun to operate to change! It has obvious operational limi-

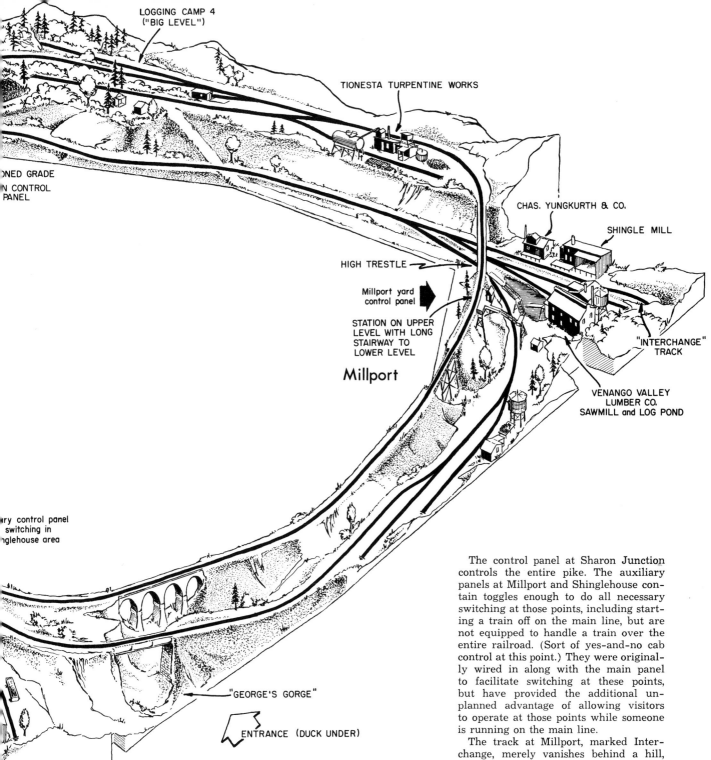

LOGGING CAMP 4
("BIG LEVEL")

TIONESTA TURPENTINE WORKS

ONED GRADE
N CONTROL
PANEL

CHAS. YUNGKURTH & CO.

SHINGLE MILL

HIGH TRESTLE

Millport yard
control panel

STATION ON UPPER
LEVEL WITH LONG
STAIRWAY TO
LOWER LEVEL

Millport

"INTERCHANGE"
TRACK

VENANGO VALLEY
LUMBER CO.
SAWMILL and LOG POND

ry control panel
switching in
nglehouse area

"GEORGE'S GORGE"

ENTRANCE (DUCK UNDER)

Livingston

tations, but I think this could be true of any pike I built 10 years ago even if I had drawn a complete plan. In other words, what I would have planned in the way of operation then would not fit my tastes now in every respect. As it stands, by altering the scheme of things as I went along, I have evolved a sort of backwoods railroad which I get a kick out of running, and operation objectives have

grown just as the railroad has grown.

The pike is about 48″ above floor level (at Millport) at its lowest point; the highest track elevation (Big Level at Camp 4) is about 55″ above the floor. The railroad occupies an area some 11 feet square. Three sides are against the wall; the fourth side (right side on the sketch) adjoins the cellar stairs.

The entrance (where you duck under the two bridges at George's Gorge to get into the center of the pike) is at the foot of the cellar stairs. The jogs in the layout, like the one at Millport, are where the thing was literally built around and over cabinets, etc.

The control panel at Sharon Junction controls the entire pike. The auxiliary panels at Millport and Shinglehouse contain toggles enough to do all necessary switching at those points, including starting a train off on the main line, but are not equipped to handle a train over the entire railroad. (Sort of yes-and-no cab control at this point.) They were originally wired in along with the main panel to facilitate switching at these points, but have provided the additional unplanned advantage of allowing visitors to operate at those points while someone is running on the main line.

The track at Millport, marked Interchange, merely vanishes behind a hill, ostensibly connecting the Millport area with another yard 'somewhere nearby' and another railroad.

Motive power (as of today, that is — I seem to be an incurable horse trader) consists of a Shay which I have had ever since PFM came out with them; a Climax which I sold to Yungkurth 2 years ago and just brought back into the fold via a trade; a United Ma & Pa 2-8-0 (somewhat modified, courtesy Kemtron); a United Reno 4-4-0 (likewise); a scratchbuilt 0-4-0; a Ken Kidder 0-4-0T (also rebuilt); and a 44-ton GE diesel switcher.

Wow — didn't mean to write this much. Enough for now.

Regards,

Bill Livingston

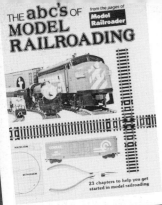

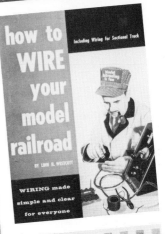

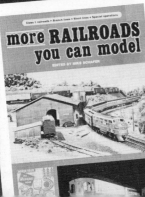